T0292881

Exposing Pay

Exposing Pay

Pay Transparency and What It Means for Employees, Employers, and Public Policy

PETER BAMBERGER

OXFORD
UNIVERSITY PRESS

OXFORD
UNIVERSITY PRESS

Oxford University Press is a department of the University of Oxford. It furthers the University's objective of excellence in research, scholarship, and education by publishing worldwide. Oxford is a registered trade mark of Oxford University Press in the UK and certain other countries.

Published in the United States of America by Oxford University Press
198 Madison Avenue, New York, NY 10016, United States of America.

Library of Congress Cataloging-in-Publication Data
Names: Bamberger, Peter, author.
Title: Exposing pay : pay transparency and what it means for employees, employers, and public policy / Peter Bamberger.
Description: New York, NY : Oxford University Press, [2023] | Includes bibliographical references and index.
Identifiers: LCCN 2022040660 (print) | LCCN 2022040661 (ebook) | ISBN 9780197628164 (hardback) | ISBN 9780197628188 (epub) | ISBN 9780197628195
Subjects: LCSH: Wages. | Equal pay for equal work. | Pay equity.
Classification: LCC HD4909 .B34 2023 (print) | LCC HD4909 (ebook) | DDC 331.2/1—dc23/eng/20220901
LC record available at https://lccn.loc.gov/2022040660
LC ebook record available at https://lccn.loc.gov/2022040661

DOI: 10.1093/oso/9780197628164.001.0001

1 3 5 7 9 8 6 4 2

Printed by Sheridan Books, Inc., United States of America

Contents

Preface

Were It Only So Simple

> Talking about salary is one of the last conversational taboos. You may know about your colleague's sex life, your friend's drinking problem, or what your neighbor really thinks of her mother-in-law. But you probably don't know what they take home in each paycheck.
> —Margaret Littman (2001, p. 39)

It's all a matter of timing. In 2005, I was teaching a course in Human Resource Management to a group of MBA students. At the start of my (intended) lecture on compensation and benefits, one of my students, a software engineer who had just founded his own start-up, told me that he intended pay in his company to be transparent. He wanted to know my opinion on the matter. "Is pay transparency a good thing or a bad thing?" he asked. Recognizing the complexity of the issue, I pitched the question back to the class. An hour of intense student debate later, I had yet to give my opinion on the matter, largely because I didn't really hold an opinion one way or the other. I needed to learn more.

I went back to my office and searched for research on the topic. I managed to dig up several studies from the late 1960s and 1970s, but found little in terms of empirical evidence, let alone *recent* empirical evidence. My curiosity now fully piqued, I decided to embark on a systematic line of research aiming at determining whether, indeed, pay transparency was a good thing or a bad thing. Soon after I published my first findings (in 2010), there was a tidal wave of interest in the topic. What happened? Why the sudden interest?

For nearly all of us, pay or remuneration is an important aspect of our work lives. The pay we receive in return for our labor is meaningful because it plays an important role in determining our quality of life: how and where we live; how we plan for the future; and what kinds of goods, services, or experiences we can obtain to enrich our life and the lives of those we care for. Every time we consider buying a product or service or making some sort of investment, the constraints imposed by our pay on our ability to meet our needs and desires remind us of the *absolute* value of our remuneration. This absolute value of pay is meaningful in that it can shape our actions, potentially motivating us to (for instance) work more hours, ask for a raise, or start looking for a new job.

But pay is meaningful in other ways as well. For instance, it may influence decisions regarding how we invest in and allocate our human capital resources, opting to study machine learning as opposed to philosophy, or choosing to build a medical career with a focus on plastic surgery over family medicine. Similarly, pay may impact our sense of self-esteem, self-control, and self-worth, or the trust we place in others, such as our employers. These other meaning-making influences of pay are largely *relativistic* in nature. That is, pay takes on additional meanings because we tend to compare our own pay with that of others. And we do this through a broad lens. We ask not only "How does my pay compare with that of others doing the same or similar work in my organization?" but also "How does my organization rate against others in terms of the average or median rate of pay for work similar to mine?" and "How does the average or median rate of pay in my job compare with the pay associated with other positions in my organization?"

In order to accurately engage in such comparisons, we need to be able to access timely, relevant, and accurate information regarding the earnings of those doing jobs similar to ours in our own and other organizations, as well as those in jobs contributing more or less to our organization than the job we perform. Information on how pay-related decisions are made in our organization might also be helpful, not only so that we know whether we're being paid fairly and equitably but also to help us decide whether it's worth spending an extra hour at work to impress our boss (with the expectation that we'll see a bigger bonus as a result), as opposed to spending that time with family and friends.

While the internet and pay-related apps such as Glassdoor and PayScale have greatly democratized access to pay information, timely, relevant, and accurate pay information—even about one's *own* remuneration, or the organization's pay-related decision-making, let alone specific details of others' pay—often remains difficult to obtain. This puts employees at a distinct disadvantage when it comes to making employment decisions or negotiating pay with a potential or current employer. Economists refer to disparities in information resources between parties engaged in a potential or actual exchange as *information asymmetry*. They note that such asymmetries, broadly speaking, create an imbalance of power in transactions and potentially skew the decision-making of the weaker party. Sociologists and psychologists specifically study pay-related information asymmetries, with the former interested in how such asymmetries may foster inequality and entrench disparities based on characteristics such as gender or race, and the latter in how they can influence individual perceptions and attitudes, which in turn may drive or constrain different organizational attitudes and behaviors.

Although the question of pay-related information asymmetries (and pay fairness more generally) has attracted a lot of attention in the media and policy circles in recent years, the issue is far from new. Even the Bible makes reference to pay fairness: "Do not take advantage of a hired worker who is poor and needy, whether that worker is a fellow Israelite or a foreigner residing in one of your towns" (Deuteronomy 24:14–15). By the 19th century, the Industrial Revolution—and with it the emergence of large, complex organizations—intensified the salience of such issues. Indeed, by the start of the 20th century, employers, labor leaders, and policymakers were engaging with one another over such issues as employees' right to (a) know the criteria and processes by which pay is allocated in their organization; (b) receive information regarding average or median rates of pay for particular positions in their company, or even individual employees' actual pay; and (c) share or discuss their own pay information with others.

Fast-forward a century, and the same stakeholders are continuing to struggle with the same questions. The main difference between now and then is that we now have a small but growing body of empirical research able to inform and guide decision-making on these questions. In particular, during the past two decades, scholars from economics, psychology, sociology, management, and law have explored the issue from different angles, aiming to get a handle on the possible implications (and in particular, possible unintended negative consequences) of various transparency-related reforms. One set of questions concerns how pay transparency might impact interpersonal and labor–management relations in organizations. For example, might pay transparency lead employees earning less to resent those earning more, impairing teamwork and cooperation? Might managers respond by compressing the wage scale (i.e., reducing pay differentials between jobs or between employees in similar jobs), and what would this mean for the organization? Other questions concern the broader economic ramifications of pay transparency at a societal level, particularly if this is mandatory. Might mandatory wage transparency lead generally to wages becoming higher (e.g., by spurring labor market competition and boosting compliance with minimum wage and overtime requirements) or lower (e.g., by facilitating employer collusion or fueling capital market pressures to reduce labor costs)?[1] A third set of questions relates to ethical concerns. Do the public benefits of reducing pay information asymmetries trump employee privacy interests? Should compensation and benefits be treated as "trade secrets," and if so, might we not be violating the rights of employers by mandating the release of such information?

There is no shortage of opinions on such matters. Indeed, for decades, leaders in industry, government, labor, and academia have been debating the merits and costs of reforming conventional (largely secretive) approaches to managing pay-related information. Those favoring more transparent pay policies and processes, whether voluntary or mandated, offer a number of important arguments. First, they argue that pay transparency exposes discriminatory wage disparities, putting employers at risk of pay discrimination litigation and motivating them to, at the very least, reduce the growth in such disparities (Estlund, 2014; Ramachandran, 2012). In contrast, opacity in pay information "permits employers to exploit historical and societal discrimination (e.g., the tendency of certain demographic groups to bargain less aggressively for their own gain)" (Ramachandran, 2012, p. 1045).

Second, proponents of pay transparency argue that efficient labor markets, critical to a healthy economy, can be ensured only if both parties to an exchange are able to bargain freely on the basis of full information. Just as *employers* need to know competitive rates in the labor market in order to secure the human capital assets they require, *employees* need such information in order to effectively weigh their labor market options. Specifically, they must be able to assess (a) the fairness of their pay relative to that of their co-workers, (b) their future wage prospects within the organization, (c) the criteria and processes that will underlie any pay adjustments, and (d) how different positions in the organization are valued.

Third, some (e.g., Estlund, 2014) argue that greater transparency regarding vertical pay dispersion in firms (i.e., the differential in pay between positions at the top and bottom of the wage scale) could generate shareholder and consumer pressure to address what some might view as unjustifiable inequality. The resonance of this argument has been growing in recent years as executive pay (including options exercised) relative to that of the typical

---

[1] These questions were proposed by Estlund (2014).

worker has ballooned: from 20:1 in 1965 to 30:1 in 1978, 121:1 in 1995, and 386:1 in 2018 (Mishel & Wolfe, 2019). Finally, proponents argue that more transparent pay practices have the potential to boost employee performance, enhance employee trust in management, force management to be more accountable for (and be able to justify) pay differentials, and reduce undesired employee turnover (Colella et al., 2007; Belogolovsky & Bamberger, 2014; Alterman et al., 2021).

In contrast, those opposing pay transparency and in favor of retaining more restrictive pay communication policies and practices argue that pay information is "commercially valuable proprietary information that should be protected as a trade secret" (Estlund, 2014, p. 792). Indeed, as Bierman and Gely (2004) note, "Human resources professionals believe that properly designed employee compensation programs can represent a source of company competitive advantage" (p. 177). Accordingly, the release of such pay information could potentially facilitate "poaching" by an employer's competitors. In addition, they argue that releasing information about wages (particularly person-specific wages) is likely to generate jealousy and resentment, potentially creating a toxic environment or, at the very least, undermining efforts to boost team cohesion and collaboration. Of course, poaching may not always be a bad thing, at least from the perspective of the poached employee. Furthermore, one could argue that perceptions of unfairness and concomitant resentment can arise even when pay is secret. Nevertheless, as discussed in Chapter 3, there may indeed be reason to expect envy and resentment to be more persistent under conditions of transparency.

A third argument against pay transparency is that it may violate individual privacy rights. As noted by Ramchandran (2012),

> People in the United States often think it is dirty to talk about money. They associate money with status, and it is impolite to talk about status, or reveal it overtly. Thus, pay transparency may simply make some people uncomfortable. (p. 1068)

And if that's the case, can employers unilaterally violate such rights by disclosing employees' pay without their permission? Ramchandran (2012, p. 1069) argues that individual rights to maintain "malleable" social conventions that ultimately facilitate discrimination need to be balanced against the rights of discrimination victims and society as a whole.

Finally, proponents of pay secrecy argue that transparency is likely to motivate managers to compress employee pay (i.e., reduce the magnitude of pay
differentials between those contributing more and those contributing less to
the firm). To the extent that such differences in pay are justifiable, compression is likely to result in the inefficient allocation of reward resources, in that
those contributing more to the value of the firm are not rewarded appreciably
more than those contributing less. Moreover, this could result in what labor
economists call a negative sorting effect, with higher contributors leaving the
organization for a competitor better able to reward strong performance.

Clearly, both sides offer reasonable arguments. However, until recently, these arguments have been based more on conjecture than empirical evidence. Accordingly, the aim of this book is to shed light on recent
findings regarding the consequences of pay communication in order to offer
evidence-based insights into how pay communication policies and practices
may impact outcomes relevant to individuals, organizations, and the broader
societies in which they operate. I review these findings and integrate them
with rich new qualitative findings based on the experiences of employees and
managers in enterprises that have experimented with alternative pay communication strategies. My objective is to help a wide range of stakeholders
better understand the potential implications—whether intended or not—of
pay communication policies and practices. In short, this book aims to deliver
a long-overdue response to the question—"Is pay transparency a good thing
or a bad thing?"[2]—that student asked me back in 2005.

But before delving into that question and exploring the potential
implications of pay transparency, I answer the other question posed previously, namely, What happened? Why the sudden tidal wave of interest in
pay communication? Accordingly, I start by discussing how the issue of pay
communication emerged and examining the forces driving its contemporary relevance. Specifically, in Chapter 1, I draw from historic documents
and the work of labor historians to better understand how the question of
pay communication surfaced in the context of the Industrial Revolution.
I also examine recent shifts in demographics, employment relations, and
even technology as possible forces driving the contemporary debate over the
merits of pay transparency, as well as how these forces have come together in
the past decade to completely transform the regulatory framework underlying pay communication in numerous countries, states, and territories. On

[2] Now, whenever I am asked that question, I offer a simple answer: "Yes!"

the basis of this historical and regulatory context, in Chapter 2, I introduce some of the theoretical frameworks that have been used to understand and explain pay communication phenomena and their potential implications.

In Chapters 3–6, I demonstrate how these theoretical frameworks help us make sense of findings from dozens of empirical investigations. In Chapter 3, the focus is on findings regarding how various forms of pay transparency affect individual-level outcomes such as task performance, envy, contextual performance (i.e., soliciting help from or providing assistance to others), counterproductive work behavior, and intentions to remain with or leave the organization. In Chapter 4, I shift my attention to the organization-level implications of pay transparency, and specifically to how pay communication may influence the nature and distribution of rewards in the organization, organizational or unit-level climate, productivity, and rates of employee turnover. Chapter 5 adopts a similar focus on the implications of pay transparency, but this time at the level of society. Accordingly, in this chapter I review the evidence regarding whether and how pay transparency impacts economic inequality, labor mobility, and labor force well-being, and I ask how regulatory efforts regarding pay communication have impacted economy-wide pay disparities. In Chapter 6, I turn to the issue of employee pay disclosure and exchange, focusing on the ways employees may disclose pay information to one another and the factors influencing such behavior. In this chapter, I pay particular attention to research on employee privacy concerns and the efficacy of restrictive pay communication policies and practices.

In the book's final two chapters, my focus is on what these findings might mean for practice, policy, and research. Accordingly, in Chapter 7, I discuss the experiences of organizations that have actually experimented with different pay transparency policies and practices, presenting the insights of their managers and employees on the factors critical to the success of such efforts, as well as what they view as the most significant advantages and disadvantages of the approach adopted in their organizations. To conclude, Chapter 8 highlights some of the policy reforms that have been proposed to address pay communication concerns, and it identifies issues and questions that remain ripe for further scholarly examination.

I would be remiss in ending this preface without acknowledging those who helped make this book become a reality. First, I thank all of those with whom I have collaborated over the years in conducting research on pay communication, namely Tamar Verach, Elena Belogolovsky, Valeria Alterman, David

Wagner, Jason Shi, Mo Wang, Jackie Koopman, Ilanit Simantov-Nachlieli, Man-Nok Wong, Bonnie Cheng, Leon Lam, Michelle Brown, John Shields, and Paul Bliese. Second, I am grateful to Shir Erlichman for her assistance in securing materials that enriched what would have otherwise been a very dull and dry literature review. Similarly, I express my thanks to Meira Ben-Gad for editing this volume. Also deserving thanks are my editors at Oxford University Press, Abby Gross and James Cook, and the anonymous reviewers to whom they turned for input regarding the framing of the book and its final manifestation. Finally, to my wife Ellen and my three amazing children—Zach, Sarah, and Noa—who, each in their own way, gave me the support and love without which this book would have remained just a well-intentioned dream. It is to them that I dedicate this work.

1

The Historical and Legal Context of Pay Communication

Pay, and particularly *others'* pay, is a topic of interest to all of us. Although we may deem it inappropriate to ask our boss what others in the organization are earning, that doesn't mean we wouldn't like to know. Nor is this due merely to curiosity. Knowing the figures on others' paychecks is important because, lacking such information, it's difficult for us to assess how fair our own pay is, whether we are justified in seeking a raise, or whether it's worth our while to seek our fortune in some other organization or career. Moreover, we might look favorably upon greater transparency in pay-related matters not only as employees but also as citizens. Greater pay transparency might serve as a means to (a) better ensure that labor markets efficiently match individuals with those employers most able to leverage their talent; and (b) make it more difficult for employers to discriminate, whether intentionally or not, against women, minorities, and other disadvantaged groups with respect to pay.

But although we as *individuals* may have an interest in knowing about the pay of others, as *employers* we would probably prefer to keep mum (Bernstein, 2017). There are several reasons for this. First, pay information is often deemed private, and widespread disclosure of individuals' pay could potentially infringe on employees' privacy. Second, such information could get into the hands of our competitors, giving them insights into our cost structure, and perhaps providing a basis to poach our talent. Third, such information might make some employees envious of others, with damaging effects on cooperation and teamwork. Finally, *pay information asymmetry* (a situation in which one party [e.g., employers] has greater pay-related knowledge than its exchange partner [e.g., employees]) can give employers a significant advantage with regard to negotiating pay. Enhanced pay-related knowledge could give employees a platform to negotiate higher rates of pay—which could lead to an upward spiral in labor costs, harming employers' ability to compete, retain existing levels of employment, or provide a reasonable rate of return to investors.

Exposing Pay. Peter Bamberger, Oxford University Press. © Oxford University Press 2023.
DOI: 10.1093/oso/9780197628164.003.0001

Clearly, the question of pay information asymmetry in general, and pay transparency in particular, is complex, if not downright contentious. As demonstrated in this book, theory and empirical research offer important clues as to how managers, labor leaders, and policymakers may want to balance the competing interests and concerns noted above. However, before exploring this research, it makes sense to first understand the historical and legal context within which the contemporary debate is nested and the forces driving what appears to be a movement toward increased pay transparency. Accordingly, my objective in this chapter is to summarize the treatment of pay information asymmetry by employers, labor leaders, scholars, and policymakers during the past century and to isolate some of the primary historical forces that have likely contributed to the recent surge of interest in pay communication.

I begin by presenting a historical analysis of the role of information asymmetry in employment relations in the United States and other countries. Within this broad context, I then review the emergence of compensation and benefits management as a discipline, how approaches to it have changed over the decades, and how these changes provide a framework for understanding the recent emergence of pay communication as a critical issue in employment relations. In this chapter's third section, I use this historical backdrop to identify some of the factors potentially driving the emergent centrality of pay communication as a critical aspect of rewards management, as well as a surge of legislation promoting the adoption of more transparent pay practices in many countries throughout the world. I conclude the chapter by reviewing these legislative efforts and discussing some of the main types of regulatory interventions that have recently been adopted or that are under current consideration.

Pay Transparency in the Context of Contemporary Labor–Management Relations

Although research on pay communication is a relatively recent phenomenon (with the initial empirical studies appearing only in the 1960s), public discourse regarding the transparency of pay information can be traced to the debates over industrial democracy emerging at the start of the Industrial Revolution. Documenting this debate in the United Kingdom at the end of the 19th century, Sidney and Beatrice Webb (1897) wrote that employee voice in the workplace is "a necessary element in the democratic state" (p. 825) and that the sustainability of political democracy is questionable when "autocracy rules economic relations in general, and the workplace in particular" (p. 840). At the same time as they were espousing trade unions as a critical institution for ensuring employee voice in turn-of-the-century Britain, other institutions aiming to pursue the same objective had already begun to emerge across Europe. For instance, by the start of World War I, works councils were well established in Germany, as were factory councils in Italy (Gumbrell-McCormik & Hyman, 2019). Underlying all of these labor institutions was the idea, promoted by the Webbs (1897), that the (low) cost of labor should not serve as a basis for enterprises to gain a competitive advantage. However, to effectively execute on this idea of democratizing the workplace, labor leaders required access to employer financial information (e.g., profits and executive pay), which the latter were not anxious to share.

In the United States, employment relations were dramatically transformed during World War I, with its associated labor shortage and demands for increased production. Institutional economists such as John Commons, industrial engineers such as Frederick Taylor, and legal scholars such as Louis Brandeis all promoted the idea that enterprises might enhance their productivity and competitive advantage by viewing employees as assets and empowering them to take a role in deciding certain aspects of workplace relations (Kaufman, 2001). In his book *Industrial Goodwill*, Commons (1919) laid out an alternative strategy for managing labor that he defined as the "citizenship" approach (it subsequently became known as welfare capitalism). Kaufman (2001) describes how, where the dominant approaches of the day positioned the employer as "a dictator . . . who unilaterally determines the labor practices in the workplace" (p. 516), in Commons' proposed alternative,

> like citizens in a democracy, [employees] are given a voice in the determination of the terms and conditions of employment and are protected from arbitrary and capricious actions of management (the "rulers") by a system of due process in the shop. (p. 56)

Commons proposed worker representatives (i.e., unions) or employer-sponsored shop committees (similar to the German works councils) as a practical means to implement such a model.

Between the two world wars, American employees became increasingly involved in decisions regarding the terms and conditions of employment through growing union representation and collective bargaining. Collective bargaining enabled employees, via their elected representatives, to have a voice in determining issues relating to wages and benefits, as well as work scheduling and assignments, safety and health, and even subcontracting and technological change. However, already in the early years of collective bargaining, unions learned that their effectiveness at the negotiating table was contingent upon their ability to secure information that would allow them to better justify their demands, namely employer financial information. Only by getting management to "open the books" could unions substantiate their claims that employees were deserving of the rewards demanded, as well as delegitimize employer claims of an inability to pay. As in Europe, American employers had little interest in sharing information that would potentially strengthen the hand of their bargaining opponent.

Accordingly, by the 1930s, many countries had adopted legislation and established institutions aimed at regulating matters relating to collective bargaining. For instance, in the United States, the National Labor Relations Act (1935) established a set of rules to guide union organizing and collective bargaining, and it set up the National Labor Relations Board (NLRB) as the institution charged to adjudicate disputes over the regulatory regime. Among the issues the NLRB had to address were employers' reluctance to negotiate over matters for which they believed that they held "managerial prerogative" and to disclose information to the union relevant to the issues being negotiated. Indeed, already in 1936, just a year following the passage of the NLRA, the NLRB ruled that "the communication of facts peculiarly within the knowledge of either party is of the essence in the bargaining process" (Bellace & Gospel, 1983, p. 59), reinforcing the idea suggested by Cox and Dunlop (1950) that efforts to deny unions information undercut a "cardinal principal" of collective bargaining, namely that "employees are entitled to participate '*effectively*' in determining wages, hours, and other terms of employment affecting their interests and welfare" (p. 405). It is now well-established in the United States that unions have the right to receive information "relevant and necessary" to bargaining and to their administration of a contract, such as wage-related information. Unions also have the right to information substantiating employer claims of an inability to pay (*NLRB v. Truitt Manufacturing Co.*, 1956).

Despite the passage of legislation in the United States and Europe mandating the disclosure of certain forms of bargaining-relevant information to unions and works councils (for a review, see Bellace & Gospel, 1983), questions over the rights and obligations of employers concerning such disclosures remain as relevant today as they were nearly a century ago. From the perspective of unions, access to information is central to their ability to negotiate effectively. Employers, for their part, argue that "the statutory obligation to disclose information to unions is an invasion of managerial prerogatives" (Bellace & Gospel, 1983, p. 58) that jeopardizes commercial secrecy and confidentiality and impedes effective decision-making. Most likely, however, what really underlies employers' disquiet over the obligation to disclose are concerns that such disclosure may weaken their bargaining power vis-à-vis labor (Amernic, 1988). Are such concerns justified?

At least two studies suggest that they may be, or more precisely, that organizational financial transparency indeed shifts power dynamics within organizations. In a study of 100 manufacturing firms conducted in the 1980s, Kleiner and Bouillon (1988, p. 613) found that relative to companies not disclosing information to employees, average compensation at comparable firms that did disclose at least some information was 2 percent higher.

More recently, Rosenfeld and Denice (2015) argued that financial information asymmetries "privilege" certain actors or groups of actors over others (e.g., executives over employees or shareholders) when claiming returns on labor or organizational assets. Accordingly, they hypothesized that "opening up an organization's books to select workers or groups of workers may shift power downward in negotiations over the distribution of pay by spurring claims for higher pay or legitimating existing claims" (p. 1046). To test this conjecture, Rosenfeld and Denice used archival data on 27,000 workers employed in nearly 3,500 British workplaces, sampled to be representative of the British workforce, who were asked about the financial disclosure practices of their employers (at both the work unit/firm and individual levels). Taking into account a large number of potential confounding factors such as firm profitability, Rosenfeld and Denice found that hourly earnings were at least 8 percent higher among those indicating high or very high levels of financial information sharing (approximately 40 percent of participants) compared with low or very low levels (just over 25 percent of participants). Replicating a finding initially reported by Kleiner and Bouillon (1988), they also found no significant productivity differences associated with varying levels of information sharing. This is important in that if the wage differences are not attributable to any heightened motivation or productivity effect, it is likely that the observed effect may indeed be driven by the employees' enhanced bargaining power.

It would be wrong to conclude from these studies that requiring employers to provide financial information to employees or their representatives necessarily gives the latter an undue advantage. Rather, recognizing that, as noted by Estlund (2011), "information asymmetries confer a bargaining advantage on the more informed party" (p. 372), it's probably more accurate to conclude that such obligations simply reduce labor's inherent bargaining *dis*advantage. That is, if anything, this brief review of the history of labor's battle for greater access to enterprises' financial information reinforces Ferrante and Rousseau's (2001) contention that "workers who understand the company books and their contribution to the bottom line can bargain quite differently than those lacking such information" (p. 112).

Drilling Down: The Emergence and Changing Nature of Compensation and Benefits Management

If the establishment of a discipline is defined by the founding of a professional organization, then compensation and benefits management as a professional discipline is a relatively recent phenomenon. The field's professional association—the American Compensation Association—was only established in 1955. The same year saw the publication of one of the first major texts on compensation, David Belcher's *Compensation Administration*. But as suggested by the short survey of contemporary labor history above, debate over the remuneration of labor and how to administer such remuneration precedes that by several decades.

Prior to World War I, pay in industrial enterprises (along with recruitment, selection, and training) was largely the responsibility of supervisors. Supervisors set production standards as well as rates of pay, largely compensating employees on the basis of a piece-rate system, or in other words, as a function of their output (a rudimentary form of what is now called pay for performance). Indeed, more than 60 percent of manufacturers responding to a 1920 National Industrial Conference Board survey reported using piece rates, and 80 percent of all workers were employed in plants where piece rates were used. Little was offered outside of cash compensation (Milkovich & Stevens, 2000). However, World War I ushered in innovations in rewards management as an element of Frederick Taylor's "scientific management." According to Walter Matherly (1926), the war made it "imperative to adjust the industrial machine to meet the wartime demands of the

Allies for supplies and munitions. When the United States decided to enter the conflict, the improvement and conservation of human resources became all the more important" (p. 256). Immediately following the war, the need for workforce stability, concerns about increasing labor militancy, and an interest in driving increased consumer demand led a number of large firms such as Ford and Proctor & Gamble to adopt many of the ideas proposed by Taylor and his disciples, including offering workers guaranteed wages based on hours worked rather than output produced, and providing them with rudimentary economic security in the form of such benefits as medical insurance and pensions (Balderston, 1935; Kaufman, 2001).

The Great Depression and World War II led to the widespread adoption of such principles, forming the core of the "Great Social Contract" (Kochan, 2000) that transformed employment relations in the United States and much of the industrialized world. With unemployment at 30 percent in 1939, payrolls half or a third of what they were a decade earlier (i.e., prior to the massive Wall Street sell-off in October 1929), and the rapid growth of industrial unionism, governments established regulatory frameworks designed to usher in more stable forms of employment relationships. This new governing regime left enterprises little choice but to shift the nature, form, and administration of remuneration. In the United States, legislation—including the Social Security Act (1935), the National Labor Relations Act (1935), and the Fair Labor Standards Act (1938)—was accompanied by mechanisms (e.g., the War Stabilization Board of World War II) designed to stabilize the economy and control wage increases. This broad-scale transformation in employment relations, with its focus on labor stability in return for employment security, was largely grounded on the principles of rationality and predictability promoted earlier by Taylor and the welfare capitalists (Kaufman, 2001). Accordingly, as noted by Milkovich and Stevens (2000), "By the late 1940s, compensation had moved from the individual contract, incentive, market-oriented system of the early 1900s to a system embedded in regulated bureaucracies" (p. 10). With the focus on long-term employment relations and economic security, this employment framework, characterized by labor economists as an "internal labor market" approach, shifted away from cash-based remuneration tied to *individual* performance and toward hourly remuneration based on the relative contribution of the *job* to the organization, along with a focus on non-cash forms of rewards, including health insurance, pensions, and pay for time not worked (Bamberger, Biron, et al., 2014).

This focus on predictability and pay equity was further reinforced by the introduction of additional regulatory frameworks as part of the 1963 Equal Pay Amendment to the Fair Labor Standards Act and Title 7 of the Civil Rights Act of 1964. Emerging from this new employment relations regime was a set of standard rewards management practices, summarized by Belcher (1955) in what was effectively the first textbook on contemporary compensation administration. In this book, mentioned earlier, Belcher makes reference to pay levels and ladders, with differentials between levels established on the basis of internal equity (i.e., the relative contribution of a given job to the value of the firm) and executed on the basis of such techniques as job analysis and job evaluation. Belcher did not dismiss the need for pay to be market competitive and to reward individual contributions, and his book also introduced analytic approaches—salary surveys and individual merit charts—for taking these considerations into account. But with well over 30 percent of the workforce in the United States (and far higher proportions in Europe) employed under the terms of collective agreements, and with standard, job-based hourly wages replacing individual incentives (in the United States, incentives accounted for a mere 12 percent of total compensation in 1950; Milkovich & Stevens, 2000), remuneration for most was relatively transparent, and any individual variance within pay levels was driven largely by employee seniority or tenure.

Yet over the decades, the role of individual contributions in compensation considerations has once again come to prominence. Individual incentives rose from 12 percent of total compensation in 1950 to more than 25 percent by the end of the 1970s. By the 1990s, the Conference Board, along with various compensation consulting companies (e.g., Towers Perrin), could report that well over one-third of U.S. enterprises were using individual performance-based bonuses and other performance-based incentives (Milkovich & Stevens, 2000). As of 2010, 42 percent of jobs in the United States were characterized as ones in which remuneration was incentive-based (e.g., sales commissions and piecework) or included some "non-production bonus," based on some subjective assessment of individual performance or contribution (Gittelman & Pierce, 2015). Several factors have been noted as having played a role in driving this shift back toward individual performance-based remuneration, including (a) a shift in employment from manufacturing (dominated by pay based on hourly wages) to services (with many in this sector compensated on the basis of salary), and hence forms of work with greater outcome variability and employee discretion; (b) the wide-scale availability of well-educated baby boomers (thus reducing firms' reliance on internal labor markets); and (c) heightened global competition and globalization, which have forced enterprises to adopt "high-performance work systems" (Kristal et al., 2020; Milkovich & Stevens, 2000). But one of the most fundamental drivers of this return to pay for individual performance was undoubtedly the global decline in union density and the proportion of the workforce covered under collective agreements (Arrowsmith & Marginson, 2011; Kristal et al., 2020).

This contemporaneous decline in union-based employment with a return toward individual, performance-based pay is notable in that these two trends likely play an important role in explaining the rising interest in pay communication. Here's why. Already in 1923, in an early volume on employee compensation, Daniel Bloomfield noted that the effectiveness of an incentive plan is contingent upon the degree to which the plan meets seven main considerations, three of which are the following: (a) promoting confidence and understanding between the employer and employees, (b) informing participants as to the factors affecting their payments and incentives, and (c) involving participants in administration of the plan. Bloomfield (as well as Belcher [1955], and William Whyte [1955] some 30 years later) suggested that plans lacking these components are likely to "foster a lack of trust and cooperation" between labor and management (Milkovich & Stevens, 2000, p. 10). Unions' insistence that pay be standardized by job (with any individual variance based on objective determinants of contribution such as seniority), as well as their involvement in setting the terms of job-based remuneration, increased the likelihood of all three of these conditions being met. However, by the 1980s, a drastic reduction in the number of workers covered by collective agreements, combined with a movement away from internal labor market employment arrangements, created a context in which individual-level factors (e.g., subjectively appraised performance) were becoming increasingly central in determining pay and the "participants" (i.e., labor) had less insight into (let alone control over) the processes determining their pay.

So Why the Current Interest in Pay Transparency?

Early Moves Toward Pay Transparency

Media references to issues of pay transparency prior to the 1980s are extremely limited, with the exception of those linked to three widely reported incidents or scandals. The first of these—the *Vanity Fair* case—involved the right of employees to disclose their pay to one another. The case, as reported by Steele (1975, pp. 102–103), involved Robert Benchley and his fellow writers at the magazine. On October 14, 1919, the *Vanity Fair* management published a policy memo stating the following:

> It has been the policy of the organization to base salaries on the value of services rendered. We have, therefore, a long established rule that the salary question is a confidential matter between the organization and the individual. It is obviously important that employees live up to this rule in order to avoid invidious comparison and dissatisfaction. Recently several cases have come to the notice of management where employees have discussed the salary question among themselves. This memorandum should serve as a warning that anyone who breaks this rule in the future will be instantly discharged.

According to Steele, Benchley responded the next day with his own memo:

> We emphatically resent both the policy and wording of your policy memorandum of October 14. We resent being told what we may and what we may not discuss, and we protest against the spirit of petty regulation which has made possible the sending out of such an edict.

That same day, Benchley and colleagues reportedly strolled around the office casually swinging signs from their necks on which their salaries were clearly written. The management of *Vanity Fair* surrendered and dropped their policy forbidding employee discussions of pay.

Ten years later, the media began to report on a brewing scandal regarding excesses in executive pay at Bethlehem Steel and American Tobacco (Mas, 2016). The growing pressure emerging from this media coverage led to the 1932–1933 Pecora hearings and culminated in a Senate resolution mandating that the Federal Trade Commission report the names of listed enterprises whose executive officers held more than $1 million in assets. As Mas notes, 877 such enterprises were listed in the subsequent report, the details of which were published in *The New York Times* in February 1934. This report, together with a separate Harvard Business School report on executive pay in the retail sector (J. Baker, 1939), "fueled further disgust with executive pay levels" (Mas, 2016, p. 8). However, legislators hesitated to set limits on executive pay or to pass laws facilitating the prosecution of individual cases in which executive pay seemed counter to shareholder interests. Instead, they opted to use the weapon of mandatory public disclosure in the form of the Securities and Exchange Act, which required publicly listed enterprises to disclose the pay of their three highest paid executives—"a less intrusive measure that would allow public scrutiny to curb CEO pay" (Mas, 2016, p. 11). Yet, although the intent was to incentivize more limited increases in executive pay by creating a backlash among shareholders, in fact, as noted by Mas, the impact was precisely the opposite. With comparisons between enterprises greatly facilitated, executives and boards felt justified in raising executive pay in order to secure or retain what was perceived as the best talent, and executive salaries generally ratcheted up as a result of the new disclosure regulations.

The third historical event relating to pay transparency occurred just 1 year later, with the passage of the National Labor Relations Act. As noted earlier, one section of this law required employers to bargain in good faith, with these provisions subsequently being interpreted as requiring employers to provide their union bargaining partners with access to information relevant to the issues being negotiated, such as enterprise financial data. But a second section of this law (namely Section 7) emerged as the foundation for one key aspect of pay transparency in the United States (Bierman & Gely, 2004), namely what Fulmer and Chen (2014) refer to as pay communication transparency (a term that is discussed in greater detail in Chapter 2). This section of the law reads as follows:

> Employees shall have the right to self-organization, to form, join, or assist labor organizations, to bargain collectively through representatives of their own choosing, and to engage in *other concerted activities* for the purpose of collective bargaining or *other mutual aid or protection* [italics added].

Using this section of the National Labor Relations Act, initial court rulings in the 1950s (e.g., *NLRB v. Babcock & Wilcox Co.*, 1956) affirmed the right of *unions* to distribute to employees employment-related information pertaining to a union-organizing campaign, noting that "the right of self-organization depends in some measure on the ability of employees to learn the advantages of self-organization from others."

However, it was not until the 1970s that questions emerged regarding the extension of this landmark decision in *NLRB v. Babcock & Wilcox Co.* to cases involving *individual* employees discussing their pay with others.

Specifically, in *Jeannette Corp. v. NLRB* (1976), the U.S. Court of Appeals ruled that the Jeannette Corporation had violated Section 7 of the National Labor Relations Act when it discharged an employee, Cheryl McNeely, for discussing wages with other employees, on the grounds that her behavior had the potential to elicit "jealousies and strife among employees." Since then, numerous other cases involving employee wage disclosures have made their way to adjudication, with the NLRB and the courts consistently ruling against employers seeking to enforce broad, and often informal, pay disclosure prohibitions. For example, in the 1989 case of *Brookshire Grocery v. Mark Moise*, the NLRB found in favor of Mark Moise, who was terminated by his employer for sharing with colleagues information on wage increases that he happened to come across during the course of his duties. The NLRB ruled that Moise's employer could not prohibit employees from discussing wages, and it mandated his reinstatement. A year later, in *Service Merchandise Company, Inc. v. Priscilla Jones*, the NLRB again ruled against the employer for enforcing a company policy forbidding all wage-related discussions. As a remedy, the company was required to revise its policy and post the following statement at each of its locations: "The company will not distribute, maintain, or enforce rules prohibiting you from discussing your wages or other terms or conditions of employment with others."

Despite such consistent rulings, and the passage of similar legislation at the state level, employers in the United States still overwhelmingly "encourage" their employees to refrain from discussing or disclosing even their own pay information with co-workers. Data collected by the Institute for Women's Policy Research show that 41 percent of private companies continue to actively discourage employees from talking about pay on the job, and another 25 percent formally prohibit pay discussions under threat of disciplinary action (Hayes, 2017). Only 17 percent of private companies in the United States explicitly allow employees to discuss their pay at work (Hayes, 2017).

Forces Driving Scholarly Interest in the 1960s and 1970s

In addition to the first cases of individual employee pay disclosures discussed previously, the 1960s and 1970s saw some of the first scholarly research on pay communication, with the publication of studies by Edward Lawler (1965, 1966, 1967), Milkovich and Anderson (1972), and Schuster and Colletti (1973). The studies by Lawler, along with Milkovich and Anderson's (1972) article, provided initial explorations of the degree to which managers accurately assess the pay of their supervisors and colleagues under conditions of pay secrecy. I present a more thorough review of these studies and their findings in Chapter 3, but suffice it to say here that according to these studies, managers tend to overestimate the pay of their peers and underestimate the pay of those hierarchically superior to them. The study by Schuster and Colletti (1973) examined the attitudes of professional employees toward pay secrecy versus greater transparency and found their "respondents divided about equally regarding preferences for pay secrecy" (p. 39). But what's most interesting for our purposes here is what motivated this seminal line of research on pay transparency in the first place.

Although research had already shown that comparisons with referent others influence employee attitudes toward pay (Adams, 1963; Festinger, 1957; Patchen, 1961), Lawler (1965) observed that little was known as to how employees conduct such comparisons, particularly in contexts in which comparative pay information is largely unavailable. Accordingly, a primary motivation was to examine the effect that "secrecy policies ... have on the accuracy with which managers perceive the pay rates of their comparison groups" (pp. 413–414). In addition, based on the conjecture that managers may perform better to the degree that they accurately comprehend the factors that determine their pay, Lawler (1966) also sought a better "understanding of managers' perceptions of the pay plans to which they are subject" (p. 274). Lawler argued that although collective bargaining does not restrict management's ability to impose performance-based incentives on exempt or salaried (i.e., professional, technical, and managerial) employees, such incentive programs may be limited in their effectiveness because white-collar employees typically lack an understanding of how performance and pay are linked in their organization. As evidence of this, Lawler (1966) cited Chalupsky's (1964) finding that one-third of scientists in research organizations were unaware that their salary increases were performance-based. Finally, Lawler was motivated by an interest in demonstrating the link between pay transparency and organizational effectiveness. As he told me, "I thought that secrecy leads to bad pay decisions because it reduces the need to justify decisions" (personal communication, January 16, 2021).

The timing of this emergent interest in pay communication is not surprising, as it coincided with the return to remuneration based substantially on individual incentives for a growing proportion of the U.S. workforce

(Milkovich & Stevens, 2020), itself driven by the two labor market shifts previously mentioned—the decline of the manufacturing sector and the decline in union influence. As shown in Figure 1.1, at the end of World War II, the private-sector labor force in the United States was roughly evenly split between service and manufacturing, at 48 percent each (with the remaining 4 percent in agriculture). By 1970, less than 40 percent of the workforce was engaged in manufacturing; and by 1980, services accounted for more than 70 percent of the private-sector workforce. Moreover, in the United States, the composition of the service sector shifted over the same years, from subsectors that were more heavily unionized, such as communications and transport, to sectors such as financial and business services, which were (and remain) largely union-free and which employed a greater proportion of staff on a salary basis (Visser, 1991).

The decline of union influence involved not only a failure of union membership rosters to keep up with the growing labor force (i.e., lower union density) but also the increasingly smaller proportion of the workforce employed under collective bargaining agreements. With respect to the former,

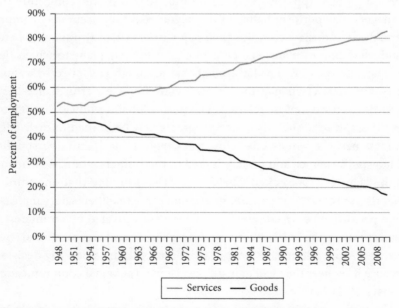

Figure 1.1 Private-sector employment as percentage of total private employment: 1948–2010.
Source: Johnson (2012).

union membership in the United States peaked at approximately 36 percent just after World War II, declining to 25 percent by 1980 (Cornfield, 1986). Even in the heavily unionized manufacturing sector, the percentage of unionized workers declined from 51.3 percent in 1956 to 39.9 percent in 1978. A similar decline in the proportion of employees covered by collective agreements occurred during the same period, with approximately 40 percent covered by such agreements in the mid-1950s, declining to 35 percent in 1960, 30 percent in 1970, and 25 percent in 1980 (Organisation for Economic Co-operation and Development, 2021).

Given the difficulties inherent to monitoring and controlling work processes in the rapidly growing service sector, managers increasingly turned to financial incentives as a means to ensure individual contributions (Bamberger, Biron, et al., 2014; Eisenhardt, 1989). The fact that, particularly in these growing employment sectors, collective agreements were more the exception than the rule made it easy for them to do so. However, with performance outputs less quantifiable in the service sector, organizational psychologists such as Lawler began to question the assumed motivational effects of incentives and, indeed, to point to their possible disincentivizing implications—for example, the possibility that subjective assessments could lead to perceptions of unfairness (Adams, 1963) or that unclear effort–reward contingencies could make employees doubt their chance of ever being rewarded (Vroom, 1964).

Yet, while such concerns appear to have laid the theoretical foundations motivating Lawler, Milkovich and Anderson, and a handful of other scholars to begin exploring whether and how pay transparency might address some of these problems with individual incentives, their research had little impact on either employers or policy. Access to pay information, and pay communication more generally, remained largely restricted.

Heightened Public Awareness and Regulatory Action in the New Millennium

The factors that drove initial scholarly interest in pay communication in the 1960s and 1970s intensified over the following 50 years. Throughout the world, union density continued to decline (in the United States, it fell to 10.3 percent overall in 2019 and just 6.2 percent in the private sector), while employment in the service sector continued to rise, topping 80 percent in

2019 (U.S. Bureau of Labor Statistics, 2020). However, two other period-relevant trends likely underlie the recent tidal wave of interest in pay communication: a growing public discourse on employment discrimination and the information technology revolution, which has facilitated the sharing and exchange of pay information.

In the United States, concerns regarding discrimination in employment led to the adoption of two important pieces of legislation in the 1960s. The first of these was the Equal Pay Act of 1963, which amended the 1938 Fair Labor Standards Act by prohibiting employers from paying different wages based on sex (although it did not preclude discrimination in hiring). Specifically, this law required employers to remunerate men and women equally when they engaged in work requiring "equal skill, effort, and responsibility and performed under similar working conditions." A year later, with the passage of the Civil Rights Act (and in particular, its Title VII clauses), the federal government expanded its protection against employment discrimination to include a wider range of activities (including hiring) and a broader range of ascribed individual characteristics, including race, color, religion, sex, and national origin. It also created an agency mandated to administer the law, namely the Equal Employment Opportunity Commission (EEOC). Similar legislation was enacted in the United Kingdom in the 1970s, including the U.K. Equal Pay Act (1970), the Sex Discrimination Act of 1975, and the Race Relations Act of 1976.

These legislative initiatives played a significant role in enabling women and minorities to enter occupations previously dominated by males and members of ethnic majorities (i.e., Whites). Yet, perhaps because some courts have been reluctant to hold employers liable for market-based pay discrimination (Adler, 2021) or discrimination resulting from social factors, such as the fact that women and minorities often negotiate less aggressively (Hegewisch et al., 2011; Ramachandran, 2012), they failed to fully address the problem of gender and ethnic pay disparities. It is true that the gender pay gap in the United States has declined substantially. As shown in Figure 1.2, the median earnings of women, without controlling for various compensable factors such as job title and years of experience, rose from just 64 cents for every dollar earned by men in 1980 to 85 cents in 2018 (Barroso & Brown, 2021). According to Chamberlain et al. (2019), in 2019 women in the United States earned approximately 79 cents for every male-earned dollar, or 95 cents per male dollar when controlling for age, education and experience, job title, employer, and location (a figure still greater than that of the gender

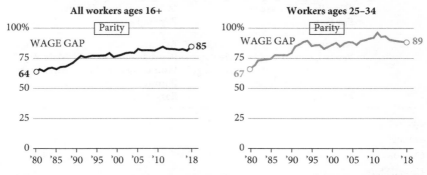

The gender pay gap is narrower among young adults than among workers overall
Median hourly earnings of U.S. women as percentage of men's median among...

Figure 1.2 The gender pay gap in the United States: 1980–2018. Estimates are for civilian, non-institutionalized, full- or part-time employed workers with positive earnings. Self-employed workers are excluded.
Source: Pew Research Center (2021).

pay gap in several other Western economies, such as the United Kingdom and Canada; Table 1.1). Yet, although these differences may appear small, particularly because they appear immediately when young workers enter the labor force (e.g., a 2021 report by the National Association of Colleges and Employers found that newly minted female college graduates earned an average of $52,266 in 2020, compared to $64,022 for their male peers [Sheen, 2022]), when aggregated across a 40-year career, they can amount to a difference equivalent to hundreds of thousands of dollars (Payscale, 2020a; Sheen, 2022). Racial disparities remain as well, with Black males earning 87 cents on average for every dollar earned by White males in 2018, and Hispanic males earning 91 cents for every dollar earned by White men (SHRM, 2020).

A second force driving heightened public interest in pay communication was technological in nature. With the growth of the internet, detailed and accurate pay data, once available only to employers willing and able to fund pay surveys, have become available to all. The founding of Glassdoor in 2007, and the ability of individuals to anonymously and securely exchange personal pay data with one another, has made employer restrictions on employee pay disclosure largely irrelevant, thus drastically reducing the degree of pay information asymmetry experienced 100 years ago by Robert Benchley at *Vanity Fair*. Indeed, Karabarbounis and Pinto (2018) report that between 2010 and 2017, annual user salary entries (required for salary

Table 1.1 The Gender Pay Gap by Country

	"Unadjusted" Base Gender Pay Gap		"Adjusted" Base Gender Pay Gap	
	Average Cents/ Pence Earned by Women per Dollar/ Pound/Euro of Male Earnings	Percentage Male Pay Advantage	Average Cents/ Pence Earned by Women per Dollar/ Pound/Euro of Male Earnings	Percentage Male Pay Advantage
Australia	0.85	15.1	0.97	3.1
France	0.88	11.6	0.96	3.7
Canada	0.84	16.1	0.96	4.0
United States	0.79	21.4	0.95	4.9
United Kingdom	0.82	17.9	0.95	5.0
Singapore	0.87	12.8	0.95	5.2
Germany	0.78	22.3	0.94	6.4
Netherlands	0.81	18.9	0.93	6.6

Source: Glassdoor Economic Research (http://www.Glassdoor.com/research/gender-pay-gap-2019).

searches) increased from approximately 290,000 to approximately 1,100,000 on Glassdoor alone.

As a result of these various forces, by 2009, the political ecosystem in the United States and other countries was ripe for regulatory attention to the question of pay communication. In the United States, the Lilly Ledbetter case was the straw that broke the camel's back, unleashing a series of executive orders and legislative initiatives over the course of the Obama administration, all aimed at regulating employer restrictions on employees' pay-related knowledge and communication.

Ledbetter was the lone female supervisor among 16 male supervisors for Goodyear Tire in Alabama. When she joined the firm in 1979, she signed an employment contract barring her from discussing her pay with her co-workers. In 1998, 2 years after winning a Top Performance Award, she received an anonymous note listing the names of four supervisors and their monthly salaries, including her own. Ledbetter was earning $3,727 per month, compared with $4,286 to $5,236 a month for the other three supervisors named in the note. Ledbetter sued Goodyear for employment discrimination under Title VII of the Civil Rights Act (see above), arguing that a series of discriminatory evaluations early in her career (in 1979–1981) had kept her pay artificially low. Nearly 10 years after her initial claim, the case reached the Supreme Court. In 2007, the Court accepted Goodyear's argument that Ledbetter's claim fell outside the statute of limitations, which was set at 180 days from when any discriminatory decisions on pay had been made. As a result, years of gender-based pay discrimination evidence was deemed inadmissible. Justice Ginsberg, in a dissenting opinion, noted that it was up to Congress to rectify this loophole in the law. Two years later, in early 2009, Congress passed the Lilly Ledbetter Fair Pay Act, which subsequently became the first law signed by President Obama. It specified that the 180-day statute of limitations under Title VII would reset with each new paycheck affected by that discriminatory action, thereby allowing evidence dating back to the initial act of discrimination underlying the unfair payment (which may have been years prior). Nevertheless, the law imposed a 2-year cap on potential penalties so that even if an employee can show evidence of 10 years of pay discrimination, the award can only "correct" for the most recent 2 years (Ramachandran, 2012).

The New Regulatory Landscape

The Lilly Ledbetter Fair Pay Act, together with the growing consensus around the need to address gender-based pay discrepancies more generally, triggered several waves of intense regulatory action in the United States and throughout the world aimed at making pay more transparent, and thereby reducing the asymmetry in pay information deemed to facilitate pay discrimination. Although it is beyond the scope of this review to discuss the details of all of the regulatory actions taken, Table 1.2 highlights some of the more prominent examples of laws regulating pay communication throughout the world. Here, I briefly summarize the primary actions taken in the past decade in the United States and a number of European countries.

United States

Following the enactment of the Lilly Ledbetter Fair Pay Act, President Obama and Congressional Democrats attempted to expand regulatory oversight of private-sector pay communication restrictions by proposing

Table 1.2 Chronology of Pay Transparency Legislation in Selected Countries

Law	Year Legislation Was Passed	Country of Origin	Brief Explanation
Equality Act 2010	2010	United Kingdom	Includes legal victimization provisions protecting employees who seek or disclose pay information and a ban on contractual "gagging" clauses.
Civil Service Act (CSA)	2012	Estonia	Stipulates disclosure of the remuneration of state officials (basic salary, variable pay, and other income) via publication on the state's official website. According to the CSA, this should include a guide to the applicable pay conditions. However, regulations to this effect have not yet been drafted.
The Workplace Gender Equality Act 2012	2012	Australia	Requires non-public-sector employers with 100 or more staff to submit a report to the Workplace Gender Equality Agency in April or May each year for the preceding 12-month period.
Gender Pay Gap Act	2012	Belgium	Requires private-sector enterprises with at least 50 employees to report every 2 years on gender-segregated mean basic pay and allowances for each employee category, job level, job evaluation class (if applicable), seniority, and education level.
Equal Pay Act	2016	Denmark	Extends a preexisting requirement to report wage statistics for companies with at least 35 employees by reducing that number to 10 employees. The law does not specify additional requirements for the pay report other than that it has to be sufficient for dialogue with the employees' representatives.
Labour Code 2016	2016	Lithuania	Obligates companies with 20 or more employees to inform works councils and trade unions of pay levels broken down by gender.
Act on the Transparency of Pay	2017	Germany	Promotes gender equality in pay. Provides for the individual right to information about remuneration paid to peers for organizations with more than 200 employees.

Table 1.2 Continued

Law	Year Legislation Was Passed	Country of Origin	Brief Explanation
Law Prohibiting Pay Discrimination Between Men and Women	2017	Peru	Prohibits wage discrimination between men and women in equivalent or identical categories or functions. Companies are required to keep tables detailing employee categories and functions.
Equality Act— Gender Pay Gap Information Regulations	2017	United Kingdom	Requires all enterprises with more than 250 employees to publish information relating to the gender pay gap in their organization.
Swedish Discrimination Act	2017	Sweden	Institutes a mandatory gender pay survey and analysis to be performed by employers, leading up to a gender wage action plan or a written pay audit report.
Pay Equity Act	2018 (in force as of August 31, 2021)	Canada	Requires employers to draft and post pay equity plans for the purpose of identifying and resolving gender wage gaps. The plans must follow a strict set of criteria, which obliges organizations to: identify job classes, determine if gender predominance exists in those job classes, evaluate work, calculate compensation, and compare compensation. Much of the work is to be done by a committee comprising employees who will be given access to the pay information they deem necessary. Upon completion of the above tasks, employers must increase compensation for the predominantly female job classes that are comparatively underpaid within 3–5 years of the law's effective date.
Pay Transparency Act	2018	Province of Ontario, Canada	Requires employers to report their pay practices to the Ministry of Labor and authorizes the appointment of compliance officers to investigate whether employers have complied with the Act. The Act has yet to be implemented.

(continued)

Table 1.2 Continued

Law	Year Legislation Was Passed	Country of Origin	Brief Explanation
Sunshine List Legislation	Initiated in Ontario in 1996	Most of the Canadian provinces	Requires some form of salary disclosure for top public sector earners, including those employed by federal Crown corporations such as the Bank of Canada or Via Rail Canada.
Equal Pay Law	2018	Iceland	Requires enterprises with more than 250 employees to obtain Equal Pay Certification every 3 years, proving that they pay women and men equally. To obtain the certification, employers must show compliance with the "Equal Pay Standard," a protocol developed jointly by Iceland's unions, the employers' confederation, and government officials. Companies failing to receive the certification can be fined.
Royal Decree—Law 6/2019	2019	Spain	Requires companies to keep a wage register by professional category and gender available for review by employee representatives. In addition, companies with more than 50 employees must provide justification when the average pay for employees of one gender is at least 25% above that of the other.
Amendment to the Equal Pay for Male and Female Employees Law, 1996	2020	Israel	Expands 1996 legislation covering state/public entities to apply to all employers with more than 518 employees. From June 21, 2022, firms must prepare an annual report analyzing employees' average salary by gender, job role, and ranking, and publish the average percentage pay gap by gender and employee group.

Sources: Estonia, Belgium, Denmark, Lithuania, and Sweden: European Commission (2021); Australia and Germany: Demand Pay Transparency (2021); United Kingdom: Queen's Printer of Acts of Parliament (2010); Canada: Canadian Legal Information Institute (2021), Comartin (2018), and Doolittle (2021); Iceland: Workplace Justice (2020); Peru: Lewis et al. (2018); Israel: Mercer (2020).

the Paycheck Fairness Act. Key provisions in this legislation (proposed in early 2009) aimed at prohibiting employer retaliation against employees for discussing pay-related matters and requiring the EEOC to collect from employers data on the sex, race, and national origin of employees along with their pay information for use in the enforcement of federal laws prohibiting pay discrimination. Congressional filibusters and procedural debates led to four separate attempts at passage from 2010 through 2014, all ending with votes largely along party lines, and all ending in failure.

In response, the Obama administration took steps to achieve similar, but more limited, policy objectives on the basis of several executive orders. The first of these (Executive Order 13665) put federal contractors at risk of losing their contracts if found to discriminate against employees "who inquire about, discuss, or disclose their own compensation or the compensation of other employees or applicants." The second, the "Fair Pay Safe Workplaces" Order (Executive Order 13673), required that contractors disclose violations of federal labor laws and executive orders addressing wage and hour, safety and health, collective bargaining, family and medical leave, and civil rights protections. This executive order was rescinded by President Trump in April 2017. Finally, in 2016, President Obama signed a Presidential Memorandum instructing the EEOC to expand Form EEO-1 (requiring federal contractors with more than 50 employees, and all employers with more than 100 employees, to report on their employment of women and minorities) to include information on rates of pay broken down by race, gender, and ethnicity. The requirement to complete the expanded form was to have gone into effect in September 2017. However, in August 2017, President Trump suspended the initiative indefinitely. Notably, Executive Order 13665 (which prohibits contractors from retaliating against employees who disclose their pay to others) was never rescinded by the Trump administration.

With Congress failing to address growing public concerns about gender pay discrepancies, legislators at the state level also began to fill in the gap (Figure 1.3). To date, 25 states (including New York, Michigan, Illinois, and California) and the District of Columbia have enacted pay transparency legislation (Trusaic, 2022). In 15 of these states, the law pertains to virtually all employees, whereas in 10 states, certain employees are exempt (e.g., domestic service workers and employees of religious organizations) (Bölingen, 2021). The laws enacted are, for the most part, aimed at ensuring that employees

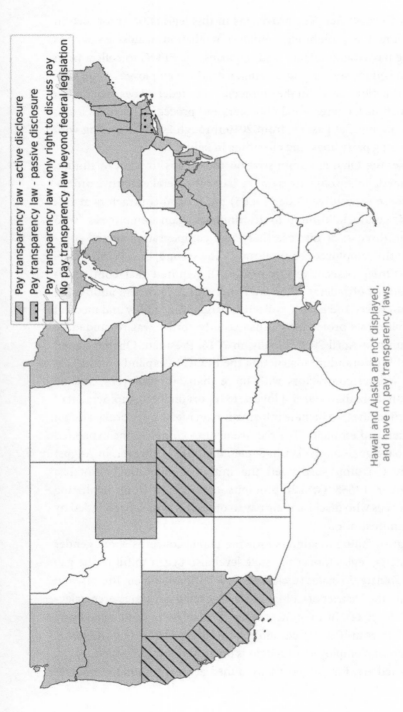

Figure 1.3 U.S. States — Pay transparency laws and aspect of pay communication. Twenty-five states have enacted pay transparency laws granting employees the right to discuss pay. Given extant federal laws (e.g, Executive Order 13665; NLRA) already guaranteeing such rights to non-exempt employees, these state laws merely extend such rights to employees exempt from federal coverage (e.g., supervisors and managers). Only one state, Colorado, mandates active disclosure of pay-related information (i.e., disclosure of pay rates or ranges, as well as bonuses and benefits). Passive disclosure (Connecticut and Rhode Island) mandates that employers provide pay rates or ranges to candidates or employees requesting such information for the position to which they are applying or currently fill.

Source: Bölingen (2021).

receive (in writing) the basic terms of employment (e.g., their wages and hours), prohibiting employers from asking job candidates about their wage history, and barring employers from discriminating against employees who engage in pay disclosure behavior or who refuse to sign employment contract provisions requiring them to refrain from such behavior. For example, New York State's Wage Theft Prevention Act, passed in 2011, requires all employers to provide written notice of rates of pay, including overtime and manner of payment (e.g., hourly, weekly, or piecework-based), at the time of hiring and then annually and whenever the terms change (Estlund, 2011, p. 784). More recently (and effective as of January 2020), the state of New York and 20 other U.S. states and territories prohibited all employers from asking prospective employees about their salary history and compensation. Section 1197.5(k) of the California State Labor Code serves as an example of a regulation protecting employee pay disclosure. It specifies that "an employer shall not prohibit an employee from disclosing the employee's own wages, discussing the wages of others, or inquiring about another employee's wages." Similarly, Sections 232(a)–(c) of the California Labor Code prohibit employers from requiring,

> as condition of employment, that an employee refrain from disclosing the amount of his or her wages, or that an employee sign a waiver or other document purporting to deny the employee the right to disclose the amount of his or her wages; additionally, an employer may not discharge, formally discipline, or otherwise discriminate against an employee who discloses the amount of his or her wages. (California Legislative Information, n.d.)

Finally, Colorado is the first state to require companies with even a few employees to disclose the expected salary or pay range for each open role they advertise, including remote positions (i.e., positions filled by Colorado residents for out-of-state employers). However, as shown in Figure 1.3, two other states (Rhode Island and Connecticut) have adopted legislation requiring employers, at minimum, to comply with employee or candidate requests for such information (Bölingen, 2021), and as of November 1, 2022, employers in New York City (with four or more employees) will also need to state a position's minimum and maximum salary when advertising a job, promotion, or transfer opportunity.

Europe

Several European countries took steps to promote pay transparency well before the Obama initiative of 2009. In Norway, for instance, income tax transparency, allowing Norwegian citizens to inspect the paper tax returns of their friends and neighbors, has been in practice since 1863 as a means to discourage tax avoidance. In 2001, these data were made internet accessible, thus enabling Norwegians to quickly and easily peek at the earnings of their neighbors, co-workers, supervisors, and leaders (hence the nickname, "Norway's Peeping Tom Law"). Searchers are unable, however, to view a breakdown of earnings by employer; and since 2014, individuals whose tax records are inspected are notified that their record has been viewed. Denmark took a more conventional approach. Its Act No. 562 was adopted in June 2006 and came into force a year later. This law aimed "to promote visibility and information about wage differentials" by requiring employers with a minimum of 35 employees (and at least 10 employees of each gender in any given occupation classification code) to annually either provide employees and their representatives (but not the public) with access to gender-based wage statistics or disseminate an internal report describing how wages are determined and laying out an action plan for the implementation of equal pay (Bennedsen et al., 2019).

More widespread regulatory action in Europe was prompted by the European Commission's release of pay transparency guidelines (Recommendation C(2014) 1405 final) in 2014 (Veldman, 2017). Among other things, these guidelines recommended that members states adopt regulations

- guaranteeing an employee's right to request information on gender pay levels for the same work or work of equal value;
- requiring employers to report on average gender pay levels by category of employee or position;
- requiring employers to conduct audits on pay and pay differentials on grounds of gender; and
- requiring employers and employee representatives to discuss gender pay disparities at the appropriate collective bargaining level.

As noted by Veldman (2017), within just a few years, the first of these recommendations (on employees' right to request information) had been implemented by three countries (Finland, Ireland, and Norway); the second (the reporting requirement) had been adopted by five (Austria, Belgium, Denmark, France, and Italy); the third (the auditing requirement) by three (Finland, France, and Sweden); and the fourth recommendation, on collective bargaining, had been implemented by five countries (Finland, France, Sweden, Belgium, and Germany).

Since 2017, a number of other European states have adopted pay transparency legislation consistent with these guidelines. The broad outline of legislation adopted in some of these countries is presented in Table 1.2, in chronological order, with a map showing the broad distribution of different forms of pay transparency legislation throughout Europe (Bölingen, 2021) presented in Figure 1.4. Two countries that have adopted broad-scale pay transparency legislation since 2017 are the United Kingdom and Germany. In April 2017, the United Kingdom extended the Equality Act 2010 (which made it illegal for employers to discriminate or retaliate against employees for discussing pay) by requiring all enterprises with more than 250 employees to annually publish information relating to the gender pay gap in their organization. Under these regulations, organizations are required to report (a) differences in the average hourly rate of pay to male and female employees, (b) differences in the average bonus paid to male and female employees, (c) the proportion of male and female employees receiving bonuses, and (d) the proportion of male and female employees in each quartile pay band. A copy of each year's report must be sent to the UK's Equality and Human Rights Commission, and it must be made available to the public through the employer's own website for at least 3 years from the date of publication.

Similarly, in the same year, the German National Parliament passed the Transparency in Wage Structures Act (*Entgelttransparenzgesetz*), which covers organizations with more than 200 employees. The act gives those employees the right to secure from their works council (or employer if no works council exists) the following peer pay information: (a) the median gross monthly pay of a relevant comparison group (e.g., employees of the other gender) containing at least six members and performing comparable work, (b) a breakdown of this information for up to two specified wage components (e.g., base salary and bonus payments), and (c) the criteria used to determine their own remuneration as well as the remuneration for the same/comparable work by others. However, no penalties are imposed on employers that fail to follow the law's requirements, and the information that employers are required to disclose is limited and relatively uninformative (Gobel et al., 2020). In a study of the early implications of this law, Gobel

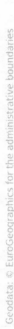
Geodata: © EuroGeographics for the administrative boundaries

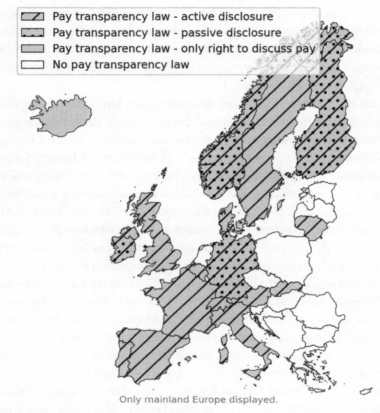

Pay transparency law - active disclosure
Pay transparency law - passive disclosure
Pay transparency law - only right to discuss pay
No pay transparency law

Only mainland Europe displayed.

If both outcome/process transparancy and right to discuss pay are presribed by law, only active/passive transparency displayed.

Figure 1.4 European States—Pay transparency laws and aspect of pay COMMUNICATION. Seventeen of the 32 European states have a pay transparency law. Eleven states have at least one pay transparency law that excludes some actors and/or is limited to enterprises employing more than a minimum number of individuals. Active disclosure of pay-related information (mandated in 16 states) involves the required disclosure of pay rates or ranges, but typically only to employee representatives or state agencies. Passive disclosure mandates that employers provide pay rates or ranges to candidates and/or employees requesting such information for the position to which they are applying or currently fill.

Source: Bölingen (2021).

et al. (2020) found that employee information requests were rare. They also found that relative to companies exempt from the law due to their size (150–200 employees compared with 201–250 employees in the non-exempt study sample), rates of employee-to-employee pay disclosure were higher, but employee self-reports of pay satisfaction were lower.

In March 2021, the European Commission (2021) released a new proposed directive to advance pay transparency in Europe. If adopted, it would expand the guidelines recommended in 2014, making obligatory for employers with 250 or more employees such practices as the following:

- Internal reporting on pay differences among female and male workers in the same category
- Ensuring the right for employees to request pay information concerning other workers performing work of similar value
- Prohibiting employers from asking about pay history
- Requiring employers to disclose salary ranges to job applicants, even prior to an interview
- Shifting the burden of proof regarding gender pay discrimination on to employers
- Conducting an equity audit (called a "joint pay assessment") in cases in which the gender gap in the same category of workers is more than 5 percent and not justifiable based on objective, gender-neutral factors. This audit will have to include the following:
  - An analysis of the proportion of female and male workers in each category of workers
  - Detailed information on average female and male workers' pay levels
  - Identification of any differences in pay levels between female and male workers in each category of workers
  - The gender-neutral justifications for pay differences between female and male workers performing the same work/work of equal value
  - Measures to address the gender pay gap if pay differences are not justified based on objective, gender-neutral criteria

Conclusion

As is evident from Table 1.2, the past decade has seen a burst of regulatory action throughout the world aimed at addressing the issue of pay information asymmetry as a means to reduce gender and ethnic pay discrepancies. These regulatory efforts have been contentious, to say the least. Indeed, as is evident from the case of the United States, regulatory progress in many jurisdictions can be described as one step forward and two steps back. Nevertheless, from a historical perspective, there is no doubt that in many areas of the world, employees have greater access to pay information than in the past. As I've described in this chapter, the current trend toward greater pay transparency likely stems from a variety of interrelated factors, including changing workforce demographics, growing popular unwillingness to accept gender- or ethnicity/race-based employment disparities, the changing nature of work, and advances in information technology. These factors have made it increasingly difficult for employers to control employee pay information disclosure, and they have put pressure on employers to "open the books"—or at least to be more transparent about the means by which pay is determined. The following chapters of this book examine the potential implications of this shift toward enhanced pay transparency and less restrictive pay communication, first from a theoretical perspective (Chapter 2) and then from a multilevel empirical perspective (Chapters 3–6).

2

Pay Communication

Core Concepts and Theoretical Underpinnings

Among compensation researchers and practitioners, the topic of pay communication has long fallen under the broader rubric of pay or salary/wage administration, a concept referring to the collection of practices and procedures used for planning and distributing employee remuneration. Although pay communication has long been a contentious issue, as a focus of systematic and scientific inquiry, it has been—at least until recently—one of the most under-researched aspects of compensation generally and pay administration in particular (Gupta & Shaw, 2014). It has also been one of the most underemphasized areas of activity for compensation practitioners. Fewer than half the respondents to a 2012 WorldatWork survey reported pay communication as a central focus of their activity (Fulmer & Chen, 2014), and in a 2020 survey (WorldatWork–Mercer, 2020) nearly a third said that the issue's importance in their organization had either decreased or remained the same.

One explanation for this may be that scholars and practitioners have lacked a common vocabulary when discussing pay communication. With different studies focusing on and measuring very different aspects of pay communication, and no broadly accepted conceptualization or standard of measurement, until recently the subfield lacked the foundation needed for systematic empirical investigation. Accordingly, a primary goal of this chapter is to suggest a comprehensive definition of pay communication, as well as a conceptual framework for making sense of this concept's core dimensions. This is important because, as we'll discover in subsequent chapters, there is increasing evidence that pay communication can have very different consequences depending on the particular aspect or dimension of interest.

Another explanation for the relative neglect of pay communication as a subdomain in compensation research may have been the absence of a theoretical framework logically linking pay communication policies and

Exposing Pay. Peter Bamberger, Oxford University Press. © Oxford University Press 2023.
DOI: 10.1093/oso/9780197628164.003.0002

practices to pay outcomes. Until recently, it was commonly believed that pay system outcomes were largely a function of the design of these systems, with implementation factors—such as how these systems are administered and employee pay-related knowledge and understanding—viewed as irrelevant, or at least unlikely to have any significant effect (Fulmer & Chen, 2014). Furthermore, given that pay was almost universally kept private and confidential (at least outside the collective bargaining context), scholars most likely rightly assumed that there was too little variability in communication policies and practices to exert any meaningful influence on employee attitudes or behavior. Indeed, given this assumption of broad-scale secrecy, much of the early research on the topic (e.g., Lawler, 1965, 1966, 1967; Milkovich & Anderson, 1972) was limited largely to examinations of employee pay-related knowledge and specifically the degree to which employee perceptions of others' pay were calibrated with what these others earned in reality. Thus, a second aim of this chapter is to present a variety of theoretical perspectives that may offer insights into how, when, and for whom varying forms and degrees of pay communication might matter.

Definition and Dimensions of Pay Communication

Throughout the years, those interested in the issue of pay communication have related to it using any number of terms, including pay openness, pay transparency, pay secrecy, pay knowledge, and pay disclosure. However, terms such as transparency, secrecy, or knowledge can conceivably be applied to various forms of pay-related information. For example, when one suggests that an organization is more transparent about its pay or that employees have greater pay knowledge, is one referring to the processes by which pay is determined or actual pay rates? Similarly, when speaking of pay disclosure policies and practices, are we concerned about the type or amount of pay information disclosed by management, or employees' freedom to discuss pay information with others?

Broadly conceived, *pay communication* relates to organizational policies and practices governing the sharing of pay-related information and, in particular, the degree to which these policies and practices facilitate or restrict the sharing of such information. Marasi and Bennett (2016) define it as "the organizational practice that determines if, when, how, and which pay information (such as pay ranges, pay raises, pay averages, individual pay levels, and/or the entire pay structure) is communicated to employees and possibly outsiders" (p. 51). They propose that within the context of this definition, the restrictiveness of pay communication ranges along two continua, namely the restrictiveness of organizational pay communication (i.e., how much information regarding pay the organization communicates to employees and even outsiders) and the restrictiveness of employee pay communication (i.e., the degree to which employees are at liberty to communicate with one another, as well as outsiders, regarding pay-related matters). Thus, with respect to both parameters, we should not conceive of organizations as being dichotomously either pay transparent or pay secretive but, rather, as more or less pay transparent (or secretive).

Similarly, Ingrid Fulmer and associates (Fulmer & Chen, 2014; Arnold et al., 2018) have proposed that pay communication policies and practices can be positioned along different continua of communication restrictiveness. However, in contrast to Marasi and Bennett (2016), they conceptualize pay communication along *three* orthogonal dimensions, with organizations potentially adopting different information-sharing policies and practices with regard to differing forms of pay (i.e., base pay, incentive pay, and benefits) for each dimension. As shown in Table 2.1, these dimensions are as follows:

Pay outcome transparency—the disclosure of actual pay rates or levels. According to U.S. Securities and Exchange Commission regulations, all publicly traded organizations in the United States must publicly disclose each year the salaries of their CEO, CFO, and three other most highly compensated executive officers for the past 3 fiscal years, along with information about grants of stock options and stock appreciation rights; long-term incentive plan awards; and pension plans. Pay

Table 2.1 Dimensions of Pay Communication

Dimension	Focus
Pay outcome transparency	Disclosure of actual pay rates or levels
Pay process transparency	Degree to which organizations share information with employees about how pay is determined, and the factors considered in deciding to pay some positions or individuals more than others
Pay communication transparency	Extent to which employees are free to solicit pay information from one another and/or share their own pay information with others

rates and levels for individuals in jobs covered by collective bargaining agreements are publicly disclosed in those agreements. But what about other executives or individuals not covered by a collective agreement? Organizations sharing information about mean/median pay or salary ranges for certain jobs or particular pay levels offer a degree of pay outcome transparency, but certainly less than that offered by organizations which publicly disclose the pay received by individual employees in all organizational positions.

Pay process transparency—the degree to which organizations share information with employees about how pay is determined, and the factors considered in deciding to pay some positions or individuals more than others. Pay process transparency is greater, for example, in organizations that share details about how merit increases or bonuses are determined (e.g., how different factors are weighted) than in organizations that simply report the factors taken into account when considering such increases.

Pay communication transparency—the extent to which employees are free to solicit pay information from one another and/or share their own pay information with others. Although employees throughout the world often face robust normative pressures to refrain from asking about others' pay or discussing pay matters with one another, employers (as noted in Chapter 1) are increasingly limited in their ability to restrict employee pay disclosures. These limits, together with employees' ability to discreetly seek and share pay information via the internet using such services as Glassdoor and Payscale, have made this dimension of pay communication the most consistently "open" across organizations.

As noted above, not only may organizations choose to be more or less transparent along these different dimensions but also, even within a particular dimension, they may display varying policies or practices with respect to different forms of pay. For instance, a company may disclose salary (i.e., base pay) ranges for various jobs or pay levels in the organization (a moderate degree of pay outcome transparency) but no information on the range of merit increases or bonuses paid. Similarly, a company may provide extensive information about how benefits are determined but only the most general information about the processes used to determine pay raises, and no information about how the firm sets bonuses or incentive payments.

Prevalence and Drivers of Varying Forms
of Pay Transparency

Applying this three-dimensional framework, Arnold et al. (2018) surveyed nearly 500 companies in Switzerland, asking participants to rate on a 5-point scale (1 being low and 5 being high) the transparency of pay outcomes, processes, and communication with respect to base pay, pay raises, individual bonuses/incentives, team- or organization-based variable pay, and benefits. Figure 2.1 shows the results for form-specific pay outcomes. As can be seen, for most of the outcomes, employees are provided with exact individual pay information in less than 20 percent of the Swiss enterprises that responded to the question. Moreover, for each outcome, 20–40 percent of the

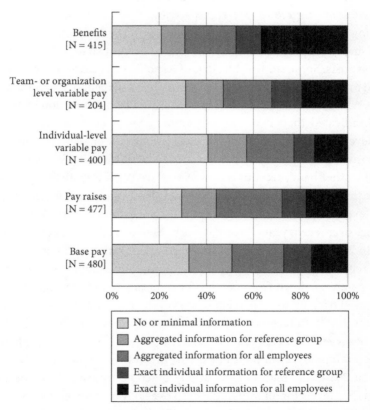

Figure 2.1 Pay outcome transparency across various pay forms in a sample of Swiss enterprises.
Source: Arnold et al. (2018).

responding organizations reported that they disclosed no substantive information to employees—not even aggregated pay data such as average range of pay for jobs at a certain level. Similar results were found with respect to pay process and pay communication transparency. Arnold et al. also found a tentative but limited trend toward greater openness: Pay transparency policies and practices across all three dimensions were largely unchanged over the previous 2 years for most of the surveyed firms, although approximately 15 percent of firms reported reduced restrictiveness (i.e., greater transparency) with respect to pay outcomes and processes.

Overall, analyses of pay transparency throughout the world—most of them less detailed than that of Arnold et al. (2018)—paint a similar picture. For instance, a 2019 LinkedIn global survey of talent professionals found that only 27 percent of the companies represented by these professionals offered some degree of pay transparency. Two-thirds of these reported sharing salary ranges with candidates early in the hiring process, 59 percent shared ranges with employees, and 48 percent shared ranges publicly on job posts. Some studies, like that of Arnold et al. (2018), show a hesitant trend toward greater openness. For example, 53 percent of respondents to a 2018 Willis Towers Watson survey of nearly 2,000 organization in 48 countries indicated their firms were "planning on or considering increasing the level of transparency around pay decisions, a challenging task given the growing complexity of pay decisions" (Willis Towers Watson, 2018a). On the other hand, recent surveys of WorldatWork members representing more than 300 largely U.S.-based privately held enterprises found relatively low levels of pay process and outcome transparency, with little positive change over recent years (WorldatWork–Mercer, 2020). As shown in Figure 2.2, in 2018 only 42 percent of surveyed organizations provided information regarding the design of their compensation system (i.e., pay process transparency), down from nearly 50 percent in 2010 (although this figure increased back up to 46 percent of surveyed firms in 2020; WorldatWork–Mercer, 2020). In terms of pay outcome transparency, in 2018 only 38 percent of surveyed enterprises furnished employees with data on the base pay range for employees in their pay grade, down from approximately 45 percent in 2014. The highest level of pay outcome transparency (disclosing actual pay levels for all individual employees) was reported by only 1 percent of participating enterprises in 2020 (down from 2 percent in 2019 and from 5 percent just 2 years prior to that; WorldatWork–Mercer, 2020). Furthermore, a 2018 study by the Institute for Women's Policy Research

Information Shared with Employees About Their Individual Salaries

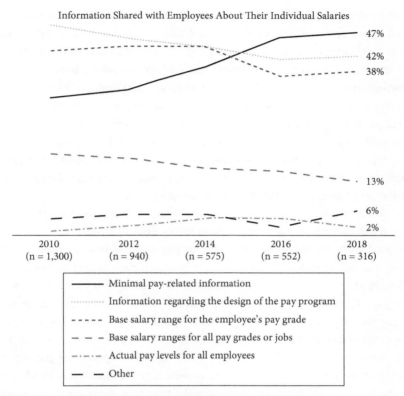

Figure 2.2 Pay process and outcome transparency in U.S. firms.
Reprinted with permission from WorldatWork (2019).

found that among private employers in the United States, 41 percent discourage wage and salary discussions, and 25 percent outright forbid it (Westfall, 2019).

What may account for the variance in pay transparency policies and practices? As highlighted in Chapter 1, the regulatory landscape for pay transparency has been shifting throughout the world in recent years, with many countries, states, and territories mandating employers to make pay more transparent, or at least adopt less restrictive pay communication practices. In some countries and regions, as noted previously, these laws simply make it illegal for employers to contractually restrict employee pay disclosures. In others, they go so far as requiring employers to disclose detailed pay information, particularly where there are gender pay disparity concerns.

But even within countries and regions, there may be substantial variance in pay communication policies and practices across enterprises. Using their Swiss employer data, Arnold et al. (2018) attempted to identify the drivers of such variance. They found that pay process transparency—that is, whether firms disclose how base pay, pay raises, and bonuses/incentives are determined—is associated with the proportion of the organization's workforce possessing a university-level education. Similarly, they found that pay outcome transparency—whether firms disclose exact levels of individual base pay and/or pay raises—is more prevalent in public (versus private) organizations, in enterprises with a higher percentage of unionized employees, and in larger firms (in terms of number of employees).

Overall, beyond Arnold et al. (2018) and a few other studies, there has been very little research on the regulatory, industry, and organizational factors associated with organizational variance in pay communication policies and practices. But anecdotal, case-based evidence suggests that enterprises may take steps to be more pay process- and outcome-transparent when faced with pay gaps linked to factors such as gender or race (Castilla, 2015). Indeed, as suggested in Chapter 1, heightened regulatory attention to pay equity disparities has motivated many organizations to be proactive in identifying pay discrepancies. This in turn has led to the development of pay equity audits—a policy-capturing tool that applies regression analysis to identify the factors potentially underlying internal differences in pay across the workforce and to differentiate those which are justifiable on business grounds from those based on demographic attributes (Sheen, 2019). Organizations that conduct such audits are often quite transparent about their results. They take steps to document the efforts made to address any unjustifiable pay gaps identified and leverage them for brand-building as well as using them to increase management accountability and prevent "creep" back toward unwarranted gaps.

Furthermore, anecdotal evidence suggests that some organizational leaders are eager to adopt more transparent pay policies and practices as a tool to transform their organization's culture and promote collective buy-in to climates characterized by integrity, trust, fairness, and openness (Trotter et al., 2017). For instance, according to Whole Foods co-CEO John Mackey, the early adoption of greater pay outcome transparency at this large grocery chain was driven by an interest in boosting employee trust in management. As he wrote in his blog in 2010, "Creating transparency and authentic communication is an ongoing challenge that every organization faces. We must continually strive to remove the barriers that prevent them, knowing that we can't maintain high levels of organizational trust without transparency and authentic communication." (For more on Whole Foods' approach to pay transparency, see Chapter 7.) Thus, the within-industry variance in pay transparency policies and practices may be explained, at least partially, by the growing prevalence of business models demanding high-commitment cultures (Bamberger et al., 2014a). Leaders of organizations that adopt such business models may view more transparent pay systems as helping establish and reinforce more open and trust-oriented organizational cultures, thereby enhancing employee commitment and normative buy-in.

Why Should We Care? Theoretical Underpinnings of the Impact of Pay Transparency

As noted previously, recognition of pay communication as a critical element of compensation and benefits management is a recent phenomenon. Indeed, until fairly recently, many rewards management researchers and practitioners assumed that to the extent that rewards influenced outcomes, such as the ability to attract and retain talent, they did so largely as a function of the *design* (rather than *administration*) of the pay system. So what changed? As noted in Chapter 1, the regulatory, normative, and institutional shifts motivating greater attention to pay communication also turned the attention of researchers (e.g., Lawler, and Milkovich and Anderson) to employees' pay knowledge and, especially, their *perceptions* about pay. Given that communication is a central influence over both knowledge and perceptions, an increased focus on pay communication and the mechanisms linking pay communication to employee understandings of pay was the logical next step. Accordingly, we next turn to the theoretical mechanisms proposed as potentially underlying the influence of pay communication on pay-related attitudes and behavior (Table 2.2).

Equity and Fairness Theories

Scholars who deal with compensation and benefits are familiar with the "pay model," a framework suggested by Belcher in the 1950s which served as the basis of Newman et al.'s *Compensation*, the primary textbook used

Table 2.2 Key Theories Associated with Pay Communication

Theory	Key Researchers (Year)	Underlying Proposition	Application to Pay Communication
Equity theory	Adams (1963)	Assessments of fairness are grounded in comparison of one's own ratio of rewards to contributions to that of comparison others. When those ratios are out of balance to one's detriment, individuals seek to restore balance by securing an increased reward, decreasing contribution, or seeking alternative employment.	More transparent pay can expose objective inequities. More restrictive pay communication can signal deceptive or aversive intent and thus generate perceptions of inequity.
Expectancy theory	Vroom (1964)	Motivational effects of pay are contingent upon (a) the subjective value of the payment (valence), (b) the expected probability that effort will result in achieving the target required for payoff, and (c) the expected probability that achieving the target will in fact yield the expected payout.	More restrictive pay communication can diminish the accuracy of the estimated probabilities associated with target achievement, and payout.
Heuristics–certainty effect	Tversky & Kahneman (1983)	Automatic tendency to overweight outcomes that are certain relative to those that are just probable when making judgments.	Pay comparisons that are based on concrete, transparent data (as opposed to estimated on the basis of uncertain signals) are more vivid and more difficult for individuals to dismiss or rationalize away, thus, if aversive, having a greater potential to elicit strong reactions.
Heuristics–completive mindset	Van Lange & Van Doesum (2015) Van Doesum et al. (2016)	Individuals with a more competitive mindset assume a zero-sum game in their relations with others, thus striving to beat out others in goal-oriented behavior.	More transparent pay practices may automatically trigger a competitive mindset among employees by presenting vivid, undeniable data that activates feelings of interpersonal competition. Result may be less thoughtfulness toward one's peers and greater social hostility.

Heuristics–psychological entitlement	Campbell et al. (2004)	Certain stimuli can create a sense that one is more deserving of preferential treatment than others.	When pay outcomes are more transparent, those benefiting or losing may each unconsciously frame themselves as more entitled, with implications on how they interact with others.
Uncertainty management theory	Lind & van den Bos (2002)	Individuals are naturally driven to seek and process information aimed at mitigating such uncertainty triangulating across multiple justice cues, and preferring to deny more aversive cues if possible.	Although more secretive pay policies and practices may signal potential employer unfairness with regard to pay, employees' inability to verify such concerns deters them from drawing inferences of unfairness.
Compensation activation theory	Fulmer & Shaw (2018)	Compensation design characteristics, including pay communication policies and practices, serve as situational cues that have the potential to activate personality-based social motives, and thus to elicit certain attitudes and behaviors.	Pay design features promoting competition have the potential to activate status-seeking motives among individuals who are predisposed to be more competitive or equity-sensitive. For them, greater pay outcome transparency may direct attention to the pay of those viewed as direct competitors, eliciting attitudes such as envy, or behaviors such as enhanced personal effort or counterproductive work behavior.

for more than 35 years to train compensation practitioners (and as of this writing, in its 13th edition [Newman et al., 2016]). The pay model specifies three main objectives of any pay system: efficiency, compliance, and fairness. Fairness underlies most of the approaches suggested by the pay model, the logic being that if rewards mechanisms are unfair or drive unfair outcomes, they are likely to undermine efforts to attract, motivate, and retain talent. But although it may be possible to specify some universal and objective notion of fairness, people's attitudes and behaviors tend to be driven by their *perceptions* of (un)fairness. These perceptions of fairness often depend on our frame of reference. After all, it is impossible to ascertain what is fair without comparing ourselves to some relevant set of "others," a practice commonly known as *social comparison* (Festinger, 1954).

Social comparison is at the root of equity theory (Adams, 1963). Equity theory proposes that assessments of fairness are grounded in a simple equation, namely how my own ratio of returns (e.g., compensation) to contributions (the economic value of my work) compares with that of some referent other. When those comparative ratios are equal, all is good and I am potentially motivated to join, contribute to, and stay with whatever effort or organization I am concerned with. But when those comparative ratios are unequal and favor some "other," it is likely to generate a negative and even aversive emotion that may drive me to action.

Hirschman (1970) lays out three main action alternatives. First, I may try "voicing" my feelings—for instance, expressing my frustration to my boss and asking for a raise. If that fails, I may opt to "exit"—to look for another job offering either more pay for the same effort or the same pay for less effort. Finally, if reasonable employment alternatives are not available, I may opt to suffer in silence. In Hirschman's typology, this last is a form of loyalty. However, both equity theory and empirical evidence suggest that employees who demonstrate this form of "loyalty" may actually seek unilaterally to re-establish balance in the comparative fairness ratio through some other means—for example, by reducing their own effort or by increasing their return through various forms of petty theft (Greenberg, 1993). Indeed, I recall as a young professor returning from a conference and submitting my travel receipts to a university administrator whose job it was to review these receipts. On my asking why she held some of the receipts up to the light, she explained, "We need to do this because some faculty members try to 'supplement their pay' by submitting doctored receipts." Several years later, it gave me great pleasure to hear that this same administrator was fired for being caught on video stealing paper, printing toner, and other office supplies, with her excuse being that she was only trying to make up for the failure of the university to pay her what she was worth!

Building on equity theory, the pay model is designed to ensure that pay systems systematically take into account comparisons of reward/contribution ratios between (a) a focal *job* and other positions within the same organization ("internal equity"), (b) a focal *job* in one's own organization and similar positions within comparable organizations ("external equity" or competitiveness), and (c) a focal *person* in a particular position and others in that position in the same organization ("employee equity"). In determining an employee's pay, organizations collect information about these three comparison sets and choose a pay level that reflects the appropriate balance for each. In contrast, when we as individuals assess the fairness of our own pay, we take a more "gestalt" perspective. That is, most of us do not systematically evaluate the fairness of our pay across each of these three comparison domains. Indeed, even if we wished to undertake such comparisons, in most cases we would be unable to access the precise information on others' rewards and contributions needed to do so.

So what do we do instead? We "guesstimate" based on the information available to us, in the same way the neighbors of Jerry Seinfeld's parents did in a wonderful episode of *Seinfeld*, the iconic comedy series. In that episode, Jerry visits his parents in Florida and takes them out for dinner, with his father driving them to the restaurant in the new Cadillac that Jerry has just given him for his birthday. They arrive at the restaurant just as his parents' neighbors from the condo development (where Jerry's father is the newly elected president) are exiting. One of the neighbors comments, "Hey, you know you missed the early bird special," while another asks suspiciously, "New car?" The innuendo is obvious: The neighbors are convinced that Jerry's father, in his new position as condo president, is skimming funds from the condo budget.

Just like the neighbors of Jerry's parents, employees also draw inferences where they can in order to glean the comparative information needed to inform their perceptions of the fairness of their pay. When information regarding pay processes and outcomes is less available, employees may automatically draw inferences from the information they do have: what vehicle their boss drives or where their co-workers go on vacation. These examples are sometimes known as *weak signals*—bits of unrelated information that by themselves may not convey much but that can offer clues to more useful knowledge. But as Frank (1985) suggests, such "weak signals" may mislead employees' pay-related impressions. Frank notes that in the context of information asymmetry, individuals attempting to distill others' pay status tend to ground their inferences in observation of others' "positional goods"—"things whose value depends relatively strongly on how they compare with things owned by others," such as vehicles and clothing (Frank, 1985, p. 101). Because positional goods are precisely those highly observable goods on which individuals tend to overspend, individuals may tend to overestimate the pay of others.

Why do we tend to rely largely on inferences from information suggesting *un*fairness? Social psychologists offer several possible explanations. One is that evolution has led us to place greater weight on negative (relative to positive) stimuli and information, what Baumeister et al. (2001) label as "bad being stronger than good." A second reason is that when we compare ourselves to others, we tend to do so in an upward direction. As noted by Buunk and Gibbons (2007), "Individuals generally prefer to compare with others who are thought to be slightly better off, providing support for Festinger's well-known notion of 'upward drive'" (p. 4). Furthermore, the mere fact that an organization has in place highly restrictive pay communication practices may be taken as an indication that the organization has something to hide. Indeed, building on Lind's (2001) fairness heuristic theory, Colella et al. (2007) suggest that in the absence of other information, employees may base their fairness assessments about pay outcomes (what is often referred to as distributive fairness or justice) on judgments about other aspects of fairness, such as the fairness of organizational procedures (procedural justice) or the fairness with which information is made available (informational justice). As they note, "If procedural and informational judgments are negative (likely because information is being withheld), then distributive judgments should be negative as well" (p. 59). Finally, perceptions of a negative imbalance or unfairness may result from a tendency to overestimate our own performance or contribution and/or to externalize any performance deficit of our own, while attributing any deficit in others' performance to them personally. Simply stated, if you fail, it's your fault; if I fail, it's a problem with the system, or my manager, or someone else. Given that we are all potentially susceptible to such self-efficacy and fundamental attribution biases (Jones & Harris, 1967; Ross & Sicoly, 1979; Kruger, 1999), it comes as no surprise that in the absence of pay-related information, we are likely to perceive our pay as unfair.

In summary, many of those taking an equity perspective to theorize about the possible effects of different pay communication practices have conjectured that more limited access to pay information is likely to be associated with employee perceptions of pay unfairness. And to the extent that perceptions of unfairness can drive the "corrective" behaviors noted previously (e.g., turnover and decreased effort; Greenberg, 1990; Cowherd & Levine, 1992; Ambrose, 2002), these theorists suggest that pay secrecy could drive a variety of undesirable employee behaviors and organizational outcomes.

Expectancy Theory and Employee Instrumentality Perceptions

No less central than equity theory to our understanding of the motivational effects of pay is Victor Vroom's (1964) expectancy theory. This theory posits that the motivational effects of pay are contingent upon (a) the subjective meaning attributed to the payment (i.e., the "valence" or motivational signal strength of the reward for the recipient), (b) the expected probability that effort will result in achieving the target required for payoff, and (c) the expected probability that achieving the target will in fact yield the expected payoff. With most employees' pay at least partially contingent on their contribution (i.e., performance), an understanding of the performance–pay relationship (the degree to which incremental increases in performance yield incremental increases in some reward) is critical for estimating the utility of marginal effort—that is, making choices about how much additional effort to exert on the job (Heneman et al., 1988). This link between the (perceived) performance–pay relationship and individual task performance is well-established in the motivation literature (e.g., Vroom, 1964; Naylor et al., 1980) and has been widely demonstrated (Kanfer, 1990).

Understanding the nature of performance–pay contingencies strictly on the basis of one's *own* experience is difficult in that it demands the consideration of multiple performance–pay events, which for any single individual can typically only be inferred over time. In contrast, information on the pay associated with varying levels of co-worker performance facilitates employees' timely estimation of performance–pay relations (Naylor et al., 1980). However, under conditions of pay secrecy, it is more difficult for employees to estimate the nature of the relationship between one's contribution and one's pay. This leads some employees to rely on their environment for (often weak) signals that might furnish insights into the nature of pay-related contingencies. And as exemplified by the *Seinfeld* episode described previously, some of these signals may be open to misinterpretation.

Moreover, as also suggested above, pay secrecy—and the information asymmetry it generates—may signal a heightened risk of managerial opportunism or deceptive intent (Wanasika & Adler, 2011; Williamson, 1975). That is, although employers may have objectively valid and positive reasons to restrict pay communication (e.g., to avoid jealousy among co-workers), pay secrecy leads employees to assume the worst (Peeters & Czapinski, 1990; Baumeister et al., 2001). This, in turn, may exacerbate the risk that weak signals used to estimate performance–pay contingencies will be misinterpreted, because weak signals tend to be interpreted "in accordance with preconceived notions" (Connelly et al., 2011, p. 55). For example, we have seen that in the absence of other information, employees may base inferences regarding performance–pay contingencies on their perceptions of procedural or informational fairness (Greenberg, 2003). But as Colella et al. (2007) suggest, if these are viewed in a negative light (a likely outcome when information is being withheld), "then distributive judgments are likely to be negative as well" (p. 59).

The net result of all this, as suggested by Lawler (1965, 1967) and others (Milkovich & Anderson, 1972), is that when employees draw inferences from the weak pay-related signals around them, they tend to overestimate the pay of their co-workers and underestimate the pay of those hierarchically superior to them. By perceiving the upper boundary of pay dispersion as lower and the lower boundary as higher, individuals effectively compress the *perceived* range of pay associated with varying levels of contribution.

Given this reduction in the perceived range of pay, although rewards may still be perceived as monotonically increasing as a function of performance, the strength of this relationship is likely to be diminished. That is, to the degree that pay secrecy leads to implicit compression of the perceived range of pay, it reduces performance–pay instrumentality perceptions—the belief that increased effort is likely to generate a commensurate increase in rewards. Thus, principles of expectancy theory offer an additional mechanism through which pay communication may impact such outcomes as task performance and even talent retention (Belogolovsky & Bamberger, 2014).

Heuristic and Automatic Mechanisms

The equity- and expectancy-based mechanisms discussed up to this point rely on two common assumptions. The first is that restrictive pay communication policies and practices place employees in a situation of information asymmetry—a situation in which "different people know different things" (Stiglitz, 2002, p. 469)—and so provokes an automatic or unconscious search for compensatory information as a way to reduce uncertainty (in this case, uncertainty as to whether the employee is being treated fairly by their employer). This tendency of individuals to search for and glean insight from signals in their environment in situations of information asymmetry is a core element of Stiglitz's (2002) signaling theory. The second assumption is that inferences drawn from such compensatory information are likely to be subject to an unconscious tendency to overweight negative information (Peeters & Czapinski, 1990; Baumeister et al., 2001). From an equity theory perspective, such negative biasing may lead employees to conclude that they are being treated unfairly. From an expectancy theory perspective, it may lead them to conclude that performance–pay contingencies make their contributions less instrumental in driving rewards than they are in reality. These two assumptions are important because they suggest that pay communication policies and practices can elicit, without conscious reflection, cognitions that can shape employee attitudes and behaviors (Belogolovsky & Bamberger, 2014). Several theories offer insights as to whether, when, and how this may occur.

Among the dozens of heuristics identified by researchers (Kahneman, 2011), the *certainty effect* is most tightly linked to how pay communication may unconsciously impact employee attitudes and behaviors. The certainty effect captures people's automatic tendency to overweight outcomes that are certain relative to those that are just probable when making judgments. This is relevant to the question of pay communication in that more transparent pay policies and practices, by allowing for *realistic* comparisons (driven by difficult-to-dismiss, concrete facts), create situations of greater certainty. In contrast, policies and practices that are more restrictive allow for only *constructive comparisons* driven by dismissible, ambiguous information inferred from data of uncertain accuracy and reliability (Goethals et al., 1991; Goethals & Klein, 2000).

The certainty effect suggests that because realistic comparisons are based on objective and concrete facts that offer a high degree of information vividness, these comparisons are more salient and thus have potential to elicit stronger affective reactions (Nisbett & Ross, 1980; Kahneman, 2011). Accordingly, the realistic comparisons associated with pay transparency are likely to foster strong emotional reactions, whether joy (when the comparison puts one "ahead" of others) or envy (when the comparison puts one "behind" others). In turn, there is extensive and consistent evidence that beyond individuals' conscious and reflective behavioral responses to such emotions, these emotion reactions can also have automatic effects on human behavior (Isen, 1984; Porath & Erez, 2007).

No less important, the certainty effect suggests that the concrete facts on which realistic comparisons are based make it difficult for individuals to dismiss the inference as possible error (Tversky & Kahneman, 1983). This reinforces the salience of the comparison, particularly when its outcome is negative—that is, the individual concludes that they are deprived relative to the comparison other. Likewise, research on information ambiguity (Van Dijk & Zeelenberg, 2003) suggests that the constructive comparisons fostered by pay secrecy can allow people to discount, rationalize, or dismiss any resulting sense of relative deprivation. In combination, these two arguments imply that under conditions of pay transparency, where comparative information is difficult to discount or rationalize away, even a relatively low degree of perceived relative deprivation may produce outsized emotional reactions, including frustration, hostility, or envy. In contrast, although secrecy may, as discussed above, lead individuals to overweigh negative signals suggesting pay unfairness, it may also facilitate the discounting and even dismissal of such perceptions. As discussed in subsequent chapters, the certainty effect and the related notion of information vividness have been central to studies that examine how transparency may impact a variety of individual attitudes and behaviors, and even organizational-level outcomes.

Building on the certainty effect, and remaining within the realm of automatic cognitive processes, more transparent pay policies and practices have other potential implications. Regardless of the nature of the information revealed, the simple vividness of realistic comparisons may unconsciously give rise to particular attitudes and beliefs, which can then affect employees' behavior in ways that are not necessarily good for the employee or the organization. Two of these attitudes and beliefs are particularly relevant, namely a competitive mindset and a sense of psychological entitlement.

Competitive Mindset

We can define *mindset* as an individual's implicit theory about the links between means and ends. Accordingly, individuals with cooperative mindsets link positive outcomes for themselves to positive outcomes for a collective, and they strive for the greater good (Kelley & Thibaut, 1978; Simmons et al., 1988). In contrast, individuals with a more competitive mindset assume a zero-sum game in their relations with others (i.e., gains for others are at one's own expense), and they strive for their personal benefit and to beat out others in goal-oriented behavior (Deutsch, 1949; Van Knippenberg et al., 2001). Consistent with the literature on social mindfulness and social hostility (Van Lange & Van Doesum, 2015; Van Doesum et al., 2016), a colleague and I (SimanTov-Nachlieli & Bamberger, 2022) propose that more transparent pay practices may trigger a competitive mindset among employees by intensifying feelings of ongoing interpersonal competition, particularly when at least a portion of that pay is contingent (as is the case in most organizations) on individual performance (see also Milkovich et al., 2013; Belogolovsky & Bamberger, 2014). By prompting employees to view their co-workers less as colleagues or teammates and more as rivals, activation of a competitive mindset may lead to a workplace atmosphere characterized less by social mindfulness (i.e., being thoughtful of others) and more by social hostility (Van Doesum et al., 2016; Van Lange & Van Doesum, 2015). Several studies in social psychology offer evidence in support of such an effect. For instance, Moyal and Ritov (2020) demonstrated that individuals placed in competitive (vs. noncompetitive) settings showed less prosocial behaviors toward others in subsequent, ostensibly unrelated tasks.

Psychological Entitlement

Another automatic cognitive outcome potentially elicited by pay outcome transparency may be a feeling of *psychological entitlement*. More precisely, by giving employees information about their compensation relative to others, pay transparency could produce a sense that one is more deserving of preferential treatment than others (Campbell et al., 2004). Interestingly, the direction in which this effect might occur is unclear. In one paper, Schurr and Ritov (2016) found that winning a prior competition (or simply recalling that one had won some prior competition) was associated with a higher level of deceptive behavior toward an unrelated other (cheating in a coin toss). Schurr and Ritov posited (and found) that psychological entitlement largely explained this effect, with individuals who had won a competition convincing themselves that it was okay for them to engage in behaviors they would normally consider unethical or otherwise unacceptable. However, others have posited (and found) that those who *lose* competitions tend to feel more entitled, on the grounds that a sense of entitlement is greatest when one feels wronged (Zitek et al., 2010). Thus, the evidence is mixed. Nonetheless, it does appear that when pay outcomes are more transparent, either winners or losers—or both—may unconsciously frame themselves as more entitled, with potentially problematic behavioral implications for their peers and the organizations employing them.

Integrative Mechanisms

So far, this review has highlighted theories which assume that pay communication policies and practices affect HR outcomes on the basis mainly of either conscious reflection by employees (equity and expectancy theories) or largely unconscious, automatic effects (the certainty effect, competitive mindset, and psychological entitlement). However, it is quite likely that pay communication policies and practices affect employee attitudes and behaviors through mechanisms integrating both automatic and reflective processes. Two theoretical frameworks offer insights into how these processes may come together to link pay communication with pay outcomes, namely uncertainty management theory (UMT) and compensation activation theory (CAT).

Uncertainty Management Theory

Uncertainty management theory (Lind & van den Bos, 2002) proposes that uncertainty about fairness serves as the primary driver linking pay communication to employee actions. This theory offers a comprehensive, social–cognitive framework for understanding when and how individuals respond to fairness uncertainty (Alterman et al., 2021; Simantov-Nachlieli & Bamberger, 2021). UMT posits not only that pay represents a central domain of fairness uncertainty for many employees but also that such pay-related fairness uncertainty is both aversive (Fiske & Taylor, 1991; Jost, 1995) and salient (Van den Bos et al., 1998). Accordingly, UMT suggests that employees may naturally be driven to seek and process information aimed at mitigating such uncertainty. Furthermore, as a social–cognitive theory, UMT suggests that to maximize predictive validity, models of attitudes and behaviors elicited by varying pay communication policies and practices must take into account not only reflective, calculative parameters but also more automatic, heuristic processes.

Consistent with the signaling notions already introduced, UMT suggests that individuals tend to triangulate across *multiple* justice cues and that when fairness information is uncertain (as is the case under more restrictive pay communication conditions), individuals rely on uncertainty-related fairness heuristics (i.e., cognitive biases that arise when justice cues are uncertain), such as status quo preservation heuristics, to form a global fairness assessment of how well they are being treated. However, consistent with systems justification theory (Jost, 1995) and the certainty effect described above (Tversky & Kahneman, 1983), UMT explains that status quo preservation heuristics occur as "people try to justify rather than challenge the existing status quo" when there is fairness uncertainty (Van den Bos & Lind, 2002, p. 48). In other words, the theory proposes that in the absence of hard evidence that they are being treated unfairly, people tend to dismiss or deny more aversive justice cues. This tendency to discount fairness information is particularly relevant when the fairness uncertainty is also explicit, as is very likely the case with pay secrecy (i.e., employees are aware that pay information and conversations are being withheld or restricted; Colella et al., 2007). Thus, for example, although more secretive pay policies and practices may signal potential employer unfairness with regard to pay, employees' inability to verify such concerns deters them from drawing inferences of unfairness. This may explain why in many cases, despite pay secrecy being suggestive of "sinister intentions" on the part of an employer, we fail to see an impact on outcomes such as performance or turnover via employee fairness perceptions. At the same time, UMT offers an explanation as to how more transparent pay communication policies and practices may be associated with diminished performance or higher turnover intentions, or other such adverse employee outcomes, by making it difficult or impossible for employees to dismiss evidence of unfair treatment. We explore this phenomenon in greater detail in Chapter 3.

Compensation Activation Theory
Compensation activation theory also integrates automatic and reflective processes in order to link pay practices and policies more generally (and not just those concerned with pay communication) to a variety of employee attitudes and behaviors. CAT, developed by Ingrid Fulmer and Jason Shaw (2018), suggests that compensation design characteristics, including pay

communication policies and practices, serve as situational cues that have the potential to activate personality-based social motives and thus to elicit certain attitudes and behaviors. Among the social motives that may be activated by compensation design characteristics are self-protection, affiliation, status via social dominance, and status via mastery. To illustrate, CAT proposes that design features which promote competition and relative comparisons across workers have the potential to activate status-seeking motives, particularly those based on social dominance—but only among individuals who are predisposed to be more competitive or equity-sensitive. Accordingly, for such individuals, greater pay outcome transparency may direct attention to the pay of those viewed as direct competitors, eliciting attitudes such as envy or behaviors such as enhanced personal effort or counterproductive work behavior.

Conclusion

We began this chapter by suggesting that to better make sense of the research on pay communication, it was first necessary to engage in a bit of "conceptual cleanup." We did so by adopting the three-dimensional framework proposed by Fulmer and Chen (2014) and Arnold et al. (2018) for pay communication policies and practices, namely pay outcome, pay process, and pay communication transparency. We then examined different theoretical mechanisms that might underlie or explain how more versus less restrictive practices and policies affect employees' pay-related attitudes and behavior. In the following chapters, we will show how these theoretical underpinnings can help us make better sense of often inconsistent findings regarding the implications of pay transparency.

Our discussion in the next three chapters focus on how pay communication policies and practices may affect outcomes at the individual, organizational, and societal levels. Here, we consider the various reflective and automatic processes at the core of the theoretical frameworks just reviewed. As suggested in this chapter, in understanding how pay communication policies and practices affect employee attitudes and behaviors, we have little choice but to consider both those reflective processes of which employees are conscious and those more automatic processes that may influence the inputs to these reflective processes.

3

Pay Transparency and Employee Perceptions, Attitudes, and Behavior

With the theories presented in Chapter 2 to guide our inquiry, we begin our exploration of the implications of pay transparency (i.e., pay outcome, pay process, and pay communication transparency) at the micro level, focusing on individual employees and their peers and teams. We first examine how restrictive pay communication policies and practices may affect employee pay perceptions and knowledge and why these effects matter. We then examine how and when pay communication may affect a variety of employee attitudes, such as fairness and trust. These effects are summarized in Table 3.1. Understanding these perceptual and attitudinal effects is important because they provide us with a better basis for probing how, when, and why pay communication may impact behavioral outcomes, including employee task and contextual performance, counterproductive work behavior, and ultimately withdrawal behavior (retention versus turnover). These behavioral implications are summarized in Table 3.2.

Impact of Restricted Pay Communication on Employee Pay Perceptions

Years ago, before I began to research pay communication, I received an email that contained an attachment but no text. The subject line read "Data Requested." Of course, such subject lines tend to be associated with computer viruses and malware, but the sender was the associate dean, and I was way too curious to just delete it. In fact, no data were being requested. Instead, it was a spreadsheet *providing* the salary data for all of my colleagues and administrative staff in the school. Seconds later, another email arrived from the associate dean—this time, clearly frantic—imploring all us unintended recipients of the previous email to delete it without opening the attachment, and if we had already opened it, to immediately close and expunge it. I did in

Exposing Pay. Peter Bamberger, Oxford University Press. © Oxford University Press 2023.
DOI: 10.1093/oso/9780197628164.003.0003

Table 3.1 Implications of Pay Transparency on Employee Perceptions and Attitudes

Outcome	References	Population Studied	Key Findings
Pay-related perceptions	Lawler (1965, 1967), Milkovich & Anderson (1972) Cullen & Perez-Truglia (2018b)	Managers in public and private sector in North America Bank employees in Asia	Indiviiduals overestimate pay of peers and underestimate pay of superiors
Satisfaction	Futrell & Jenkins (1978)	Pharmaceutical sales personnel in North America	Pay outcome transparency is associated with greater improvement in pay, promotion, and job satisfaction (relative to pay secrecy) but greater decline in supervisory satisfaction.
Justice/ fairness	Belogolovsky & Bamberger (2015) SimanTov-Nachlieli & Bamberger (2021)	Israeli engineering students Employees from United States, United Kingdom, and Canada (recruited via Prolific)	Outcome pay transparency positively associated with distributive justice only for those more equity sensitive. Pay process transparency is positively associated with procedural and distributive justice, but pay outcome transparency's association with distributive justice depends on one's pay relative to others.
Envy	Bamberger & Belogolovsky (2017)	MBA students in Singapore	No main effect, but for those more collectivistic, pay transparency is associated with greater envy.
Trust	Montag-Smit & Smit (2020) Alterman et al. (2021)	MTurk workers (United States) MBA students in China	Restrictive pay process and communication are associated with lower trust. Pay transparency–trust relationship depends on distributive justice perceptions.

fact delete the spreadsheet, but only after staring at the numbers and being shocked by two things: First, that I had grossly underestimated the earnings of some of my senior colleagues and second, that I had grossly overestimated the earnings of some of my peers.

Table 3.2 Implications of Pay Transparency on Employee Behavior

Outcome	Reference	Population Studied	Key Findings
Task performance	Futrell & Jenkins (1978)	Pharmaceutical sales personnel in North America	Outcome pay transparency associated with increase in job performance.
	Bamberger & Belogolovsky (2010)	Israeli engineering students	Task performance rose for those in pay transparent condition but fell for those in secrecy condition. Effects were particularly strong for those more interpersonally competitive.
	Bamberger & Belogolovsky (2014)	Israeli engineering students	Pay secrecy has an adverse effect on individual task performance, particularly when performance is subjectively evaluated and assessed on relative basis.
	Blanes et al. (2011)	German piecework employees	Productivity is positively associated with employee knowledge of their relative position in pay distribution.
OCB	Marasi et al. (2018)	MTurk workers (United States)	Greater levels of pay secrecy reduce engagement in OCB operating via informational justice.
	Bamberger & Belogolovsky (2017)	MBA students in Singapore	Pay outcome transparency has an indirect, negative effect on helping via envy.
CWB	Marasi et al. (2018)	MTurk workers (United States)	Pay transparency is inversely associated with CWB operating via informational justice.
	SimanTov-Nachlieli & Bamberger (2021)	Employees from United States, United Kingdom, and Canada (recruited via Prolific)	Pay *process* transparency is inversely associated with CWB against the organization and peers via procedural and distributive justice. But pay *outcome* transparency is positively associated with CWB for those at the bottom of the pay distribution and inversely associated with CWB for those at the top of the pay distribution.

CWB, counterproductive work behavior; OCB, organizational citizenship behavior.

It turns out that my poor estimations of my colleagues' paychecks were not so unusual. In fact, studies have consistently shown that employees' perceptions of others' pay tend to be well off the mark. Indeed, some of the first studies on pay secrecy were aimed at estimating precisely how off-mark these employee perceptions may be, and in what direction. Studying seven organizations—three in the public sector and four in the private sector (in the food, chemical, utility, and aerospace industries)—in the early 1960s, Edward Lawler (1965) wanted to know whether managers have an accurate picture of other managers' pay. Whereas the three public sector organizations made public the pay ranges (although not average or median rates of pay) for all positions, the private organizations all followed a policy of strict pay secrecy, with not even pay ranges disclosed (p. 415). After securing average salaries for all managerial positions in all seven organizations, Lawler asked managers in each company what they believed to be the average yearly salary of managers (a) at their present level, (b) one level above them, and (c) one level below them.

In the public organizations, managers tended to overestimate the pay of those one level below them (by an average of $340) and those at the same level (by an average of $161). The error in their estimate of earnings for those above them was only $24 (a small amount, even in the 1960s) and not statistically significant. In the more pay-secretive private firms, although managers also tended to overestimate the pay of those below them, the average error was $475—more than 35 percent higher than the (mis)estimates of their peers in the public sector. For managers at their own level, respondents' estimates were not significantly different from actual pay (with an average overestimate of $64). However, the private sector managers grossly underestimated the pay of those one level above them, by an average of $425. More than 62 percent of the private sector managers underestimated the pay of their superiors one level above (whereas only 27 percent of the private sector managers overestimated their superiors' pay).

Two years later, Lawler (1967) repeated this study with a new set of 110 managers in a different private sector manufacturing enterprise. This time, he assessed how managers perceived the pay of those both one and two levels above or below them in the organizational hierarchy. Overall, the findings point to a similar pattern: Managers again overestimated the pay of those at or below their level, and they underestimated the pay of those at levels above them. Particularly interesting, however, was the magnitude of the misperceptions. Whereas the mean absolute errors as a percentage of the estimated salary were 10.3 and 13.3 with regard to managers two and one levels below, respectively (i.e., average overestimates of $540 and $290, respectively), the mean absolute error was greater than 15 percent of the estimated salary for those one or two levels above them. Managers underestimated the salaries of those one level above them by an average of $1,208 and of those two levels above them by an average of $4,980! Based on these findings, Lawler concluded that even if employees are compensated on the basis of objective equity, more restrictive pay communication practices lead employees to perceive that their contributions are less valued (and compensated) by their employers than they are in fact, and so may adversely impact both motivation and talent retention.

Lawler's findings have since been replicated by others. For example, Milkovich and Anderson (1972) reported similar findings even among managers in a company characterized by somewhat less restrictive pay communication practices, in which employees had access to information on the salary range and median pay of positions in their own pay grade (although not of those in other pay grades). Cullen and Perez-Truglia (2018a) not only replicated Lawler's finding but also offer several meaningful extensions to his discovery. First, despite conducting their study some 50 years later, examining comparative pay misperceptions among a wide range of employees (not just those in managerial positions), and conducting their study in a large Asian bank (rather than in North America), Cullen and Perez-Truglia report a pattern of findings remarkably similar to that found by Lawler (1965, 1967). As in the private sector organizations studied by Lawler, salary information was not disclosed, and the bank discouraged employee discussions about pay. And as in the private sector organizations studied by Lawler, misperceptions of *peer* pay were found to be relatively low and, most important, unslanted, whereas perceptions of managerial pay were off by a substantial amount. Specifically, although employees on average overestimated their peers' pay, the overestimation was just 2.5 percent, the mean absolute difference between the perceived average and the actual average was just 11.5 percent, and approximately the same proportion of employees underestimated their peers' pay as overestimated it. In contrast, consistent with Lawler's findings, only 12 percent of the bank employees estimated the pay of those one level above them within 5 percent of the actual figure, with a mean absolute error for perceived manager salary of 28 percent, more than double that for peers (11.5 percent). Most significantly, misperceptions of managerial pay were slanted, with the average employee underestimating managerial pay by over 14 percent.

Second, whereas Lawler could only speculate as to what his results might mean with respect to employee motivation and retention, Cullen and Perez-Truglia (2018a) actually assessed this impact. Consistent with Lawler's expectations, in terms of task motivation, they found that increasing the already (slightly) overestimated perceptions of peer pay by a further 1 percent would decrease hours worked by nearly 1 percent (p. 3). In contrast, a similar 1 percent increase in (underestimated) manager pay would result in a small but statistically significant increase of 0.2 percent in the number of hours worked (p. 3). Similar negative/positive effects were found with respect to the impact of an increase in peer/manager salaries with regard to both the number of emails sent (an alternative indicator of effort) and sales performance (where relevant). As Cullen and Perez-Truglia state, "When they find out that their managers earn more than they thought, employees work harder, on average. In contrast, employees do not work as hard when they find out that their peers earn more" (p. 2). Taken as a whole, these findings suggest that overestimation of peer salaries and the more substantial underestimation of managerial salaries may be detrimental to employee motivation.

Note that Cullen and Perez-Truglia's findings offer little support for the second part of Lawler's speculations, namely that pay misperceptions would affect employee retention. Specifically, in their study, a further increase of 1 percent in perceived peer salaries was associated with a statistically significant but very slight increase (just a quarter of a percentage point) in the probability of an employee leaving the company. That is, a higher perceived peer salary demotivates employee retention, as Lawler proposed, but in a manner that is hardly noticeable. A similar 1 percent increase in perceived manager salary (i.e., reducing the degree of underestimation) is associated with a reduced probability of employee turnover, but this reduction is even smaller (0.02 percentage points) and statistically insignificant.

In summary, more than 50 years of consistent evidence from very diverse employee populations indicates that more restrictive pay policies lead employees to misjudge the pay of others in their organization. Moreover, the evidence points to an overestimation of how much peers and those in lower pay grades are earning and underestimation of the sums those in higher pay grades are taking home. Intuitively, such findings suggest that more restrictive pay communication practices may have adverse implications for employees and those employing them. First, as suggested by Lawler and supported by the evidence presented above, it may reduce perceptions of pay fairness, as well as pay satisfaction and motivation to perform. Second, it may weaken employee commitment to the organization and increase turnover intentions, although based on the findings of Cullen and Perez-Truglia, such effects may be complex and less than robust. Finally, logic suggests that pay secrecy may encourage employees to negotiate for pay raises that may not be objectively justified, thus potentially creating employer-directed feelings of resentment, frustration, and perhaps even distrust among employees when their requests for a pay raise are rejected. Some of the implications of pay communication restrictiveness for employee attitudes are explored in the next section, and implications for key employee behaviors are discussed in the sections following it.

Attitudes: Job Satisfaction, Justice/Fairness, Envy, and Trust

The impact of pay transparency on employee work attitudes is equivocal, with some studies suggesting that pay transparency results in more positive attitudes and others suggesting the opposite. A closer look at the literature suggests that these seemingly inconsistent findings in fact make sense, for two reasons. First, pay transparency's impact on work-related attitudes depends on the particular aspect of pay transparency examined (pay process, outcome, or communication transparency). Second, the implications of pay transparency may vary from attitude to attitude. That is, pay transparency may boost job satisfaction (a positive attitudinal outcome) but also trigger or exacerbate malicious envy (a negative attitudinal outcome).

Implications for Job Satisfaction

Initial research on how pay transparency might influence employee attitudes followed up on Lawler's conjecture that relative to pay secrecy, pay transparency would give rise to greater job satisfaction. In one of the few field experiments conducted on the implications of pay communication, Futrell and Jenkins (1978) designed and executed an experimental field study with a sample of approximately 500 pharmaceutical sales employees.

Approximately 30 percent of the employees (152 salespeople in three of the company's nine sales districts) were randomly assigned to a pay transparency (experimental) condition, and the remainder were assigned to a secrecy (control) condition. Both groups completed an initial survey capturing satisfaction with their pay, the firm's promotion policies, their superiors, their co-workers, and the work itself. A month later, partial pay outcome transparency was introduced for the experimental group. Sales personnel in this condition were given the mean rates and range of pay for varying levels of seniority in the company, as well as relative performance scores and the firm's low, average, and high merit increase rates. After a year, the attitude survey was repeated for employees in both groups. Statistical tests showed that relative to the initial survey, those in the pay transparency condition experienced a significantly greater increase in pay-, promotion-, and work-related satisfaction than those in the more secretive control condition. However, the former also experienced a significant decline in satisfaction with their supervisor relative to the time prior to the introduction of pay transparency, whereas there was no such decline for those in the pay secrecy condition. The study's authors speculated that the poor supervisor satisfaction findings likely reflected the very partial nature of the transparency condition, in which employees were given pay outcome and performance data but were not informed of the criteria underlying relative appraisal scores or how they might improve their standing in the future. Both of these factors are associated with employee justice perceptions.

In contrast, Pfeffer and Langton (1993) argue that people "prefer to remain ignorant, particularly of an unfavorable location in the distribution of organizational rewards" (p. 386), and that as a result, greater information about the dispersion in wages is likely to be associated with *lower* levels of job satisfaction. Focusing on the dispersion of wages among members of academic departments, and noting that pay tends to be more open in public (versus private) colleges, they posited and found the adverse effect of wage dispersion on employee satisfaction to indeed be greater among academics in public institutions. That is, people in public institutions exhibited greater dissatisfaction when salaries were more dispersed. Accordingly, whereas—as suggested by Futrell and Jenkins (1978)—pay transparency may *directly* enhance job satisfaction, in contexts in which pay is widely dispersed among organizational members, greater knowledge of such dispersion may diminish job satisfaction, particularly for those at the lower end of the pay range.

Implications for Fairness and Justice Perceptions

More recent research has focused on employees' attitudes that could theoretically serve as a mechanism linking pay communication to specific behavioral outcomes. As noted in Chapter 2, equity theory continues to play a central role in explaining the behavioral implications of pay communication policies and practices (e.g., Colella et al., 2007). Accordingly, much of the recent research on pay transparency's attitudinal effects has focused on employee perceptions of fairness, justice, or equity.

Organizational justice is considered to be an overarching concept capturing four main justice dimensions. *Distributive* justice captures the degree to which resources are allocated in a manner "consistent with implicit norms for allocation such as equity or equality" (Colquitt, 2001, p. 386). *Procedural* justice is the degree to which organizational procedures and decision-making are characterized by consistency, lack of bias, correctability, representation, accuracy, and ethicality (Colquitt, 2001, p. 386). *Interpersonal* justice is fostered when others are treated with respect, propriety, and sensitivity, and *informational* justice relates to whether any explanations provided are comprehensive, reasonable, timely, and truthful (Colquitt, 2001; Greenberg, 1993). At first glance, pay transparency may be thought of as facilitating all four aspects of justice or equity. For instance, pay outcome transparency should make those responsible for pay allocation decisions more accountable, and thereby drive more equitable pay structures and eliminate disparities incompatible with implicit merit-based norms of allocation. For similar accountability reasons, pay process transparency should boost procedural justice. Pay process and communication transparency should enhance informational and interpersonal justice by providing more comprehensive insights into how pay-related decisions are made and justified, and by respecting individuals' right to discuss (solicit and share) pay-related information with others.

However, these effects may not be as simple and straightforward as just suggested. For instance, policies that give employees access to others' personal pay information may violate the latter's right to personal privacy and thus be deemed as harming rather than promoting informational and interpersonal justice (Smit & Montag-Smit, 2018). Furthermore, it is *subjective perceptions* of justice that ultimately shape employee behavior, and these perceptions themselves may be grounded in different norms of resource allocation that vary from one subculture to another within the same organization. Keeping in mind the certainty effect discussed in Chapter 2, pay outcome transparency has the potential to amplify perceptions of pay *un*fairness by making allegedly unfair allocations more vivid and difficult to dismiss. Thus, pay outcome transparency can in some cases actually add fuel to the fire of injustice.

Empirical studies are beginning to shed further light on how pay communication policies and practices may impact employee justice perceptions. First the good news. Some experimental evidence indicates that at least one form of pay transparency, namely pay process transparency, has largely beneficial implications for perceptions of procedural and distributive justice. In a recent field study of 321 American, British, and Canadian citizens working at least 20 hours per week in the private sector, SimanTov-Nachlieli and Bamberger (2021) asked study participants to complete measures of process and outcome pay transparency as well as their perceptions of procedural and distributive justice. They found pay process transparency to have a significant positive correlation with both procedural justice ($r = .39, p < 0.01$) and distributive justice ($r = .27, p < 0.01$) and—in multiple regression analyses—to explain more than one-fifth of the variance in perceptions of both justice forms.

Looking more broadly, however, findings with regard to the effects of pay transparency on distributive justice are less clear. In an experimental study, Belogolovsky and Bamberger (2015) posited and found the impact of pay transparency on distributive justice perceptions to vary as a function of individual competitiveness—a stable and trans-situational disposition capturing the "desire to win in interpersonal situations" (Houston et al., 1992, p. 1153). Building on the idea that (a) in assessing distributive fairness, what matters for more competitive individuals is that their pay exceeds that of relevant others, and (b) in the absence of pay information, individuals upwardly bias their pay estimates for comparison peers (Lawler, 1965, 1967; Milkovich & Anderson, 1972), Belogolovsky and Bamberger argued that pay secrecy should be inversely associated with distributive justice perceptions and that this should be particularly true for more interpersonally competitive individuals. Consistent with this theorizing, in an experimental study comparing complete pay outcome transparency (i.e., participants could see the performance-based pay received by others) to complete secrecy, they found a significant ($p < 0.05$) negative main effect of pay secrecy on distributive justice perceptions. Moreover, as hypothesized, this main effect was driven largely by the more competitive participants. As shown in Figure 3.1, the slope of the total effect of pay condition on distributive fairness

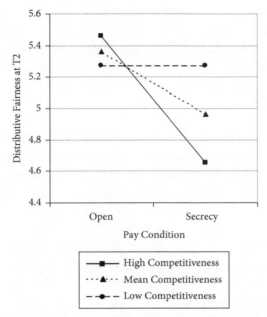

Figure 3.1 Moderation of the effect of pay condition on distributive fairness.
Reprinted with permission from Belogolovsky and Bamberger (2015).

perceptions for participants with low competitiveness scores (i.e., 1 standard deviation [SD] below the mean) was relatively flat (estimate = .00; $p > 0.10$). In contrast, for those with high competitiveness scores (1 SD above the mean), the slopes were steep and significant (estimate = –.80; $p < 0.01$).

Belogolovsky and Bamberger's (2015) findings, although notable, compared two rather extreme situations, namely complete pay outcome transparency with complete secrecy. Furthermore, participants in this lab experiment, all students, were told that their pay would be entirely based on their *objectively* assessed task performance relative to their peers. But how generalizable are these findings to real-life situations in which individuals experience varying degrees of pay outcome transparency, and in which the merit-based underpinnings of pay differentials may be uncertain? In the field study noted above, SimanTov-Nachlieli and Bamberger (2021) posited that rather than varying as a function of individual disposition, the impact of pay outcome transparency on distributive justice perceptions should vary as a function of individuals' level of pay relative to that of comparative peers. They assessed participants' self-perceived pay rankings as follows:

Think of a ladder with 10 rungs representing where employees in your organization, doing similar jobs or contributing the same level of value to the
organization as you do, stand in the pay range. At the top of the ladder are
the employees who have the highest pay. At the bottom are the employees
who have the lowest pay. Between 1 (bottom rung) and 10 (top rung), where
do you think you stand on this ladder?

Based on participants' responses to this question, the researchers found that
perceived pay position indeed moderates the effect of pay outcome transparency on perceived distributive justice. Pay outcome transparency was
associated with *lower* perceived distributive justice among participants who
positioned their pay below that of referent others. In contrast, among those
perceiving their pay as higher than that of others (1 SD unit above the mean),
there was a positive—but not statistically significant—association between
outcome pay transparency and distributive justice perceptions.

In a second study, approximately 400 employed Israeli online panel
members were told that they would be paid on the basis of their subjectively evaluated performance in an online task. Participants were divided
into four distinct experimental conditions: three pay outcome transparency
conditions in which the participants were paid (a) far less, (b) a little less,
or (c) more than their peers; and one pay outcome secrecy condition. As
shown in Figure 3.2, following their task performance, they received pay
information accordingly. Compared to those assigned to the secrecy condition, pay outcome transparency resulted in significantly lower distributive justice perceptions for those in the two lower paid conditions (lowest
for those paid far less). In contrast, compared to those assigned to the secrecy condition, pay outcome transparency resulted in significantly higher
distributive justice perceptions for those in the condition in which they
observed they were paid more than their peers. The condition assignment
by itself explained nearly 30 percent of the variance in distributive justice
perceptions.

Taken together, these studies indicate that pay outcome transparency may
have mixed effects on employees' perceptions of distributive justice. Where
pay is understood to be a function of justifiable (i.e., objective) differences
in performance, disclosing relative pay information may have beneficial
results, particularly among those disposed to be more competitive (for
whom such comparisons are more salient). But in the majority of situations,
in which the link between performance and pay is uncertain, the findings

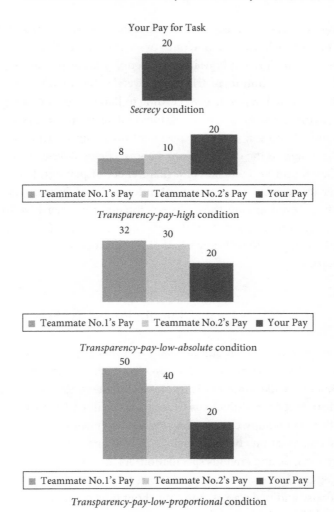

Figure 3.2 What participants were shown by condition in SimanTov-Nachlieli & Bamberger's (2021) second study.

Reprinted with permission from SimanTov-Nachlieli and Bamberger (2021).

of SimanTov-Nachlieli and Bamberger (2021) suggest that the impact of pay outcome transparency on distributive justice perceptions depends largely on employees' perceptions of where they fall relative to comparison others with respect to their pay.

As for the impact of pay transparency on the remaining justice dimensions, Bamberger and Belogolovsky (2010) examined the impact of pay outcome transparency (versus secrecy) on informational justice. Arguing that although more restrictive pay outcome practices may not necessarily limit information about how pay is awarded in theory (i.e., pay processes), pay outcome secrecy, by definition, restricts employees' access to information about how pay is allocated in practice. According to Bamberger and Belogolovsky, this may, in turn, raise employee suspicions that decision-makers have something to hide. However, in a lab experiment involving student participants, similar in design to the one mentioned above (Belogolovsky & Bamberger, 2015), they found no evidence of a main effect of pay outcome transparency (versus secrecy) on participant informational justice perceptions. Furthermore, even among those dispositionally more sensitive to unfairness (i.e., high inequity sensitivity), pay outcome secrecy (versus transparency) did not appear to have any significant impact on informational justice perceptions.

Implications for Envy

Envy is a common human emotion and one that is particularly salient in contexts—including work organizations—in which individuals compete for valued outcomes, like athletes in a sports tournament. Rewards need not be openly distributed for individuals to envy one another. For instance, in one information technology company, a software engineer explained that even everyday conversations between managers and subordinates could be the subject of intrigue and envious speculation. As he put it, "anytime our manager talked to anyone alone we would start to assume that that person was getting a raise and make an assumption about how much it was." Moreover, he claimed that this sense of envy was pervasive, impacting the productivity of the entire team. "Each time a new person was assumed to be the one getting a raise, the entire team would feel envious and work against him." So if envy and the counterproductive work behaviors that they can generate are a common consequence of more secretive approaches to remuneration, is pay transparency likely to mitigate or exacerbate such envy?

One of the primary arguments made by those opposed to pay transparency has long been that increased pay visibility and/or employee pay disclosures are likely to engender episodic envy, the negative emotion felt "when a person lacks another's superior quality, achievement, or possession and either desires it or wishes the other person lacked it" (Parrott & Smith, 1993,

p. 906). In other words, common as envy may be in the workplace, pay transparency is likely to exacerbate the situation. Recent research, building on social comparison theory and the certainty effect (discussed in Chapter 2), suggests that this concern may be well-founded.

Social comparison theory posits that humans have an inherent tendency to compare themselves with others, particularly those in a better situation than themselves, as a basis for self-evaluation and uncertainty reduction (Festinger, 1954; Wood, 1996; Buunk & Gibbons, 2007). The link between contrast-based upward comparisons and negative emotions such as envy is, as noted by Duffy and Shaw (2000, p. 4), "easy to imagine," and it has been demonstrated by others (e.g., Vecchio, 2005; Call et al., 2015). Moreover, few question that pay serves as a primary domain for social comparisons at work and, as a result, a basis for the emergence of envy (Vecchio, 2005; Duffy et al., 2012). Yet questions remain as to the degree to which transparency may influence upward social comparisons and the emotional reactions generated by them (Shaw, 2014). After all, pay need not be transparent for individuals to infer their relative pay situation. Moreover, as we have already discussed, in more restrictive pay communication situations, individuals tend to overestimate the pay of relevant others (peers) (e.g., Lawler, 1965, 1967). This, if anything, creates an exacerbated state of relative deprivation *in their minds*, and thus potentially generates greater envy in situations of more (versus less) restrictive pay communication.

While not dismissing this argument, Bamberger and Belogolovsky (2017) argued that due to the vividness of the pay information obtainable under conditions of greater pay transparency, as suggested by the certainty effect, pay transparency is likely to generate stronger feelings of episodic envy compared to pay secrecy. They conjectured that

> while pay transparency facilitates *realistic* upward comparisons (driven by hard to dismiss, concrete facts providing clear indications of one's position relative to others), pay secrecy allows for dismissible, *constructive comparisons* (driven by ambiguous information inferred from data of uncertain accuracy and reliability). (Goethals et al., 1991; Goethals & Klein, 2000, p. 660)

Furthermore, they argued that such realistic comparisons foster stronger feelings of episodic envy, for the two reasons outlined in Chapter 2: because the information vividness associated with objective, concrete, realistic comparisons makes them likely to elicit stronger emotional reactions (Nisbett & Ross, 1980; Kahneman, 2011); and because the certainty effect makes it difficult to dismiss realistic comparisons, thus reinforcing the salience of deprivation-related information (Tversky & Kahneman, 1983). In contrast, consistent with research on information ambiguity (Van Dijk & Zeelenberg, 2003), pay secrecy leads to constructive comparisons that are easily discounted or rationalized away. Accordingly, they expected that even a low degree of perceived relative deprivation would elicit stronger envy reactions under conditions of pay transparency than under pay secrecy. Moreover, because individuals with more collectivist (versus individualistic) orientations are more prone to engage in social comparison (Buunk & Gibbons, 2007), they posited that these adverse effects of transparency on envy would be amplified among the former.

Using a lab-based experimental design similar to that used in their earlier work, Bamberger and Belogolovsky (2017) tested this reasoning on 146 undergraduate business students in Singapore. The participants were randomly assigned to one of four pay communication conditions, with two conditions stable over six rounds of performance (the secrecy and transparency conditions), and the other two changing in round 4 (secret to transparent, transparent to secret). Participants in the secrecy condition (and during the secrecy portion of the changing conditions) received information only on their own level of performance and bonus pay. Those in the transparency condition (and transparency portion of the changing conditions) received information on (a) their own performance level and pay and (b) the pay (but not performance) of their fellow group members (all of whom were confederates). The results of the experiment largely supported Bamberger and Belogolovsky's conjecture. Although no main effect of pay transparency on episodic envy was found, the interaction of pay transparency with individualist/collectivist orientation was observed to significantly predict envy. Specifically, as shown in Figure 3.3, the slope of pay transparency on envy toward the highest paid other at T_2 is positive and significant for those with a strong collectivist orientation, but nonsignificant for those with a less collectivist (i.e., more individualistic) orientation.

Similar findings, indicating an adverse effect of pay transparency on peer envy, were reported by Schnaufer et al. (2018). Their longitudinal field study involved employees of a German technology company following introduction of a company-wide transparency initiative. The effects were more robust

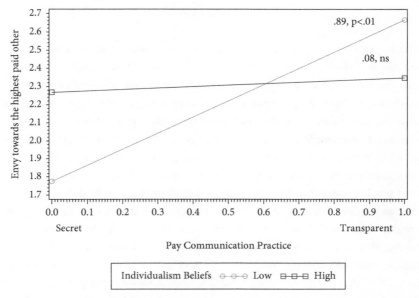

Figure 3.3 Moderating effects of individualism/collectivism on the relationship between pay transparency and envy toward the highest paid other.
Reprinted with permission from Belogolovsky and Bamberger (2017).

among employees who (a) were more sensitive to injustice and (b) had a stronger latent fear of being exploited, what the researchers refer to as "victim sensitivity."

Notably, although the two studies just described focused on the envy-related implications of pay *outcome* transparency, interviews with managers and employees suggest that similar effects may be generated on the basis of pay *communication* transparency. For instance, one of the managers interviewed as part of my research into pay transparency recounted his experiences with an extremely "pay-centric" subordinate, in what he described as an organization in which pay information was highly restricted:

Obviously, I could never tell him how much others made as that was not allowed, but I had the feeling that he periodically compared salaries with his peers. Every time I had the feeling that he was doing that comparison I would subsequently notice a drastic and sudden change in his behavior: He would hide information to try to get ahead of his peers and do other negative things that ultimately affected his career.

Implications for Trust

The implications of pay transparency for employees' trust in management are anything but clear-cut. Although it may seem intuitive that more secretive pay practices should generate suspicion and lack of trust, can we logically assume that pay transparency will have the opposite effect? Anecdotal observations collected in my qualitative research suggest this may indeed be the case. For example, one customer engagement worker who we interviewed recalled that soon after joining her company, some 12 years prior to our conversation, she learned that her co-workers were all about to receive a 25 percent pay increase. Inquiring with her supervisor, she was told that although this was indeed the case, as a new employee she was not eligible for the increase: "They explained to me that my salary had already been determined taking this new salary schedule into account, and that a merit-based increase could be expected only after my next review in a year's time." But due to a downturn in the company's fortunes and a subsequent pay freeze, that 25 percent gap remained for the next 10 years. As our interviewee stated,

> The knowledge that they were all making more than me made me very frustrated and it wasn't easy working there. I had to remind myself that my day would come to get a raise and that my work wasn't any less important.

However, her relationship with her supervisor remained unaffected, precisely because he was open with her about the pay gap, and because he did his best to work around it, supplementing her pay with "other perks."

As defined by Mayer et al. (1995), *trust* is

> the willingness of a party to be vulnerable to the actions of another party based on the expectation that the other will perform a particular action important to the trustor, irrespective of the ability to monitor or control that other party. (p. 712)

Mayer and Davis (1999) argue that employee trust in management develops over time, largely as a function of the latter's actions and decisions. Building on this idea, Montag-Smit and Smit (2021) proposed and demonstrated that human resources–related actions, specifically those related to pay communication, impact employee trust not so much via employee fairness perceptions but, rather, by affecting the motives employees attribute to the actions and decisions of their employer. Indeed, as they note, pay secrecy may drive even employees who believe they are being paid fairly to attribute negative motives to their employer, thus diminishing their trust.

Montag-Smit and Smit (2021) argue that pay transparency has both risks and benefits for employees. For example, under conditions of pay transparency, managers may feel pressure to pay all employees similarly. This can compress differentials and present a risk to pay equity (Bartol & Martin, 1989). On the other hand, by increasing managers' accountability for their pay decisions, pay transparency may be viewed as supporting overall pay fairness. Montag-Smit and Smit resolve this conundrum by arguing that different transparency dimensions may have different trust implications. More precisely, they suggest that pay process and communication transparency should be associated with greater employee trust in management to the extent that individual employees can control how much personal information about their own pay is disclosed to others. Where pay transparency involves the disclosure of individual pay (i.e., pay outcome transparency), trust in management may rise or fall depending on individuals' information-sharing preferences. Pay outcome transparency may lead to diminished trust among individuals who prefer not to share pay information or, conversely, to heightened trust in management for those with positive sharing preferences. Montag-Smit and Smit also posit that the link between pay transparency and trust is mediated by employee attributions about whether their employer's motives are benevolent or malevolent.

Montag-Smit and Smit (2021) tested this idea with a cross-sectional survey using a pooled sample of MTurk workers ($n = 197$)—that is, ordinary people who had signed up for Amazon's Mechanical Turk, an online labor market—and university employees ($n = 168$), who worked in organizations with varying levels of all three forms of pay transparency. As hypothesized, they found that pay transparency policies and practices impact employee trust in management by shaping employee attributions of the employer's motives. As shown in Figure 3.4, more restrictive pay process and communication policies were positively associated with malevolent attributions (and negatively with benevolent attributions) and, in accordance, with lower levels of trust. With respect to pay outcome transparency, no such effects were detected until individual pay sharing preferences were taken into account. When these preferences were considered, more restrictive pay outcome practices were positively associated with malevolent attributions ($b = .17$, $p < 0.01$), and hence indirectly linked with diminished trust—but only

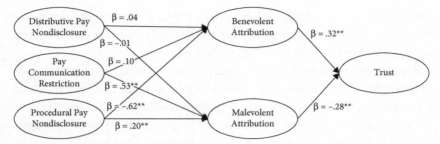

Figure 3.4 Findings from a test of an attribution-mediated model of three forms of pay transparency (outcome, process, and communication transparency) on trust.
Reprinted with permission from Montag-Smit and Smit (2020).

among employees who had more open sharing preferences. Among those with more secretive preferences, these same restrictive practices had no effect on employee attributions or trust.

Whereas Montag-Smit and Smit (2021) demonstrate that the impact of pay process and communication transparency on trust is largely positive (albeit stronger in the case of the latter among those more willing to share their own pay information), Alterman et al. (2021) argue that these effects may depend on perceptions of organizational-level differences in distributive fairness. Building on uncertainty management theory (discussed in Chapter 2), they propose that individuals may be unable to make informed fairness or trust assessments without considering some additional justice cue. They suggest that distributive justice serves as such a cue (consistent with systems justification theory; Jost, 1995), and they argue that when distributive justice is considered in the context of pay secrecy, employees are likely to dismiss aversive fairness information. They do so for two reasons. First, attributions of unfairness suggest a lack of control, which in turn can lower one's self-esteem and self-efficacy (Van den Bos & Lind, 2002). Second, they do so because they can: Given the context of pay secrecy, there is no clear evidence that pay has in fact been unfairly allocated. In contrast, consistent with the certainty effect (Kahneman & Tversky, 1979)—that is, the heuristic by which people overweight outcomes that are certain relative to those that are probable—when pay is more transparent, the vivid content of that information may make it difficult for employees to deny distributive injustice, thus eliciting more negative assessments of organizational trustworthiness.

Based on this logic, Alterman et al. suggest that under conditions of *low* distributive justice perceptions, the uncertainty associated with more restrictive pay communication (i.e., higher pay secrecy) is likely to better preserve trust levels. In other words, they argue that when employees perceive distributive justice in their organization as deficient, the relationship between pay secrecy perceptions and organizational trust is positive, with greater pay secrecy linked to *higher* trust, and greater transparency to *lower* trust. In contrast, when employees perceive distributive justice in their organization as robust, Alterman et al. posit an inverse relationship between pay secrecy and trust. This is because where pay is more transparent, perceptions of distributive justice (i.e., fair pay) likely reinforce transparency-based inferences that the organization is trustworthy, whereas in the context of pay secrecy, the uncertainty surrounding outcome-based inferences results in a more muted trust reaction.

Using a sample of approximately 200 Chinese executive MBA students (all employed) and applying a two-phase survey design, Alterman et al. (2021) initially assessed participants' perceptions of pay process and pay communication transparency in their respective firms. One month later, Alterman et al. assessed participants' perceptions of organizational trustworthiness. As expected, they found that distributive justice perceptions indeed moderate the impact of pay transparency on trust. Specifically, they found that among employees who perceived distributive justice in their organizations as high, organizational trust rose along with perceptions of greater transparency. However, among those perceiving distributive justice as low, the reverse was true: Organizational trust was positively related to pay *secrecy*, with trust higher under conditions of pay secrecy than under conditions of pay transparency.

Taken together, these studies suggest that the association between pay communication practices and employee trust in the organization is anything but simple. Transparency with regard to pay procedures and processes, as well as employee pay disclosures (i.e., pay communication transparency), is likely to elicit greater trust, but only when employees have a sense that pay is generally allocated on a fair and equitable basis. Absent this sense of underlying fairness, even pay communication practices that are seemingly benign (in terms of personal privacy) may not in fact boost employee perceptions of organizational trustworthiness but, rather, may backfire and degrade them.

Behavioral Implications: Task and Contextual
Performance at Work

As noted above, based on his seminal findings, Lawler proposed already in the 1960s that more restrictive pay practices, by distorting employees' perceptions of relative pay, adversely affect motivation and hence job performance. Equity theory (Adams, 1963) served as the basis for this conjecture, with the argument going something like this:

a. Pay secrecy distorts employees' perceptions of others' pay.
b. This distortion leads individuals to believe they are paid less than others, taking their relative contributions into account. In other words, they perceive their relative reward:contribution ratio as inequitable.
c. Employees seek to restore balance to their reward:contribution ratio by increasing their rewards and/or reducing their contribution.

Based on this logic, throughout the years, a number of studies have examined how pay communication practices and policies may impact employees' task and contextual performance.

Job Performance

Several studies have tested this equity-mediated model of the relationship between pay transparency and individual job performance or, more simply, the expectation that pay transparency is associated with higher job performance. One of the first to do so was the study by Futrell and Jenkins (1978) mentioned above, with pharmaceutical sales employees. In addition to assessing the impact of increased pay transparency on satisfaction levels, the investigators also tested for a possible impact on job performance, as assessed by the employees' supervisors. As will be recalled, the study applied a quasi-experimental design, offering sales personnel in three of the company's nine sales districts (152 of 508 sales staff) information regarding each salesperson's performance evaluation, as well as well as average salaries for different tenure categories, and low, high, and average merit increase amounts. Using a 7-point measure of performance, the findings suggest robust support for Lawler's conjecture, with a change in overall assessed job performance (from before to after the lifting of pay information restrictions) of 0.66 for those in the three experimental districts versus –0.02 for those of their peers in the six districts that maintained relative pay secrecy ($F = 74.88$, $p < 0.001$).

But what accounts for this positive association between pay outcome transparency and job performance? Futrell and Jenkins' (1978) findings of a link between pay transparency and greater job satisfaction are suggestive of a tit-for-tat explanation, in which employees reciprocate their enhanced job satisfaction by increasing their effort and contribution. Unfortunately, the study presents no direct evidence for any such mechanism. In an effort to begin to better understand the nature of the transparency–performance association, Bamberger and Belogolovsky conducted several experimental studies, using a design in which students were randomly assigned to either a pay outcome secrecy condition or a pay outcome transparency condition. In both conditions, in multiple rounds, they received a merit-based reward based on their round-specific performance relative to their peers on a simple task.

In their initial study, Bamberger and Belogolovsky (2010) combined equity theory and fairness heuristics theory (Lind, 2001) to posit that distributive fairness perceptions would explain the negative impact of pay secrecy (relative to transparency) on objective task performance. Specifically, they argued that although employees are always concerned about the fairness of their pay, under conditions of pay secrecy they have little choice but to draw inferences from other fairness indicators, such as those connected to procedural and informational justice. Assuming that rewards are directly tied to objectively assessed performance, to the extent that employees' access to pay-related information is more restricted, they are likely to draw negative inferences regarding procedural and informational fairness and to use these inferences as a basis for perceptions of distributive fairness. Equity theory (Adams, 1963) would then predict a downward adjustment of effort for employees working under conditions of pay secrecy, thus depressing their performance (relative to that of those working under conditions of pay transparency). Bamberger and Belogolovsky's findings were largely consistent with this theorizing. First, they found that although mean performance rose over the trial rounds in the pay-transparent condition (from 463.62 [SD = 143.61] to 637.42 [SD = 276.22]), mean performance *dropped* in the secrecy condition (from 606.89 [SD = 224.22] to 556.85 [SD = 281.47]). Similarly, mean distributive fairness perceptions increased over this interval in the pay-transparent condition but declined slightly in the secrecy condition. More precise tests of the indirect effect of pay secrecy (versus transparency) via distributive fairness perceptions indicated that this indirect effect was in the negative direction expected and statistically significant (low/high confidence intervals [CIs] = –80.76, –3.98), accounting for approximately 17 percent of the total effect of secrecy on task performance. Finally, moderation analyses indicated that these effects of pay secrecy on task performance via distributive fairness were amplified for—and largely driven by—those employees who were more interpersonally competitive. For those with low levels of competitiveness (–1 SD), the indirect effect of secrecy on distributive fairness was 0.00 (standard error [SE] = 22.54) and nonsignificant (low/high CIs = –45.31, 45.36), whereas for those with high levels of competitiveness (+1 SD), the expected indirect effect of secrecy on fairness was –69.46 (SE = 30.73) and significant (low/high CIs = –137.57, –18.77), accounting for 29 percent of the total effect of pay secrecy on performance.

Belogolovsky and Bamberger (2014) used a similar design to test an alternative explanation for the adverse impact of pay secrecy on individual job performance. Drawing from expectancy theory and the findings reported by Lawler in the 1960s, they posited that pay secrecy may degrade performance by adversely impacting employees' effort–pay instrumentality perceptions (what they refer to as pay-for-performance or PFP perceptions), with these effects exacerbated by any situational (rather than individual difference) factor that might weaken the expected impact of effort on rewards. More precisely, they argued that Lawler's seminal finding—that under conditions of pay secrecy people overestimate the pay of their peers and underestimate that of their superiors—effectively compresses the *perceived* (relative to the true) range of pay for varying levels of contribution. Based on expectancy theory (Vroom, 1964), this compression in perceived PFP should reduce how hard employees are willing to work, leading to diminished performance. Furthermore, this should be so particularly in situations in which (a) effort–reward contingencies are made even more uncertain, such as when performance is assessed subjectively rather than based on objective measures, or (b) performance is assessed relative to others (e.g., pay is contingent on ranked performance) rather than on the basis of some absolute criterion (e.g., meeting a minimal level of performance).

Consistent with earlier findings (Futrell & Jenkins, 1978; Bamberger & Belogolovsky, 2010), Belogolovsky and Bamberger's (2014) results show that pay secrecy indeed has an adverse effect on individual task performance. This is not to say that PFP perceptions *unconditionally* mediate the performance

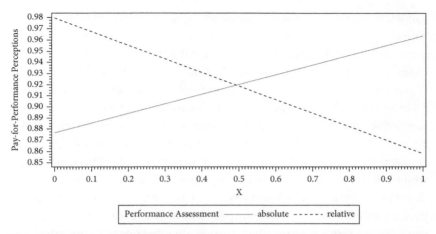

Figure 3.5 Moderation of the effect of pay communication policy (X) on subsequent instrumentality (pay-for-performance) perceptions.
Reprinted with permission from Belogolovsky and Bamberger (2014).

effects of pay secrecy. In fact, Belogolovsky and Bamberger found that these perceptions are relatively insensitive to pay transparency or secrecy when performance is assessed based on absolute criteria, but they are highly sensitive when performance is assessed on a relative basis. Interestingly, in this study, PFP perceptions were lowest under conditions of pay secrecy and the (relative) ranking-based approach to pay determination (which is the norm in most organizations) and highest under conditions of pay transparency and relative (versus absolute) criteria (Figure 3.5). This is noteworthy in that although pay–performance contingencies unbounded by some absolute standard may signal potentially higher rewards for superior performance, the uncertainties associated with relative (as opposed to absolute) criteria should theoretically heighten risk, thus potentially limiting the expected instrumentality of effort in driving rewards. The results of this study therefore suggest that in organizations in which pay is driven by one's job performance relative to a set of comparison peers, transparency may signal reduced risk, thus facilitating *higher* instrumentality or PFP perceptions.

The findings of Belogolovsky and Bamberger (2014) are important for several reasons. First, they replicate earlier findings indicating that more restrictive pay communication practices may adversely affect individual job performance. Second, they offer further insight into the motivational basis for such effects, suggesting that pay secrecy may degrade employee motivation as a function of not only reduced fairness perceptions (an explanation consistent with equity theory) but also reduced instrumentality perceptions (an explanation consistent with expectancy theory). Finally, these findings hold across the board for all employees, in contrast to studies which suggest that the impact of pay outcome transparency on job performance may be highly contingent on individual differences, such as interpersonal competitiveness (Bamberger & Belogolovsky, 2010) or narcissism (LaViers, 2019). This is valuable to know because although employers have no control over individual differences among their employees, they do have some control over the situational context within which pay-related practices take place—and particularly with how pay-determining performance is assessed. Thus, understanding the potential impact of various pay communication practices on employee performance gives employers scope for adjusting the former in ways that might improve the latter.

Other studies by behavioral economists offer additional evidence of a potential transparency boost to individual performance but hint at a subtler explanation. For example, Huet-Vaughn (2014) reports that in a study of employees paid on the basis of piecework, those who were given information about their co-workers' earnings (based on similar work at the same piece rate) outperformed by 10 percent those working under more restrictive pay information conditions. Similarly, Blanes et al. (2011) found that when piece-rate workers in a German enterprise were told their relative position in the distribution of pay and productivity, productivity rose. In both of these cases, the investigators invoke a more automatic cognitive explanation for their findings—namely that the provision of comparative pay and productivity information activates workers' incipient concerns about their standing relative to others, and so pushes them to improve their performance.

Yet although this status-based explanation is logical, neither study offers any empirical evidence to support such a mechanism. Furthermore, the generalizability of these findings may be questioned because in both studies the focus was on highly quantifiable piece-rate work. Under such a simple, objective assessment system, workers clearly understand that any gap between expected and actual performance (or pay) can be addressed merely by exerting greater effort. What happens, however, when employees are given information only about their *relative* performance and pay, especially when the nature of the work offers no standard route for improving one's performance relative to others? Barankay (2012) asked this question in a field experiment with furniture salespeople who were responsible for selling a variety of product types and brands. Prior to the experiment, all salespeople were told their performance rankings, and this information was then halted in the treatment group. Barankay observed the opposite effect from that seen by Huet-Vaughn (2014) and by Blanes et al. (2011)—namely an *improvement* in sales performance among those no longer receiving ranking information relative to their peers who continued to receive such information. The explanation: When employees performing multiple tasks are only told that their overall performance rank is lower than expected, without any guidance as to what they must do to hit the desired level, they are likely to become demoralized. In other words, although providing relative performance-related information may activate an automatic tendency for people to boost their effort so as to improve their relative position, this is only true when people can see a clear link between their effort and its rewards. When the link between effort and one's performance ranking is uncertain, people may not only fail to intensify their task-related effort but also work *less* productively, choosing instead to allocate their time and energy resources to other domains in which effort–outcome relations are more certain.

So what's the takeaway for managers? Does pay transparency bode well for individual task performance, or might it be best to stick to pay secrecy? Overall, research findings suggest that, consistent with a number of theoretical perspectives, pay transparency is indeed associated with enhanced individual task performance. Although Barankay's (2012) findings go in the opposite direction, suggesting that task performance drops with greater transparency, there is no reason to over-interpret this finding and totally dismiss the other, more consistent findings of a positive effect of pay transparency. Rather, in light of the overwhelming evidence suggesting a beneficial impact of pay transparency on job performance, it makes sense to view these results as suggesting that in situations in which performance ratings are subjective, pay transparency should be accompanied by *performance appraisal* transparency. In other words, in such cases, it may be important to tell employees as much as possible about the criteria used to assess job performance, in addition to providing the resources (e.g., training) that would allow them to better meet these criteria in the future.

Impact on Contextual Work Behavior

Contextual work behavior refers to positive and negative work behaviors that go beyond nondiscretionary task performance, specifically behaviors that "shape the organizational, social, and psychological context that serves as the catalyst for task activities and processes" (Borman & Motowidlo, 1997, p. 100). Positive contextual work behaviors typically fall under the rubric of organizational citizenship behavior (OCB), defined as employee behavior that is at least somewhat volitional and that improves the functioning of an organization (Organ & Paine, 1999). These behaviors typically encompass elements of altruism, sportsmanship, conscientiousness, and courtesy, and they take the form of helping co-workers, developing ways to help the organization function better, and volunteering for extra duties (Organ & Ryan, 1995; Podsakoff et al., 1997). Negative contextual work behavior is often referred to as counterproductive work behavior (CWB), and it is in many ways the semantic opposite of OCB (Dalal et al., 2009); it includes any volitional employee behavior that harms, or is intended to harm, the legitimate interests of an organization (Sackett & DeVore, 2001; Spector et al., 2006). Behaviors that fall under this heading include confrontational or aggressive behavior and work withdrawal. Although not a central focus of OCB and CWB research, pay systems and structures have been studied as possible influences on such behaviors. For example, research has examined how alternative forms of team-based pay may have both positive and negative influences on co-worker helping, a core citizenship behavior (Bamberger & Levi, 2009).

Conceptual discussions of how pay communication policies and practices may impact contextual behavior also point to both positive and negative effects. For example, based on social exchange theory (Blau, 1964), Marasi et al. (2018) suggest that pay transparency has a positive effect on OCB and a negative association with workplace deviance behaviors or CWB. Following the logic described earlier with respect to organizational justice, they argue that when pay communication is restricted, employees are likely to suspect the organization of engaging in unfair practices at employees' expense and to reciprocate by withholding discretionary cooperative work behaviors (e.g., OCB) and engaging in more deviant behavior (CWB). Equally, when employees are given less restricted access to pay information, they are likely to perceive such policies as indicating informational, procedural, and distributive fairness on the part of the employer and to reciprocate by avoiding any deviant behavior and boosting their engagement in organizational citizenship behavior.

Others suggest more negative effects. For instance, as discussed earlier, under conditions of greater pay outcome transparency, employees may observe discrepancies that they would otherwise not suspect or would dismiss as unlikely. Where such disclosures reinforce perceptions of distributive unfairness, the reciprocity expected by Marasi et al. (2018) may be unlikely to emerge.[1] Furthermore, as also just discussed, pay outcome transparency may lead to envy, with its pernicious effects on employee collaboration and helping behavior. In the worst cases, envious employees may actively pursue actions aimed at harming their envied co-workers. Finally, employees who believe they are underpaid may attempt to unilaterally restore equity (Greenberg, 1990) by engaging in organizationally targeted deception. Thus, by this line of reasoning, pay outcome transparency may be inversely related to helping, a central dimension of OCB, and may even be positively related to sabotage, cheating, or theft, which are central dimensions of CWB.

Three empirical studies have attempted to resolve this debate. Marasi et al. (2018) used a cross-sectional, survey-based design to test a model in which pay communication openness (a construct capturing both the degree to which employee pay communication is unrestricted by the employer and the degree to which the employer provides pay information to employees) is associated with heightened levels of OCB via enhanced informational and distributive justice perceptions. Using a sample of 611 American MTurk workers, they found no link between pay openness and either OCB or CWB via distributive justice. However, they did find the expected positive effect on OCB via informational justice perceptions. In addition, they found evidence of a weaker indirect, negative effect of pay openness on CWB via informational justice perceptions.

The second study, by Bamberger and Belogolovsky (2017), used an experimental design with a student sample to test the envy-mediated effects of pay transparency on peer collaboration. In the experiment, participants solved anagrams in return for performance-based pay, with participants randomized between open and secret pay conditions. The first part of this experiment was described earlier in this chapter, in the context of pay communication's impact on envy. But the study also had a second element, namely to assess the mediating role of envy in linking pay outcome transparency to peer helping. As noted above, in this study, Bamberger and Belogolovsky found pay transparency to have the expected positive effects on episodic envy, particularly among participants with a more collectivist orientation (i.e., a higher

---

[1] Marasi et al. (2018) note that perceptions of distributive unfairness are unlikely under conditions of pay outcome transparency because "organizations that utilize pay openness practices probably have an equitable pay structure to avoid potential conflict and pay discrimination lawsuits," whereas organization with pay structures that are (or appear to be) inequitable "are less likely to use pay openness . . . and more likely to hide the inequitable pay structure" (p. 63).

tendency to engage in social comparisons). To assess the impact of envy on helping, as part of the same experiment, participants received periodic help requests from their "teammates" (all confederates). The number of help requests from the highest paid (and thus most enviable) teammate to which the participant acceded served as the indicator of help-giving or peer collaboration. As expected, the findings showed an inverse association between the envy expressed toward the highest paid teammate and the provision of help to that individual. As shown in Figure 3.6, this negative effect was attenuated among participants who scored high in measures of prosocial orientation but amplified among those who, by disposition, were less prosocial. Combining both elements of their experimental model, they found pay outcome transparency to have a robust indirect and negative effect on peer helping via episodic envy, particularly among individuals who were more collectivistic and less prosocial in orientation.

Finally, in the SimanTov-Nachlieli and Bamberger (2021) study discussed earlier, the researchers sought to examine the role of distributive and procedural justice perceptions in explaining a possible effect of pay outcome and process transparency on CWB. As already noted, based on uncertainty

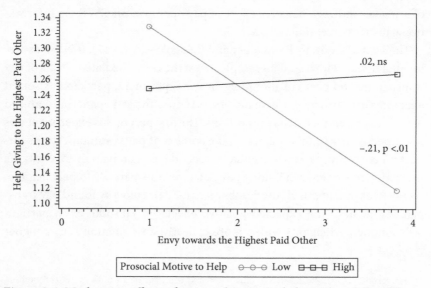

Figure 3.6 Moderating effects of prosocial motive to help on the relationship between envy toward the highest paid other and help giving to the same.
Reprinted with permission from Belogolovsky and Bamberger (2017).

management theory, they posited and found pay process transparency to be positively related to procedural justice perceptions in their survey of more than 300 North American and British private sector workers. Pay process transparency was also positively associated with distributive justice perceptions. Extending the findings of Marasi et al. (2018), they found procedural justice perceptions to be inversely associated with the frequency of self-reported CWB directed against the organization (e.g., theft) and both procedural and distributive justice perceptions to be inversely associated with CWB directed against the organization and fellow employees (e.g., aggression and sabotage).

But what about the effects of pay outcome transparency? These effects were a bit more complex. As will be recalled, the effect of pay outcome transparency on distributive and procedural justice perceptions was found to be contingent on the participant's self-perceived position on the pay ladder. For those at the top of that ladder, there was a positive association with distributive pay transparency, but for those toward the bottom, the association was negative. With distributive justice perceptions inversely associated with both co-worker-directed and organizationally directed CWB, the investigators found an effect of pay outcome transparency on both forms of CWB, contingent on pay position. For those at the high end of the pay ladder, those for whom relative pay information was more accessible reported higher distributive justice and less frequent engagement in both forms of CWB. However, for those at the lower end, the effects were precisely the opposite: diminished distributive justice and more frequent engagement in CWB directed against both the organization and co-workers. Moreover, in their experimental follow-up study, SimanTov-Nachlieli and Bamberger (2021) found that relative to those in a secrecy or high-pay transparency condition, those in a transparent but underpaid condition were more likely to cheat (i.e., steal from the investigator) and also engaged in more deceptive and unfair behaviors toward an anonymous co-participant ("co-worker").

Although the findings from these three studies suggest somewhat divergent effects, they are reconcilable. The Marasi et al. (2018) study used a broad-scale measure of pay communication openness that encompassed all three dimensions of this construct. The fact that no indirect effect via distributive justice was found suggests that the beneficial indirect effects on increased OCB and reduced deviance behavior (CWB) via informational justice were likely driven by pay process and pay communication transparency. As noted earlier, these two pay transparency practices neither impinge on employee privacy preferences nor offer the kind of pay outcome information that might be suggestive of unfair reward allocation on the part of the organization. Accordingly, to the extent that these two practices are perceived as promoting informational justice, reciprocity in the form of heightened OCB and reduced organizational-directed CWB is most reasonable. In contrast, the study by Bamberger and Belogolovsky (2017) focused strictly on how pay *outcome* transparency affects peer helping, and they examined one particular scenario in which the pay information disclosed indicates one's pay is below that of a peer. As noted by the investigators, although this sounds like a rather unique situation, it may be more common than one suspects; there is consistent evidence that individuals tend to more frequently engage in upward (versus downward) comparisons, comparing themselves more frequently to higher rather than lower earning peers (Buunk & Gibbons, 2007). Accordingly, when considering this study in light of Marasi et al. (2018), the findings suggest that whereas pay communication and process transparency may lead to increased OCB, pay outcome transparency may be problematic with respect to a central dimension of OCB, namely peer helping and collaboration.

A similar conclusion may be reached when contrasting Marasi et al.'s (2018) findings regarding CWB with those of SimanTov-Nachlieli and Bamberger (2021). Here, too, whereas the former appear to reflect the beneficial (CWB-reducing) effects of pay process and pay communication transparency, the latter highlight the more complex and problematic effects of pay outcome transparency. Although pay outcome transparency may result in diminished CWB for those at the high end of relative pay, for those at the bottom end, pay outcome transparency appears to elicit behaviors detrimental to both the organization and the employee's peers.

Conclusion

This chapter presented what some might call "the good, the bad, and the ugly" with respect to pay transparency's potential impact on employee perceptions, attitudes, and job-related behaviors. Rather than there being one common vector of outcomes, the pattern of effects varies according to the particular pay transparency policy implemented, as well as the consequence of interest. The findings presented here also suggest that pay transparency practices affect employee behavior via individual perceptions and attitudes.

In terms of what this all means for organizations, the findings presented here suggest that at least with regard to the pay outcome and pay communication forms of transparency, the risks with respect to individual employee attitudes and behaviors are limited. No study that I am aware of suggests that easing restrictions on the communication of pay processes, or allowing employees to discuss pay more openly with one another, adversely affects employee attitudes or job-related behaviors. However, the evidence presented in this chapter suggests that the robust task-related benefits of pay outcome transparency may be accompanied by potential attitudinal and behavioral risks, particularly among those falling at the lower end of pay structures. As we discuss in Chapter 4, in addition to these individual-level consequences, this combination of benefits and risks also plays out when considering the implications of pay communication at the organizational level.

4

The Impact of Pay Transparency on the Firm

Many of the individual-level consequences of pay transparency discussed in Chapter 3 can, in theory, have significant enterprise-level implications. In this chapter, we examine whether, when, and how these pay communication policies and practices might impact outcomes of relevance to the organization. We begin by focusing on potential implications of pay transparency for the firm's human capital resources and, specifically, how different pay communication practices may affect the firm's ability to attract and retain employees generally and key talent specifically. This requires an examination not only of the links between transparency and employees' motivation to remain (i.e., employee retention and turnover rates) but also of the extent to which pay transparency results in the self-selection of *certain types* of employees (what labor economists call "sorting"). Following this analysis, we turn our attention to the implications of pay transparency for performance management and pay dispersion (differences in pay levels within and across jobs or organizational levels; Shaw et al., 2002). Building on the notion that transparency heightens the socioemotional costs to managers of differentially rating their subordinates' performance, and the subsequent implications for pay dispersion, we discuss how both employees and supervisors may be incentivized to seek more particularistic and discreet ways of rewarding top performers, namely via "perks" (or, in more technical terms, idiosyncratic or i-deals). Because all of these effects can have normative implications for the firm, we also examine in this chapter the ways in which pay communication policies and practices can transform (as well as be reciprocally influenced by) organizational culture and climate. The chapter concludes by discussing the net impact of all of these enterprise-level effects of pay transparency on productivity and firm performance.

Exposing Pay. Peter Bamberger, Oxford University Press. © Oxford University Press 2023.
DOI: 10.1093/oso/9780197628164.003.0004

Pay Transparency and the Attraction and Retention of Human Capital Resources

Human resources (HR) scholars and practitioners have long argued that it is the people that make the firm (Schneider, 1987). Indeed, the resource-based view (Barney, 2001) argues that human capital, defined by Becker (2002, p. 3) as "the knowledge, information, ideas, skills, and health of individuals," is a key driver of competitive advantage. Putting these ideas together, Ployhart et al. (2014) use the term human capital resources for the individual and synergistic contributions of a firm's employees—their combined mix of energy, drive, creativity, experience, knowledge, and skills. Practitioners and scholars recognize that the loss of these individual and synergistic contributions can have devastating consequences for an organization.

Although a variety of HR policies and practices can help organizations attract, develop, effectively deploy, and retain good employees, it is well-established that compensation and benefits play an essential role in motivating talent to join and remain with the organization. For example, Cable and Judge (1994) found that pay level (not surprisingly) is positively associated with job attractiveness. Controlling for pay level per se (reflecting a situation in which different jobs offer similar levels of pay), Cable and Judge found that other pay system attributes, such as flexible benefits and individual-based (versus group-based) pay or performance, may affect individuals' job choice decisions. Similarly, Shaw et al. (1998) found levels of pay and benefits to be inversely associated with, and to explain nearly half of the variance in, voluntary turnover among the truck drivers they studied.

To some degree, these findings reflect the idea that pay levels and compensation systems are often broadly emblematic of organizational values. As Rynes (1987) states, "Compensation systems are capable of attracting (or repelling) the right kinds of people because they communicate so much about an organization's philosophy, values, and practices" (p. 190). Nonetheless, the impact of compensation and benefits on organizational success in recruiting and retaining human capital resources reflects the basic assumption that individuals seek to maximize their perceived utility in any wage–effort bargain (Akerlof & Yellen, 1990). Accordingly, when considering whether to take (or remain in) a job, all of us compare across alternative positions the actual or potential return on our labor: what we get from an employer in return for the time, energy, and other personal resources that we put into the job. This rewards/contribution comparison is at the root of equity theory

(Adams, 1963), discussed in Chapter 2. When it comes to securing human capital resources, managers have to assume that when the results of this comparison are not in their organization's favor, they will be unable to attract (and retain) the kinds of employees they want. Consistent with Albert Hirschman's (1970) classic exit, voice, and loyalty theory, current employees who perceive that their returns for the same inputs will be better elsewhere may voice their concerns and negotiate for a pay increase and, if this fails, may simply "follow the money." However, what is critical to remember here is that these equity-based comparisons are all based on *perceptions*, and as discussed in Chapters 2 and 3, the accuracy and salience of these perceptions are often influenced by the degree to which organizational pay communication policies and practices are more or less transparent.

Three main questions arise when considering how pay communication may impact an organization's ability to attract and retain human capital resources. The first concerns the degree to which pay communication policies and practices impact organizations' ability to efficiently meet their recruitment objectives. The second concerns the effect of these policies and practices on employee turnover intentions and rates. The third question concerns the degree to which pay transparency may impact the qualitative nature of these shifts in human capital resources with respect to both recruitment and retention (i.e., sorting effects).

Pay Transparency and Talent Recruitment

There is good reason to suspect that organizational pay communication policies and practices may impact the job choices made by potential candidates—and thus the organization's ability to secure the talent it seeks. There are two ways this may occur. First, as suggested by Rynes' (1987) remark quoted above, pay-related practices send signals to potential employees about the organization's "philosophy, values, and practices," and particularly the nature of its employment relations. As noted by Cable and Judge (1994), more transparent pay communication practices might be interpreted to suggest that the organization values transparency and openness more generally, has nothing to hide, and can thus be deemed a more trustworthy institution in which to "park" one's human capital. On the other hand, for those placing a high value on personal privacy, such a signal might reduce the attractiveness of the organization, thus motivating talent with such values to look elsewhere. In short, pay transparency policies and practices may influence both positive and negative attributions held by candidates about potential employers.

The second way in which pay communication may impact people's job choices is that employees may be interested not only in the potential return on their human capital in the particular position for which they are applying but also in a vector of positions within the organization. This may be especially relevant in so-called internal labor market firms, or those with a reputation for hiring from within. In such firms, many candidates will want to know not only the likely starting pay in a given position but also the probability and expected magnitude of pay increases in that position, as well as in subsequent positions for which they might qualify over time. To the degree that organizations are unable (or unwilling) to provide such information, candidates may prefer to take a position in a different firm offering less uncertainty over their future potential earnings.

Unfortunately, research has yet to examine the direct impact of pay process, outcome, or communication transparency on human resources recruitment. However, some insights may be drawn from the study of Smit and Montag-Smit (2018) discussed in Chapter 3. As will be recalled, these investigators sampled nearly 400 employed adults, with half drawn from an MTurk panel and the rest being university employees. Participants were surveyed on their perceptions of pay outcome, process, and communication restrictiveness, as well as on their attributions to these policies of benevolent and malevolent intentions on the part of the employer—for example, "My organization has the pay communication policy that it does in order to . . .": ". . . ensure that employees are paid fairly," ". . . promote employee well-being" (benevolence) and ". . . exploit workers," ". . . take advantage of employees" (malevolence). The study revealed direct effects of both pay process and communication restrictiveness on attributions regarding the employer's pay practices, with process restrictions inversely/positively associated with benevolent/malevolent attributions, and communication restrictions positively associated with malevolent attributions. As for pay outcome policies and practices, the study found restrictiveness to be positively associated with malevolent attributions only among participants with stronger preferences for pay transparency. Although these findings reflect employees' attributions about the pay practices of their current employer (and not candidate attributions regarding a potential employer), it is not unlikely that a similar pattern might be found among individuals learning about the pay communication policies and practices of potential employers. Still, we have much to learn about how pay transparency affects the ability of organizations to attract talent, the quality of the talent attracted, and the efficiency of recruitment efforts.

Pay Transparency, Turnover, and Sorting

To date, three main studies have examined the turnover and sorting effects of pay communication policies and practices. Two of these studies examined the effects of pay outcome transparency, whereas the third focused on pay process and communication transparency.

In terms of pay outcome transparency, one might assume that when individuals are exposed to information about others' pay, those who learn that they are paid less relative to similar others (i.e., employees doing similar work and/or making a roughly equivalent contribution to the organization) are likely to feel frustrated or even exploited. These employees will then have an interest in securing better employment terms, either with the same employer or elsewhere. Indeed, this is the logic underlying exit, voice, and loyalty theory (Hirschman, 1970), as well as applications of Adams's equity theory.

However, as noted earlier, several factors leave this intuitive assumption open to question. First, as previously discussed, it's not as if in the absence of concrete information about organizational salaries and benefits, employees do not think about others' pay or draw inferences from whatever information they can glean. They do! Moreover, the empirical evidence indicates that if anything, under conditions of secrecy, people perceive the pay of their peers in similar positions as higher than it is in reality. This being the case, pay transparency (relative to secrecy) could conceivably be associated with *lower* turnover. Second, exposure to the pay information of others, even others earning more than oneself, could in fact serve as an incentive to *remain* in the organization. After all, employees who learn that high performers in their peer group (much less those higher up in the organizational hierarchy) earn little more than they do could easily conclude that it may be best to look for advancement elsewhere. This effect is referred to by economists as "rational updating" (Card et al., 2012), and it suggests that learning one is paid less than one's peers can be "good news," whereas learning that one is paid more can be viewed as "bad news." Finally, in light of the evidence regarding employee attributions (Smit & Montag-Smit, 2018), whether pay outcome transparency leads to higher or lower turnover rates may depend less on employees' perceived or actual position in a pay range and more on their personal disclosure preferences. That is, under conditions of pay outcome transparency, those who are happier when information is out in the open will attribute more benevolent motives to their employer, and so may be more likely to stay with the firm. In contrast, under the same level of transparency, those with stronger preferences for privacy may assume the employer is acting with malevolent intentions and may be more likely to leave. So what does the empirical evidence suggest?

Belogolovsky and Bamberger (2014) examined the impact of pay outcome transparency on participants' intentions to remain as part of their laboratory experiment (with a student sample) discussed in Chapter 3. Study participants (N = 300) were randomly distributed into six conditions defined by a $2 \times 2 \times 2$ factorial design. Specifically, participants were assigned to one of two pay outcome transparency conditions, in which participants did (transparency) versus did not (secrecy) receive information on teammates' performance-based bonus pay in each round, as well as their own; one of two pay determination conditions, in which bonuses were distributed according to absolute versus relative performance–reward criteria; and one of two performance assessment conditions, in which performance was assessed subjectively versus objectively. In Chapter 3, we noted that relative to those assigned to the pay secrecy condition, those in the transparency condition showed more improvement in individual task performance over multiple performance rounds. We also noted there that much of this effect was explained by the difference in participants' effort–reward instrumentality (pay-for-performance [PFP]) perceptions, which were more compressed under conditions of pay secrecy, and that this effect was amplified under conditions of (a) subjective (versus objective) performance assessment and (b) relative (versus absolute) reward distribution.

A similar pattern of effects was found with regard to participants' retention intentions (i.e., intentions to remain). As shown in Figure 4.1, Belogolovsky and Bamberger's (2014) model posited an indirect effect of pay outcome transparency on participants' intentions to remain via pay instrumentality or PFP perceptions. As also shown, this model posited that the impact of PFP perceptions on retention intentions would be conditioned by the same two factors just noted, namely absolute versus relative assessment and participants' relative (versus absolute) performance level. Following three rounds of task performance (with rewards given after each round),

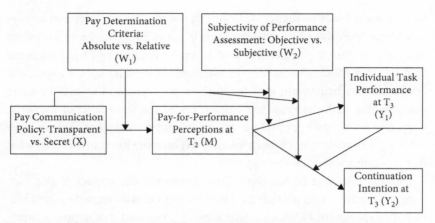

Figure 4.1 Theoretical model of the impact of pay outcome transparency on performance and withdrawal.
Reprinted with permission from Belogolovsky and Bamberger (2014).

participants were asked to indicate on a 7-point scale their willingness to participate in additional rounds of the experiment. The findings pointed to a direct effect of pay outcome communication on participants' retention intentions: After controlling for pay determination criteria and subjectivity of assessment, pay secrecy was negatively related to participants' willingness to continue in the task (estimate = $-.38$, $p < 0.05$). Moreover, as predicted, this effect was explained by participants' more compressed PFP perceptions under conditions of pay secrecy (relative to transparency), particularly among participants assigned to the objective (versus subjective) assessment condition.

Furthermore, upon unpacking the results, the investigators found that as shown in Figure 4.2, among high performers (+1 standard deviation [SD] of performance), when the assessment criteria were objective, the slope of effort–pay perceptions on intentions to continue was positive and significantly different from 0 (estimate = 3.09, $p < 0.05$). For average performers, these same objective performance assessment conditions yielded a flatter (yet still significantly different from 0) positive slope (estimate = 2.13, $p < 0.05$). But the graph also shows that this pattern disappeared under conditions of subjective performance assessment. Specifically, when performance was assessed subjectively, the PFP perceptions–continuation intentions slope was not significantly different from 0 for high, average, or low performers. In summary, the subjectivity of performance assessment and individual task

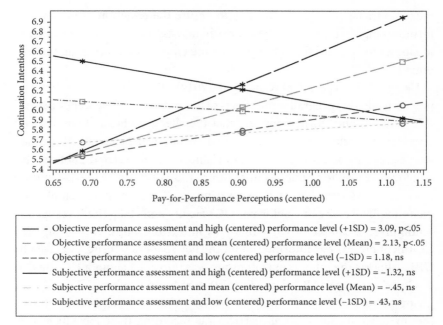

Figure 4.2 Moderation of the effect of pay-for-performance perceptions at T_2 on continuation intentions at T_3.

Reprinted with permission from Belogolovsky and Bamberger (2014).

performance jointly moderated the second stage of the mediated relationship, with the positive impact of transparency-influenced PFP perceptions on intentions to continue participating being amplified when performance assessment was objective, and with this amplification being particularly pronounced among high performers.

So what are the key takeaways from this study? First, as one might assume on the basis of expectancy theory (Vroom, 1964), pay outcome transparency may have little impact on employee turnover when performance–reward linkages are clouded by the uncertainty of subjective performance assessments. If there is little guarantee that one's contribution as an employee will be recognized, even the stronger PFP perceptions associated with pay transparency are unlikely to make it worthwhile to remain if more certain employment frameworks are available. Second, at least when applied in a PFP context, the benefits of pay outcome transparency on labor stability are likely to manifest particularly with high-performing employees. This is good news for employers because it suggests a positive sorting effect: Although pay

outcome transparency may do little to ensure the retention of poorly performing employees, at least when performance assessment is more objective,
it appears to "sort in" the better performing employees, motivating them to
remain.

Using a field experiment, Card et al. (2012) offer similar results but, im-
portantly, also (a) generalize the effects of pay outcome transparency beyond
PFP contexts and (b) demonstrate that the effects go beyond withdrawal/
retention intentions and impact actual withdrawal behavior. This study
took advantage of a court decision in California that declared public sector
employees' wages to be public information, and a decision by the *Sacramento
Bee* to set up a searchable database covering the salaries of all state employees,
including University of California (UC) faculty and staff. The investigators
randomized a sample of UC employees into two groups. One group (the
treatment group) was informed about the newspaper's website and given its
URL, whereas the other (control) group was informed about a UC site that
disclosed the pay of UC's top administrators but not other UC staff. After
giving participants approximately a week to check the suggested websites,
the investigators surveyed all participants regarding their job satisfaction
and intentions to leave and also recorded salary information, publicly available from the newspaper. Two or 3 years later, they also collected data on employee withdrawal, identifying study participants who no longer had a UC
email address.

First, simply directing participants in the treatment group to the
Sacramento Bee's salary listings resulted in an extremely large increase in
the proportion of study participants accessing that information—an indication of the success of the experimental manipulation. With respect to
the questions of interest, no main effect of exposure to peer salary information on withdrawal intentions was found. However, consistent with the
findings of Belogolovsky and Bamberger (2014), there was evidence of a
moderated effect. Specifically, for those in the treatment (transparency)
condition, participants whose pay fell below the median for their department and occupation group (and particularly those in the lowest quartile
of their pay distribution) expressed greater intentions to look for a new job.
In contrast, those with higher salaries in the treatment condition reported
job search intentions not significantly different from those in the control
condition. Moreover, participants' job search intentions were highly predictive of actual turnover 2 or 3 years later, although as knowledge about
the newspaper's salary listing became widely diffused over this time period,

the effects (in the same direction as those for turnover intentions) were significantly weaker.

These findings are interesting and important for several reasons. First, similar to the findings of Belogolovsky and Bamberger (2014), they indicate that pay outcome transparency has meaningful implications for employee turnover. Second, in contrast to Belogolovsky and Bamberger, who found a significant *positive* effect of transparency on retention with respect to PFP (i.e., bonus), Card et al. (2012) suggest a *negative* effect with respect to base pay (i.e., salaries). However, in terms of the sorting effects identified, the findings of these two studies are remarkably similar, in that both suggest that pay outcome transparency has a positive sorting effect. Whereas Belogolovsky and Bamberger found the positive effects of transparency on *retention* to be most robust among higher performing (and thus better paid) participants, Card et al. found the positive effects of pay outcome transparency on *turnover* to be most robust among those ranked toward the lower end of their pay scales (who were presumably those with subpar performance, given that movement within pay scales in the organization was largely merit-based). Thus, although the main effects of transparency on turnover may be inconsistent across these two studies, they are suggestive of the same general effect: Pay outcome transparency appears to sort-in the better performers and/or sort-out those with consistently poorer performance.

Until now, we've only reviewed the evidence regarding the impact of pay outcome transparency on employee turnover. What about the impact of the other two forms of pay transparency?

In one of the first studies taking pay process transparency into account, Shaw and Gupta (2007) posited that such transparency is instrumental in regulating the impact of pay dispersion (i.e., the spread between high and low earners) on turnover. Arguing that pay dispersion has generally positive sorting effects (i.e., reducing turnover among higher performing employees) as long as employees "have accurate information about the extent of pay dispersion and the contingencies for this dispersion" (p. 909), they posit that when such information is less transparent, this positive sorting effect of pay dispersion is more attenuated. Indeed, they suggest that due to the uncertainty, ambiguity, and distrust likely to emerge around poorly communicated pay dispersion, under such conditions pay dispersion is likely to be positively related to turnover, even among strong performers. Using data from 263 trucking companies employing differential pay based on either employee performance or seniority, they found good performer quits to be lower in well-communicated, dispersed, *performance-based* pay systems, and average performer quits to be lower in well-communicated, dispersed, *seniority-based* pay systems. However, the expected adverse effects of poor pay communication (i.e., low pay process transparency) were not statistically significant, thus raising questions about the precise mechanism underlying these effects.

Alterman et al. (2021) addressed the question of whether, when, and how process and communication transparency may impact employee turnover in two studies conducted in China. Both studies were grounded in the logic that pay process and communication transparency affect turnover via attributions of employer trustworthiness, with the attribution of low employer trustworthiness driving employee intentions to leave their current employer. In addition, the study's authors contend that the impact of such pay transparency on attributions of trustworthiness is contingent on other justice-related signals and particularly on impressions of the organization's fairness in allocating rewards (i.e., distributive justice). Building on uncertainty management theory (UMT), discussed in Chapter 2, they argue that when employees perceive greater distributive justice, pay secrecy is likely to be inversely associated with attributions of employer trustworthiness, and hence positively associated with higher turnover intentions. However, based on the certainty effect and employee tendencies to deny or dismiss what is less certain, they posit the opposite association between pay secrecy and trust attributions. That is, when employees perceive the allocation of rewards as less fair, trust attributions are likely to be higher as a function of more restrictive pay communication policies and practices.

In their first study, conducted on approximately 200 managers pursuing a part-time MBA, Alterman et al. (2021) found the association of pay secrecy perceptions and turnover intentions to indeed operate via employee attributions of organizational trust. Moreover, as they posited, this indirect effect via trust was conditioned by distributive justice perceptions. In particular, consistent with UMT's emphasis on the certainty effect, employee perceptions of pay transparency were positively associated with higher levels of organizational trust (and lower turnover intentions) when employees perceived distributive justice in the organization to be high. In contrast, consistent with UMT's status quo preservation heuristic, and as shown in Figure 4.3, when distributive justice perceptions were low, individuals perceiving greater pay secrecy attributed *greater* trustworthiness to their organization than individuals who viewed pay communication policies and practices as

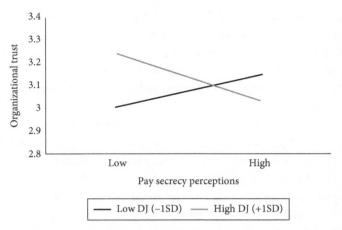

Figure 4.3 Moderating effect of distributive justice (DJ) on the relationship between pay secrecy perceptions and organizational trust.
Reprinted with permission from Alterman et al. (2021).

more transparent. This heightened sense of trustworthiness was in turn associated with lower employee intentions to leave their current employer.

In their second study, Alterman et al. (2021) focused on the association between pay secrecy policies and practices and turnover rates at the *enterprise* (rather than individual) level. Using data from 200 small, medium, and large enterprises from one province of China, they found a similar justice-moderated association between restrictive pay process and communication policies/practices, and turnover. Focusing on the conditioning role of enterprise distributive judgment climate ("shared perceptions of reward and resource distribution fairness"; Whitman et al., 2012, p. 778), they found the relationship between pay secrecy and enterprise voluntary turnover rate to be positive at moderate to high levels of distributive justice climate. In contrast, at lower levels of distributive justice climate, the relationship between pay secrecy and voluntary turnover was negative (i.e., higher secrecy, lower turnover rate) but not statistically significant. In light of the findings of their first study, the findings from this second study reinforce the notion that in a context in which employees perceive the allocation of rewards to be fair, pay process and communication transparency may be an effective means to reduce employee turnover. Indeed, their findings indicate that above and beyond other confounding factors, a 1 SD decrease from the mean in pay secrecy practices (i.e., an increase in pay process and communication transparency), combined with a 0.5 SD increase in distributive justice climate, would result in a 12 percent voluntary turnover rate. Given that voluntary turnover rates were roughly 19 percent at average pay secrecy and distributive justice climate levels, these results show that such a shift in these two focal variables can reduce voluntary turnover rates by 7 percentage points.

Although Alterman et al. (2021) examined the turnover-related consequences of pay process and communication transparency, whereas the other two studies discussed earlier (Belogolovsky & Bamberger, 2014; Card et al., 2012) focused on pay outcome transparency, there is a common underlying theme to all three studies. As noted earlier, the findings of Card et al. (2012) suggest a *positive* association between pay transparency and employee turnover (i.e., turnover intentions rose after pay transparency was introduced), whereas the findings of Belogolovsky and Bamberger (2014) indicate greater retention intentions under conditions of pay transparency (i.e., an *inverse* transparency–turnover relationship). However, as noted earlier, in both studies, transparency was linked to lower turnover-related outcomes for those at the upper end of the pay distribution, whereas for those at the lower end, transparency was either not linked (Belogolovsky & Bamberger, 2014) or positively linked (Card et al., 2012) to these outcomes. In that sense, the Alterman et al. (2021) study resolves and clarifies what might otherwise appear to be equivocal findings, suggesting that employee turnover may indeed be mitigated by greater pay transparency (i.e., less secrecy) among those perceiving high distributive justice or exposed to a positive distributive justice climate. However, among those perceiving low distributive justice or exposed to a more negative distributive justice climate, greater pay transparency is unlikely to yield any beneficial shift in individual turnover intentions or, at the firm level, voluntary turnover rates.

Pay Transparency's Impact on Pay Dispersion and I-Deals

Our examination of pay transparency's consequences to this point has focused largely on the attitudinal and behavioral responses of employees. But given that more transparent pay information increases the visibility of managerial reward-related decision-making, it is reasonable to assume that managers will also feel the effects of any shift in pay transparency policies and practices. Specifically, under conditions of greater pay transparency, managers are likely to experience a sense that their decisions are more exposed and visible to others. But how will they respond to this and, more important, what might their response mean to the organization as a whole, particularly with regard to the nature and allocation of organizational rewards?

On the one hand, one might assume that managers will respond by becoming more accountable when making pay-related judgments. After all, with greater access to pay-related information, employees should be better positioned to identify inequitable reward allocations and bring them to the attention of management. This should incentivize managers to ensure the fairness and justifiability of their pay-related decisions. As a result, one might argue that where there is variance in the contributions made by different employees in a given position, one would be more likely under conditions of pay transparency to see similar variance in pay rates. That is, the heightened visibility enabled by pay transparency should drive a tighter link between employees' contributions and their rewards. Furthermore, this greater accountability should reduce any unjustifiable forms of bias in pay decisions, such as bias related to gender or ethnicity.

On the other hand, one can imagine a situation in which managers, anticipating heightened employee scrutiny under conditions of greater transparency, take steps to reduce pay dispersion (variance in pay rates between employees doing roughly the same work). Managers may hope that by doing so, they will reduce the salience of any perceived injustice and thus limit the likelihood of employee complaints or requests for a pay adjustment (both being pecuniary costs of transparency to managers). In fact, this is not such an imaginary situation. In 2015, a Google employee named Erika Baker and some of her colleagues distributed an internal spreadsheet on which co-workers could publicly record their salaries. Google, which allows employees to discuss their pay with one another, did not intervene. According to Le Beau (2019), "between 2 and 5 percent of Google employees entered salary data, and there were multiple reports that employees tried to use the spreadsheet to get raises." But now imagine being the supervisor of one of these employees coming to you with a spreadsheet asking for a raise. How would you respond? Although you might have no choice but to adjust the individual's pay, in the next round of merit pay reviews you might try to forestall future situations of this type by ensuring that all your subordinates would henceforth receive approximately the same level of pay regardless of their performance or contribution.

In this situation, the supervisor's response would generate what economists refer to as pay compression. Pay compression is potentially problematic for the firm for two reasons. First, from a human capital resources perspective, pay compression has been linked to negative sorting effects, as higher performing employees seek employment that rewards them more equitably for their differential contribution. Second, remember the customer engagement worker mentioned in Chapter 3 who described how, despite a decade-long pay discrepancy, her boss managed to keep her loyal by ensuring she received lots of perks? To avoid such negative sorting effects, managers might seek alternative, more covert means to differentially reward deserving employees, just like that customer engagement worker's boss.

To date, three studies have tackled this question—and all suggest support for this compression effect of pay transparency. Mas (2017) investigated the impact of a shift to pay outcome transparency with respect to city managers (the highest paid municipal employees) in California. Although pay outcome transparency had already been adopted by 63 percent of cities in California prior to 2010, a California court decision in that year mandated such disclosure across the board, thus allowing the investigators to assess the salary implications of the policy shift in the context of a natural experiment. Comparing the change in managers' pay in cities that had adopted pay outcome transparency prior to the 2010 decision with those disclosing as result of the decision, Mas found that disclosure led to a decline in managers' pay of approximately 7 percent on average. The decline in wages occurred regardless of whether managers remained on the job or were replaced. And although wage cuts were larger in bigger cities (where compensation was higher to begin with), for most employees any pay cut was nominal. Indeed, cities whose managers received below median pay experienced no pay reductions at all. This pattern of reductions at the top of a pay distribution is consistent with pay compression. Moreover, the effects of this compression were very clearly detrimental for the municipal employers. Mas found that pay disclosure was associated with a 75 percent increase in voluntary turnover among city managers. Even worse, the cities that experienced turnover had difficulty finding replacements; and where replacements were found, they were less qualified than those they replaced (based on a biography analysis). Finally, Mas offers quantitative evidence that rather than being driven by heightened levels of accountability, the declines in pay were driven by more populist motives, with public officials responding to pressure to reduce what might have been viewed as excessive pay even where such pay levels were justified and warranted.

But although populism may be a reasonable explanation for these documented causal effects in the public sector, to what degree can we assume these effects generalize to non–public sector organizations, whose leaders are less subject to populist pressures? A second study, by Wong et al. (2022), suggests that although the mechanism may be different, the effects are largely the same. Wong and colleagues argue that when differences in pay between peers performing roughly the same job are made transparent, employees who feel cheated of their just deserts may respond in ways that can take a significant socioemotional toll on those responsible for determining pay levels—for example, pressuring their supervisor to adjust a performance rating, or becoming less collaborative in their work. For managers, this means having to deal with conflict, reduced morale, reduced unit performance, and perhaps even threatened turnover. Consistent with Bernstein's (2017) notion that transparency motivates "hiding," these pressures arising from the visibility of pay disparities may give managers an incentive to minimize or compress pay dispersion—at least for that form of pay over which they tend to have the greatest influence, namely variable pay, or individual performance-based bonuses and incentives (Golman & Bhatia, 2012).

Yet as noted earlier, pay compression can lead to problems of its own: specifically, negative sorting effects (where higher performing employees seek more remunerative employment) and the need to develop imaginative substitutes for direct pay arrangements. Wong et al. (2022) note that pay compression may motivate employees to seek less visible forms of remuneration, through voluntary, personalized, and particularistic agreements negotiated between employees and employers—that is, i-deals (Rousseau, 2005; Rousseau et al., 2006). These can include benefit i-deals (e.g., extra "personal days") and developmental i-deals (personalized skill and career development arrangements; Hornung et al., 2008, 2009) that are left unspecified in formal employment contracts. I-deals, being under the radar, carry lower socioemotional costs for supervisors in firms with greater pay transparency, and so employees may perceive them as more likely to actually be granted. As a result, Wong et al. posit that employees of firms characterized by more transparent pay policies and practices (and thus more compressed pay) are more likely to seek i-deals to secure what they deem to be a fair return on their contribution to the firm.

To test these hypothesized effects, Wong et al. (2022) collected data from the owners and/or general managers of 111 medical device distribution enterprises in China, along with 645 sales staff employed in these firms. These firms were all rather small, with sales staff accounting for nearly 90 percent of each firm's workforce, and all sales staff performed roughly the same set of tasks. The study focused on differentials in participants' variable pay—individual performance-based bonuses and incentives, which accounted for nearly 40 percent of employees' annual income. In all the firms, supervisors played a significant role in determining the magnitude of employees' variable pay because commissions and bonuses were contingent upon supervisor-assessed performance.

To conduct the study, Wong et al. (2022) first surveyed the owners/general managers, requesting data on the number of individuals employed by the firm, pay transparency, each employee's annual fixed and variable pay, and the firm's revenue. Approximately 1 week after responses were received from the employers, employees were surveyed and asked to provide demographic information (e.g., gender, age, education, and tenure) and to report the frequency with which they requested various forms of i-deals.

Consistent with the results of Mas (2017), Wong et al. (2022) found pay transparency to be positively related to variable pay compression ($\gamma = 0.05$, $p < 0.05$). Moreover, as also predicted, compression in variable pay was positively related to both developmental i-deal requests (requests for unique training and development opportunities; $\gamma = 0.99$, $p < 0.01$) and benefit i-deal requests (e.g., requests for unique forms of insurance and/or time off; $\gamma = 1.09$, $p < 0.01$). Indeed, pay transparency was found to explain 18 percent of the variance in pay compression across firms, with pay compression explaining, in turn, 35 percent and 18 percent of the variance in average developmental and benefit i-deal requests, respectively. Moreover, consistent with research on social comparison, which suggests that comparison information is more salient in more collectivist contexts (Gibbons & Buunk, 1999), the effects of transparency-driven pay compression on both forms of i-deal requests were found to be particularly strong among enterprises characterized by more collectivist shared norms (Figure 4.4).

Finally, in a third study (to be discussed in greater detail in Chapter 5), Cullen and Pakzad-Hurson (2019) examined data from contract workers and employers using the TaskRabbit platform, who dynamically negotiated workers' pay under varying degrees of pay outcome restrictiveness over time. In the secrecy condition, negotiations between the worker and employer

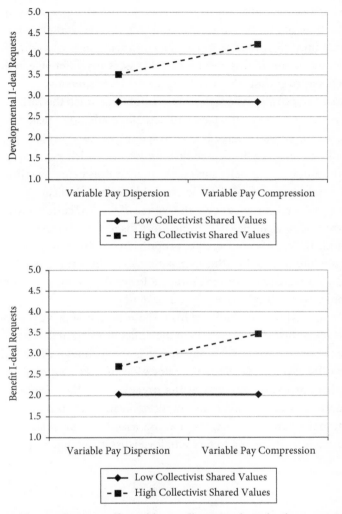

Figure 4.4 The moderating effect of firm collectivist shared values on employee i-deal requests.
Reprinted with permission from Wong et al. (2022).

remained private until the contract was executed, whereas in the transparency condition, the gig workers were co-located and tended to disclose their pay to one another. Because wages can be renegotiated upwards (but never downwards) on TaskRabbit even after a wage offer is accepted by an employer (up until completion of the contracted task), the researchers were able to capture the impact of pay transparency on changes in remuneration from the time of hire (i.e., the point at which the gig worker's wage bid was accepted) until the point at which the contracted task was completed and payment was made. In this way, they could assess any difference in the equalization of pay over time under varying levels of transparency.

To assess pay compression, the investigators examined the variance in post hoc negotiated pay (i.e., the payment actually made upon task completion) relative to the initially agreed-upon wage. Figure 4.5 displays the results. Dots falling along the 45-degree line are jobs in which pay was not raised above the amount originally agreed to, whereas dots below that line are jobs in which pay was increased for lower paid workers, indicating wage compression (reduced variance) over the course of task execution. Observations above the line indicate pay becoming more dispersed over the course of task execution. The significantly greater proportion of jobs falling at or below the 45-degree line in panel b (the transparency condition) relative to those in panel a (the secrecy condition) indicate lower dispersion (or higher compression) under conditions of pay transparency.

Taken as a whole, the findings from these studies suggest that organizational leaders should be cognizant of the difficult situation that pay transparency may create for managers and supervisors. Although these individuals are typically asked to facilitate the allocation of organizational rewards in a way that serves the interests of the organization, the adoption of more transparent pay communication practices means that in serving these organizational interests, managers may be asked to pay a significant personal price (e.g., in having to face employee dissatisfaction and direct, often

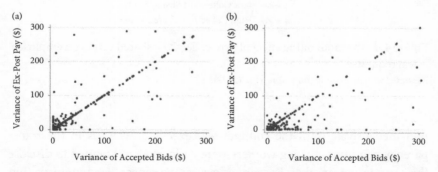

Figure 4.5 Variance in final pay versus accepted bids in secret (a) and transparent (b) conditions.

Reprinted with permission from Cullen and Pakzad-Hurson (2019).

emotion-laden appeals). As found by all three studies described above, this can create an implicit incentive for managers to make decisions that ultimately compress pay differentials. Furthermore, as Wong et al. (2022) suggest, such compression has the potential to push various other aspects of rewards underground in the form of i-deals. To counter such effects, particularly for firms characterized by more collectivist shared values, organizations may consider adopting frameworks that increase managers' accountability for pay-related decisions. Alternatively, they might consider balancing the socioemotional costs to managers of differentially rewarding employees with incentives for doing so. Such incentives might be based, for example, on evaluating and rewarding managers not only for capturing and rewarding differential employee contributions but also for doing so in a fairer and more justifiable manner.

Pay Transparency's Impact on Organizational Culture and Climate

Organizational culture and climate are amorphous concepts. Roughly speaking, *organizational climate* refers to the psychological atmosphere in an organization or organizational unit—that is, the feelings and attitudes shared by organization members. *Organizational culture* refers to the values, norms, beliefs, and taken-for-granted assumptions underlying the behavior of organization members. Organizational culture and climate may be difficult to pin down precisely, but employees typically get a feel for both not long after taking on a new job.

Jack (not his real name), an engineer, was interviewed in the context of a qualitative study my team and I conducted a few years ago. Jack recalled for us the culture of the large California-based tech company he used to work for, comparing it to that of the smaller tech firm he had recently joined. As he explained it, managers at his previous firm had a reputation for keeping their cards close to their chest, and their approach to pay was no different. Because employees could not use pay to get a sense of their standing within the company, they engaged in incessant games of competitive measurement and one-upmanship on everything else: job titles, promotions, and even office characteristics (i.e., size, with or without a window). In Jack's words, "Since their pay was anything but transparent, there was a lot of weight placed on other things like titles and offices." Jack's new company had a policy of pay transparency—something that Jack learned about only after he signed on. According to him, the difference in culture was shockingly apparent:

> I think because the company is so transparent, it almost calms everyone, or at least that's what I see with my subordinates. It's a very different culture from my previous company, it's almost like people are less capitalistic and compare themselves less.

Jack reasoned that precisely because of its pay transparency, the culture in his new company was characterized by a focus on securing "cool" projects and work offering challenge, growth, and engagement rather than on "checking to make sure that I'm earning more than the guy next to me."

Is this strong evidence that pay transparency transforms organizational culture? Clearly not. Indeed, whereas systematic and even quasi-experimental evidence suggests a causal pathway from pay communication policies and practices to such organizational-level consequences as employee turnover and pay compression, little systematic—much less causal—evidence exists with regard to pay communication's implications for organizational culture. Indeed, the association between pay communication and organizational culture presents a classic "chicken and egg" question: Does a transparent, open culture encourage less restrictive pay communication policies and practices, or vice versa?

Anecdotal, case-based evidence (such as that offered by Jack above, and the case studies presented in Chapter 7) suggests that pay transparency impacts organizational norms and values. For example, in an article surveying pay transparency's relationship with organizational culture, Barker (2019) noted that "transparency in the workplace is crucial to building trust within an organization and encouraging employees to become more actively engaged in the future of their company." Moreover, media accounts suggest that the adoption of more transparent pay practices has an impact on gender-related norms and values in organizations due to the tendency of more transparent pay practices to narrow the gender pay gap. For instance, one report quoted Mari Hegyi, director of the people team at Limeade, as emphasizing that her company's shift to more transparent pay empowered the company's employees, motivating them—and particularly those typically disadvantaged in the labor market—to advocate for themselves. In her words, "From a diversity and inclusion and equity standpoint, this has been a really cool impact of this, just enabling our women and others to ask about their compensation and to come to that table informed" (Kidwai, 2020).

Support for such a causal pathway, in which the adoption of more transparent pay communication policies and practices generates culture change in the organization, is offered on the basis of relational contracting theory (G. Baker et al., 1994, 2002). This theory suggests that employees behave toward employers in keeping with how they believe the latter are behaving toward them, and specifically whether the employer is seen as treating employees opportunistically. Based on this principle, Fahn and Zanarone (2020) propose that because more transparent pay practices amplify the costs to the employer of opportunistic behavior, increasing transparency can shift the orientations of both sides, creating a more trusting organizational climate. However, transparency can also reinforce norms of social comparison, and so give rise to a climate of malicious envy among peers. Fahn and Zanarone's theory suggests that because of these implications for employee norms and values, less restrictive pay communication policies and practices may be more suitable in some contexts (e.g., when task performance is more difficult to objectively assess) and less suitable in others (e.g., where there is a strong tendency toward social comparison). However, regardless of the outcome, the theory assumes that pay transparency shapes organizational culture more than it is shaped by it.

Support for the idea that introducing pay transparency may change the organizational climate for the better also stems from attribution substitution theory (Kahneman & Frederick, 2004; Kahneman, 2011). This theory suggests that in situations in which some target attribute is unavailable (e.g., the competence of different co-workers), people shy away from complex, reflection-based and hence effortful judgments, and instead rely on a more automatic, intuitive approach using heuristics to generalize from more easily accessible information. For example, imagine that an employee wants to ask a colleague for help or feedback on a project but wants first to ensure that person possesses the knowledge to truly be of assistance. Indeed, it is well-established that despite the obvious potential benefits of collaboration in organizations, employees can sometimes be hesitant to approach others, not only because they are fearful of the reaction (e.g., appearing stupid or being turned down) but also because they do not necessarily know to whom to turn (Lim et al., 2020). Building on attribution substitution theory, Belogolovsky et al. (2016) suggest that when employees lack information about others' expertise, they rely on cognitive shortcuts to make judgments—including assuming others' expertise on the basis of what those others earn. But as discussed in previous chapters, under conditions of relative pay secrecy, biases in perceptions of others' pay are substantial—increasing the risk of misattributing expertise to certain peers and seeking help from those less competent to provide it. Following this logic, the researchers propose that more transparent pay practices reduce such errors in the attribution of expertise and thus facilitate more effective resource-seeking. This is important from an organizational perspective in that when employees target their requests toward those most able to assist them, their experience with help-seeking is likely to be more positive, thus encouraging and reinforcing a culture of peer collaboration within the firm (Grant, 2013).

To test this logic, Belogolovsky et al. (2016) used a simulation experiment, monitoring how a change in pay communication from secret to transparent affected help-seeking over time as individuals encountered new pay-related information (the study design and population were the same as in the study by Bamberger and Belogolovsky [2017] described in Chapter 3). Participants were 146 undergraduate business students at a Singaporean university assigned to virtual work groups composed of themselves and three confederates. Participants were randomly assigned to one of the conditions specified by a 4 (pay communication conditions: secret, transparent, secret → transparent, transparent → secret) × 6 (performance phases) design with repeated measures. As in Bamberger and Belogolovsky (2017), under the transparency regime participants were informed of their own performance level and payout and the pay, but not performance, of their fellow group members (all of whom were confederates), albeit by code number rather than by name. Participants in the secret → transparent and transparent → secret conditions experienced a change in pay communication after the third performance phase. There were 38 participants in the stable secret condition and 36 in each of the other three.

The study's findings largely supported the hypotheses, showing that pay secrecy impacts help-seeking by adversely influencing how accurately participants perceived the task expertise of the highest paid group member. Specifically, the results suggest that pay secrecy complicates the sourcing of help by affecting the accuracy with which those new to a work group are able to infer the expertise of other group members. The findings also controvert suggestions that expertise perceptions tend to be "sticky" (i.e., stable). Rather, Belogolovsky et al. (2016) found that when pay communication shifted from secret to transparent midway through the experiment, participants' perceptions about the expertise of the highest paid group member became more accurate. This, in turn, increased efficacious help-seeking over time.

In summary, theory, anecdotal reports, and limited experimental evidence all suggest that pay transparency may spark a shift in both organizational climate and organizational culture. In terms of the former, the adoption of more transparent pay communication policies and practices can elicit a change in the psychological atmosphere of the organization or unit, shifting employees' shared attitudes and feelings around issues such as gender equality and procedural fairness. In terms of the latter, the adoption of more transparent pay communication policies and practices can alter the values and norms underlying other types of behavior in the organization, such as those relating to trust, voicing, and self-advocacy.

At the same time, some qualitative accounts of pay transparency experiences in specific firms suggest that organizational culture (often in the form of founder norms and values) also can *engender* less restrictive pay communication practices—or at least that the two can have a reciprocal association. By this, I mean that although transparency in pay communications may be driven by the norms and values of founders or corporate leaders, it also likely elicits further changes in the norms and values of the enterprise as a whole.

One example of an organization in which adoption of across-the-board pay transparency (pay process, outcome, and communication transparency) can be directly tied to its founding norms and values is Cogent, an Australian digital services and software development firm that is discussed in more detail in Chapter 7. According to Mark Wells, the company's CEO, Cogent is "a values-run company, and one of our values—right from the start—was transparency." Indeed, the company was established around five core values that are still listed on its website (the others, after transparency, are well-being, evolution, inclusion, and meaning). The website explains that the company's founders considered transparency an essential antecedent of trust, which itself is essential for successful long-term employee and client relationships. As noted on the website,

> We strive to be transparent in everything we do at Cogent because we believe that transparency builds trust, and trust builds Cogent. . . . By adopting openness and honesty as default, we're able to truly understand one another and the decisions we make because the reasons behind them are clear.

However, to reiterate, a reciprocal effect cannot be ruled out. More precisely, it is easy to see how (a) existing transparency norms in other organizational domains or core organizational values drive the adoption of more transparent pay practices, and (b) these less restrictive pay practices then impact the organization's culture more generally, driving the organization to make other practices more transparent, thus (c) reinforcing and expanding transparent pay practices as well. For instance, at Buffer, a social media software company that made its pay algorithm public in 2013 (when the firm had a headcount of just 13), transparency was a core value essentially from the get-go. Since that time, the company has reinforced this value, referring to it on the company's website as the foundation for "a lifestyle of authenticity and honesty, an effective way to work remotely and establish a culture of trust, a tool to help others," and a means to "make all communication clear and avoid making assumptions." Accordingly, transparency has not only been expanded to other reward-related domains but also been extended to apply to the company's diversity policies and practices (the company offers access to its diversity and inclusion data via https://diversity.buffer.com), product roadmap (via https://trello.com/b/PDIV7XW3/buffer-transparent-product-roadmap), and even some of its software code (https://github.com/buffer app). Confirming the impact that pay transparency has had on the company's culture as a whole, head of finance Caryn Hubbard told a journalist,

> I think what that does is culturally it makes conversations around career growth and opportunities at the company really more about experience and value and ambition. So the pay transparency lends [sic] to deeper, richer conversations, rather than just focusing on dollars. (Kidwai, 2020)

Implications for Productivity and Firm Performance

Up to this point, we have examined a variety of firm-level consequences of pay transparency, all of which could potentially impact firm productivity and performance. On the one hand, findings suggest that pay outcome transparency may have generally positive effects on individual task performance (see Chapter 3) as well as on employee sorting, pointing to an overall positive net effect of pay transparency on firm performance. On the other hand, as suggested by Zenger (2016), pay outcome transparency has the potential to adversely impact productivity and performance at the firm level if it demoralizes employees. Indeed, the idea that workers are less motivated and withdraw effort (i.e., work less hard) as a function of pay dissatisfaction is a core proposition of Akerlof and Yellen's (1990) fair wage–effort theorem and has substantial support in the literature (e.g., Greenberg, 1990; Krueger & Mas, 2004; Mas, 2006, 2008; Cohn et al., 2014). Recall, for example, Card et al.'s (2012) finding that pay outcome transparency lowered job satisfaction for UC employees who were paid below their reference group. Demoralization is also possible if pay transparency results in pay compression, with lower than typical or market-rate pay increases for high-performing employees. Moreover, according to the fair wage–effort hypothesis, to the extent that workers believe their actual wage is below their perceived fair wage, they may not only put in less effort but also leave their employer (negative sorting) or even withdraw from the labor market, thus potentially boosting unemployment and having adverse productivity implications for the labor market as a whole.

Unfortunately, research testing these competing predictions is limited, with the findings generated being—you guessed it!—rather equivocal. For instance, in one study, Obloj and Zenger (2017) report a net negative effect. They designed a field experiment in a European bank in which they manipulated rewards (in the form of monetary prizes) available to branch employees based on the branch's performance in selling small consumer loans. Specifically, they divided the bank's 164 outlets into four tournament conditions, with conditions varying by the value of the prizes awarded. Not surprisingly, in branches assigned to the low-value award condition, the award had a diminished positive impact on branch performance. However, the researchers also found that branch performance declined as a function of the branch's proximity or connection to branches with superior reward conditions, with the magnitude of the reduction corresponding with "how physically or socially close" these disadvantaged outlets were to the more advantaged ones. Although they lacked the data to demonstrate that those in more proximate branches compared their rewards with one another more than did employees in more distal branches, the inference that they draw from their study is that with transparency comes the potential for "in your face" (i.e., certain and vivid) inequity, with the resulting demoralization generating a system-wide decline in firm performance.

Focusing on the productivity implications of pay transparency, the findings of Bennedsen et al. (2019) also suggest that pay transparency may have, at best, mixed consequences on enterprise productivity and performance.

Adopting a novel, quasi-experimental design, these researchers drew on matched employee–employer wage data from Denmark. The Danish data are unique in that starting in 2006, Denmark required enterprises with 35 or more employees to report aggregated salary data broken down by gender and to inform their employees of any gender-based wage gaps (aggregated data are used in order to protect individual anonymity). As discussed in Chapter 5, the researchers' main focus in this study was on the impact of this law on changes in the wage gap over the subsequent years, comparing enterprises with 35–50 employees (covered by the law) to those employing 20–34 workers (exempt from the law). However, Bennedsen et al. (2019) also examined the productivity- and performance-related consequences of pay transparency.

On the one hand, relative to the exempt firms, Bennedsen et al.'s (2019) findings indicate that productivity (measured in terms of the logarithm of sales per employee) in the non-exempt enterprises (i.e., those required to make pay more transparent) declined by 2.5 percent following passage of the transparency law. On the other hand, this drop in productivity had no significant effect on enterprise profitability (a key performance indicator), in that the average employee wage (measured as the ratio of total labor costs to number of employees, again log-transformed) also declined more (a 2.8 percent greater decline) in non-exempt firms relative to the smaller, exempt firms. Still, both of these outcomes could point to diminished competitiveness (and hence the potential for an adverse impact on longer term performance) at the level of the firm, in addition to a negative externality to workers if they suffer an overall decline in pay or increase in job insecurity as a result of increased transparency. Although lower labor costs might sound like a significant benefit of pay transparency (at least to employers), if reduced average wages stem from the loss of difficult-to-replace human capital resources (i.e., loss of more productive but costlier talent rather than a growing headcount with stable wages), this might not only explain diminished productivity but also point to, potentially, a significant competitive disadvantage for these firms moving forward.

Although Bennedsen et al.'s (2019) findings regarding the impact of the 2006 pay transparency law in Denmark (described above) may, like those of Obloj and Zenger (2017), be consistent with more "dark-side" theorizing, there is little evidence that *all* forms of pay transparency are likely to generate declines in productivity and firm performance. Indeed, as noted in Chapter 3, the findings of SimanTov-Nachlieli and Bamberger (2021) suggest that pay process transparency, rather than resulting in employee demoralization, has generally positive affective consequences, particularly on employee perceptions of organizational fairness. Furthermore, anecdotal evidence suggests that even the adoption of pay outcome transparency can have beneficial implications for employee attitudes and hence perhaps for firm-level productivity and performance as well. For example, comparing the results of its annual employee engagement survey prior to and following the introduction of pay outcome transparency in 2018, Pollen (formally Verve) reported that its employees were "more engaged than ever" (Pollen, 2021). Similarly, the findings of Cullen and Perez-Truglia (2018a), summarized in Chapter 3, indicate that vertical pay outcome transparency (allowing employees to view pay rates for jobs at higher and lower levels) often results in employees discovering that their supervisors earn more than they expected, and this discovery boosts employee effort and performance.

Finally, whereas the studies by Obloj and Zenger (2017) and Bennedsen et al. (2019) were not designed specifically to assess the impact of pay transparency on productivity, a study by Huet-Vaughn (2013, 2014) aimed to test precisely that, and this study suggests largely beneficial productivity effects. Huet-Vaughn "hired" a sample of MTurk workers for what was ostensibly a real job, namely to enter bibliographic information from journal articles into a database. His employees were paid on a piece-rate basis, with a set rate for each article correctly entered. They were told that they would be employed for two periods of data entry and then, regardless of their performance, would be terminated. Employees were randomly assigned to one of two conditions, which differed in the information provided at the end of the first round: In the first, participants were told only their own earnings (control), and in the second they were also informed as to how their earnings compared with those of a group of fellow employees (treatment). Those in the treatment condition were further split into two subgroups, with half informed of their relative earnings vis-à-vis a low-performing peer group and the other half vis-à-vis a high-performing peer group. Huet-Vaughn then watched as the workers engaged in a second round of data entry, after which their employment was indeed terminated.

Huet-Vaughn found that, on average, participants' output (the number of correctly inputted bibliographic entries) was roughly 10 percent higher among the main treatment group, who received either sort of peer earnings information, compared to the control group—a significant productivity boost. When the effects were unpacked for the two treatment subgroups, it emerged that most of this productivity boost was driven by those who were informed of their earnings relative to a low-performing peer group, such that the participant ranked higher on average in the earnings distribution. Among those exposed to the earnings of the high-performing peer group (such that the participant ranked lower on average in the distribution), productivity was not significantly different from that of the control group, which received no comparison pay information. Viewing his findings as generalizable to at least the online labor market, Huet-Vaughn (2013) concludes that from a policy perspective, "when feasible, firms and governments may want to selectively manipulate the exact distribution of earnings offered as the comparison group" so as to maximize productivity benefits. That is, although there is no evidence from this study that pay outcome transparency depresses productivity, the findings suggest that the magnitude of any productivity gain may be contingent on the extent to which comparison group information emphasizes employees' positive earnings position relative to others.

Conclusion

As suggested by Nobel Prize winner Richard Thaler and Cass Sunstein in their book *Nudge* (2009), small changes in an individual's environment can trigger both reflective and automatic cognitive processes that can lead to behavioral change with broad, system-wide implications. Whereas some pay transparency interventions represent anything but small and inexpensive changes in policy and practice, other steps taken to reduce restrictions on pay communication can indeed be simple to implement, yet still have far-reaching implications. In this chapter, we reviewed some of these broader organizational implications. These are summarized in Table 4.1. As we've discussed, although research remains limited, there seems to be a clear indication that pay transparency can have positive sorting effects, attracting higher performers at the upper end of pay ranges to join and remain with the organization, while also motivating voluntary turnover among those at the lower end. On the other hand, it can also have unintended consequences on supervisory behavior that may ultimately reduce pay dispersion, something that research suggests can drive sorting in precisely the opposite direction, as well as "underground" forms of remuneration in the form of i-deals aimed at mitigating such negative sorting. We've also pointed to largely anecdotal evidence regarding the impact that pay transparency can

Table 4.1 The Advantages and Disadvantages of Pay Transparency for the Firm

Advantages	Disadvantages
Positive sorting effects (facilitating attraction and retention of high potentials and top performers) to the extent that transparency makes visible greater performance-based pay dispersion.	Negative sorting effects (attenuating the ability of the firm to attract and retain high potentials and top performers) to the extent that transparency motivates compression of pay differentials by controversy-aversive managers.
Transparency facilitates rational updating as lower paid employees, observing higher pay earned by higher performing peers, see benefits of remaining with employer as they develop their firm-specific assets.	Transparency may motivate lower paid employees to secure alternative employment that places greater value on their human and social capital.
Employees valuing openness may attribute benevolent motives to employer, and thus be more attracted to firm (i.e., facilitating recruitment) and less likely to leave.	Employees valuing privacy may attribute malevolent motives to employer, and thus be less attracted to firm (i.e., complicating recruitment) and more likely to leave.
Pay transparency increases the costs to the employer of opportunistic behavior, thus incentivizing the creation of a more trusting organizational climate.	Pay transparency reinforces norms of social comparison and competition, thus potentially giving rise to a climate of malicious envy among peers.
Equivocal evidence on productivity, but even if it is adversely impacted, this does not translate into diminished profitability.	If lower labor costs are an outcome of transparency, it may be indicative of a negative sorting effect, which, in turn, could adversely impact long-term firm performance.

have on an organization's culture and climate. Finally, studies examining the implications of pay transparency on productivity and firm performance offer largely equivocal results and highlight a variety of contingencies that might account for the mix of positive, negative, and null findings.

The effects that we have surveyed here likely represent just the tip of the iceberg. Many more effects—some stronger and some more subtle—are likely to be discovered in the years ahead. But just as pay transparency can have system-wide effects at the level of the organization or organizational unit, it may also have system-wide effects at the societal level. It is to these societal implications that we turn next.

5

Societal-Level Implications
of Pay Transparency

Currently, a majority of enterprises throughout the world continue to maintain relatively restrictive pay communication practices. Yet, as noted in
Chapter 1, governments at the national and regional/provincial levels are
increasingly becoming more activist in this domain, adopting regulations
and mechanisms aimed at encouraging greater transparency in pay-related
matters. Some governments, particularly those in the Nordic countries, have
even gone so far as to make individual income tax records (containing personal earnings data) available to citizens over the internet. Although continuing concerns over gender-based wage disparities are an important driver of
such regulatory efforts, reforms in pay transparency have also been promoted
as a means to facilitate labor mobility, ensure employee rights to collective
representation, and protect shareholders and other corporate stakeholders
from executive opportunism. But how effective have these regulatory efforts
been in achieving their broad, societal objectives, and at what cost?

In this chapter, I explore the impact of broad-scale pay transparency
interventions on the targets they were designed to impact, as well as some
of their unintended consequences. In particular, I review the evidence regarding the impact of such interventions on three main sets of outcomes,
namely the gender pay gap, inequality, and employee well-being. I begin by
presenting a quick review of the various regulatory initiatives adopted by
governments throughout the world.

Regulatory Efforts Promoting Pay
Transparency: Global Trends

In discussing Table 1.2 in Chapter 1, I highlighted two main types of pay
communication regulations: those mandating the removal of all restrictions
on employee disclosures and those requiring employers to provide pay

Exposing Pay. Peter Bamberger, Oxford University Press. © Oxford University Press 2023.
DOI: 10.1093/oso/9780197628164.003.0005

process or pay outcome information either directly to employees or to public authorities for review and (sometimes) subsequent disclosure. An example of the former is the1930s-era National Labor Relations Act in the United States, which precludes enterprises from disciplining employees for disclosing their pay to peers. Contemporary interpretations of this law mandate that employees cannot be penalized for any discussions about pay, including soliciting pay information from peers, on the grounds that such information may be crucial when workers consider the need for potential benefits or union representation. More recently, many U.S. states have adopted more direct legislation ensuring employees' rights to solicit and disclose personal pay information without fear of employer retaliation. For example, the California Equal Pay Act of 2015 states that "an employer shall not prohibit an employee from disclosing the employee's own wages, discussing the wages of others, or inquiring about another employee's wages."

Far fewer state authorities have mandated pay outcome transparency, where employers must make pay information available, although some jurisdictions (e.g., Colorado) have some form of pay outcome regulations in place. For instance, several countries (e.g., the United Kingdom, Canada, Denmark, France, Israel, and Australia) have adopted legislation requiring organizations over a certain size threshold (e.g., 35 employees in Denmark and 1,000 in France) to report or publish information about the magnitude of any gender pay gap in their company. Other countries require companies to disclose peer pay information in some cases (e.g., Germany requires such disclosures to employees who believe they are victims of gender wage disparities in firms with at least 200 employees). Finally, in the early years of this century, Norway made all tax records fully accessible to the public via the internet, allowing Norwegians to view financial data (along with year of birth and location of residence) for any taxpayer in the country.[1] Although no employer data are provided, as long as they have a name to search by, Norwegian employees can potentially view pay information for up to 500 co-workers and supervisors in their company in any calendar year. Such information can offer employees significant insight into both the vertical (between levels or jobs) and horizontal (within levels or jobs) dispersion of pay in their organization.

---

[1] Tax records have been public in Norway since the 19th century, but they were digitized and put online in 2001 (before that, Norwegians had to make a formal request in person at a tax agency to see such records). Transparency soared with further regulatory changes in 2007, which enabled any individual to access others' tax records online within minutes.

Regulatory efforts such as these should, in theory, have beneficial labor market implications. For instance, again in theory, greater access to pay information should make employers more accountable to normative pressures to eliminate pay disparities based on gender, ethnicity, or race (Castilla, 2015; Dobbin & Kalev, 2016). Greater access to pay information, especially where disparities exist, should also encourage more forceful pay negotiations among workers who might otherwise hesitate to ask for higher pay. For example, Callum Negus-Fancey, founder of the booking and events company Pollen (previously known as Verve), noted in an interview with *Forbes* that ensuring women have greater access to pay information levels the playing field with regard to salary negotiations. As he explained it, women are often hesitant about negotiating a higher salary, and when they aren't hesitant, they are often viewed as aggressive, a perception that may impede their progress within the organization even if they are hired. According to Negus-Fancey, access to pay information essentially eliminates the need for employees to improve their negotiation skills in order to secure equitable remuneration—an outcome that is mutually beneficial for both the job candidate and the employer. Finally, such information should strengthen the "invisible hand" of labor markets, fostering labor mobility and better ensuring that talent moves to those employers most in need—and thus willing to pay a premium for it (Harris, 2018).

Of course, things may not necessarily work out this way. As noted in Chapter 2, the vast majority of employees in the United States are discouraged, if not contractually prohibited, from sharing pay information (Institute for Women's Policy Research, 2014). But even removing restrictions on employee pay communication does not mean that employees will suddenly start to disclose their pay to one another. Similarly, requiring employers to report on disparities, and enabling employees to inquire about them, does not ensure that they will disappear. Recall the unintended consequences of regulatory requirements for companies to disclose the remuneration of executives, described in Chapter 1. These regulations were aimed at reducing within-firm wage gaps (between executives and lower paid workers), but in most countries they had the opposite effect: As executives gained more information about what their peers were earning, they negotiated for higher remuneration, *expanding* within-firm wage gaps (Hermalin & Weisbach, 2013; Mas, 2016). These gaps continue to grow at rates of more than 10 percent per year (de Vaan et al., 2019). Similarly, regulations enacted by the U.S. Securities and Exchange Commission in 2006 requiring the disclosure of benchmarking data—that is, peer firms used by corporate compensation committees as a basis for estimating executive pay—have done little to mitigate the growth of such wage gaps (de Vaan et al., 2019). Furthermore, critics of pay transparency argue that efforts to address gender pay disparities and inequality more generally via regulations mandating pay transparency can have costly unintended consequences, such as placing extra demands and constraints on enterprises (Obloj & Zenger, 2022), making it difficult to recruit unique talent (Bruner, 2022), violating individual privacy (Smit & Montag-Smit, 2018), and generating envy and conflicts between co-workers that might ultimately harm productivity and firm performance (Bamberger & Belogolowsky, 2017; Breza et al., 2018).

Fortunately, findings from a growing body of empirical research are beginning to shed light on the often complex and nuanced societal-level implications of pay transparency and regulatory efforts aimed at encouraging or mandating it.

Pay Transparency and the Gender Pay Gap

Much of the recent legislation in pay transparency has focused on addressing pay disparities, particularly those based on gender or ethnicity/race. Indeed, despite a concerted effort by governments in many countries and territories, gender and ethnic/racial pay gaps remain large. For example, in the United States, the gender pay gap in 2021 was 18 percent, meaning that for every dollar that a man might earn in a job, a woman doing equivalent work earned just 82 cents (Payscale, 2020a).[2] However, as shown in Table 5.1, when taking both gender and race into account, the disparity is even greater, with Black women in 2020 earning only 64 cents for every dollar earned by White men. Although the news is a bit better in much of Europe (the gender gap is 19.2 percent in Germany but only 14.1 percent on average across European Union countries [Eurostat, 2021]), it is worse in many developing countries. For example, the gender pay disparity for women in India was 34 percent in 2018 (Oxfam, 2019).

---

[2] This figure reflects the uncontrolled gender pay gap, in which the median earnings of women and men are compared without controlling for factors such as job title, years of experience, industry, location, etc. According to Payscale (2021), the controlled gender pay gap in 2020 was narrower, with women earning 98 cents for every male dollar. Notably, however, this controlled gap had not appreciably changed since 2015, even as the uncontrolled pay gap has been (incrementally) shrinking.

Table 5.1 Median Annual Earnings and Gender Earnings Ratio for Full-Time, Year-Round Workers, Age 15 Years or Older, by Race/Ethnicity, 2019 and 2020

Racial/Ethnic Background*	2020				2019 (in 2020 Dollars)			
	Women ($)	Men ($)	Female Earnings as % of Male Earnings of Same Group	Female Earnings as % of White Male Earnings	Women ($)	Men ($)	Female Earnings as % of Male Earnings of Same Group	Female Earnings as % of White Male Earnings
All races/ethnicities	50,982	61,417	83.0%	N/A	47,889	58,173	82.%	N/A
White	53,731	67,629	79.4%	79.4%	51,965	66,022	78.7%	78.7%
Black	43,209	50,525	85.5%	63.9%	41,611	46,214	90.0%	63.0%
Asian	68,442	83,173	82.3%	101.2%	57,516	76,616	75.1%	87.1%
Hispanic or Latina	38,718	45,074	85.9%	57.3%	36,561	42,037	87.0%	55.4%

Notes: White non-Hispanic alone; Black alone; Asian alone; and Hispanic (may be of any race); full-time, year-round defined as working at least 35 hours per week, and at least 50 weeks per year, Adjustment to 2019 dollars is using CPI-U-RS.

Source: Institute for Women's Policy Research analysis based on U.S. Census Bureau, "Historical Income Tables: Table P-38. Full-Time, Year-Round Workers by Median Earnings and Sex," *Current Population Survey* (Washington, DC: U.S. Census Bureau, 2021), https://www.census.gov/data/tables/time-series/demo/income-poverty/historical-income-people.html. Reprinted with permission from Hegewisch and Mefferd (2021).

Behind these economy-wide figures lie real people in real companies. For example, in October 2020, the Equal Employment Opportunity Commission (EEOC) in the United States filed suit again Dell, a major manufacturer of computers and information technology (IT) equipment. The case involved two IT analysts, Kea Golden and a male colleague, both of whom were hired at the same time, had 25 years of experience (much of it with the same employer prior to its acquisition by Dell), and carried out the same duties. However, Ms. Golden's pay was $17,000 less than that of her male colleague (EEOC, 2020). Moreover, this was not Dell's first experience dealing with pay inequality. In 2018, Dell denied liability but paid nearly $3 million in back pay and interest to the affected employees when the U.S. Office of Federal Contract Compliance Programs claimed that the company had violated equal employment opportunity rules by "discriminating against females in engineering, marketing, and sales roles" in locations throughout the country. To what degree might the adoption of pay outcome and/or process transparency practices at Dell have prevented the continuation of such gender-based disparities?

One indication that pay transparency may offer a useful means to combat gender-based pay discrepancies is that such discrepancies are substantially lower in public sector and unionized workplaces. For example, Hegewisch et al. (2011) notes that in contrast to a 23 percent gender wage gap (based on median annual earnings) for all full-time workers, in the federal government, where pay rates are transparent and publicly available, the gap is only 11 percent. Of course, we must be cautious in drawing conclusions from such comparisons because employment practices in the federal government are distinct from those common in the private sector across a wide range of other dimensions. Nevertheless, several recent studies, using rigorous designs, similarly conclude that pay transparency can have an important impact on gender-based pay discrepancies.

Using a novel field study design, Emilio Castilla (2015) tested the degree to which transparency in pay decisions impacts gender, race, and ethnicity-based pay gaps. Castilla analyzed the performance-based pre- and post-transparency reward decisions of approximately 9,000 employees in a single service organization. Prior to the introduction of transparency, women, ethnic minorities, and non–U.S.-born employees received significantly lower monetary rewards compared to U.S.-born, White male employees in the same job with the same manager and the same performance and human capital profiles. Specifically, prior to the adoption of transparent pay practices, growth in annual pay was 0.4 percent lower for women than for men, and 0.5 percent lower for African Americans and Hispanics relative to Whites, even when controlling for unit, job, manager, and performance appraisal score. This discrepancy narrowed following the introduction of pay process and pay outcome transparency procedures, such that the differences were no longer significant.

A second study, by M. Baker et al. (2019), examined the impact of public sector salary disclosure laws on university faculty salaries in Canada. These laws, adopted at different times by Canada's different provinces, make public the wages of individual faculty members whose pay exceeds specific thresholds. The study found that the adoption of such legislation reduced the wage gap between male and female faculty members by a statistically significant 2 percentage points, even when controlling for numerous employee and employer characteristics. Given that the gender pay gap was approximately 7 percent to begin with, this reduction represents a 30 percent improvement, with most of the reduction occurring as a function of increases in the pay of female faculty.

Finally, as noted in Chapter 4, Bennedsen et al. (2019) used a difference-in-differences approach with matched employee–employer wage data from Denmark in order to assess the implications of pay transparency on gender-based pay disparities. Bennedsen et al.'s findings indicate that following the law's passage, earnings of men in the non-exempt (i.e., slightly larger) enterprises grew nearly 2 percentage points slower than those in the small, exempt enterprises—a difference that is statistically significant. Pay for women in the former increased by 0.28 percentage points relative to that of female employees in the smaller, exempt firms, although this difference was not statistically significant. Taken together, the findings suggest that the legislation was effective in achieving its primary objective. The wage gap in the non-exempt enterprises closed by approximately 2 percentage points more than in the exempt enterprises, or by 7 percent relative to the pre-law mean pay discrepancy. Furthermore, firms with larger gender-based pay discrepancies appeared to be more sensitive to the passage of the law, closing the gap more aggressively than firms with smaller discrepancies. The findings also indicated that although the non-exempt enterprises hired more female employees relative to the exempt enterprises, females were no more likely to leave the non-exempt firms (relative to the exempt firms) following passage of the pay transparency law.

Implications for Labor Mobility

In Chapter 4, we reviewed research examining the implications of pay transparency on productivity, highlighting several studies suggesting rather negative effects at the level of the firm. But at the societal level, these productivity effects may be different. One of the ways that pay transparency might enhance labor productivity at the market level is if, as suggested earlier, it facilitates the movement of human capital resources to those activities in which they are able to generate the greatest return for the economy. Such movement is most likely to occur when the market for labor is competitive. In a competitive labor market, pay is a function of the true economic value of the work performed, rather than of employees' and employers' relative bargaining positions. Employers who offer pay below the level implied by the value of the work will lose their employees, but they also have no incentive to pay above this level (which may vary from firm to firm depending on how productively they employ their workers). However, in a noncompetitive labor market, some employers may have the bargaining power to set wages below the true economic value of the work performed. This may boost the firm's profits (i.e., performance), but it can also drive some workers, particularly those for whom this wage falls beneath some subjective "floor," into other activities that, although perhaps paying slightly better, fail to capture their true potential value for the economy. Worse, it can drive them out of the labor market entirely.

Noncompetitive labor markets can emerge when one employer dominates the market for a certain type of labor (e.g., the coal mining company towns of early 20th-century West Virginia); when companies enforce draconian "no-compete" clauses in employment contracts, which forbid employees from working for the competition; or when several employers collude to directly or indirectly set wages (effectively establishing a monopsony). Such collusion can arise when companies agree to no-poaching policies or set common wage practices, as did several large IT companies such as Apple and Google in the first decades of this century (Ames, 2014; Worstall, 2014).

But noncompetitive labor markets can also emerge when pay information is asymmetric or, in other words, when employers have easy access to compensation survey data but employees do not. When employees lack complete information about their pay and benefits relative to those offered by a potential alternative employer, they are simply less likely to try to improve their own earnings, either by negotiating for a raise with their current employer or by seeking a new job. Although employees have access to publicly accessible pay information from the U.S. Bureau of Labor Statistics, or from private, third-party disclosure websites such as Glassdoor or Payscale, these data are far less fine-grained and can be of lower quality than the wage survey data commissioned by employers. The upshot is that even armed with such publicly available data, employees remain largely unaware of the true distribution of wages and have little choice but to accept at face value what the employer claims to be true about the distribution of pay in the firm or labor market.

This can put workers at a significant disadvantage in negotiations. Evidence of how information asymmetry can bias negotiations in favor of those possessing greater information was first presented by Akerlof (1970) in his seminal research examining how such information asymmetry influenced the sale of used cars. Since then, Sadler and Sanders (2016) have demonstrated that asymmetric information between National Basketball Association team owners and players improved the owners' bargaining position during lockout negotiations, and, as discussed in Chapter 1, Rosenfeld and Denice (2015) revealed the impact on wage outcomes of employer financial disclosures in British collective bargaining.

From a public policy perspective, however, reliance upon employer-provided data in wage negotiations can create a situation in which employees believe it is simply not worth their while to benchmark their current pay against that offered by other employers. According to Harris (2018), in a white paper for the Brookings Institution, such beliefs impose a natural damper on labor mobility, one that is no less costly to the economy than collusion by Silicon Valley employers to "fix" the going wage for software engineers. Both harm the economy by effectively restricting the efficient movement of labor to its most lucrative activity. A scene from the popular TV show *Mad Men* illustrates how even when employees possess information about others' pay, they may be hesitant to challenge employer assertions. In one of the show's episodes, a forward-thinking 1960s advertising executive, advocating for his firm to let him start a television unit, mistakenly receives the paystub of one of his peers. Upset by what he sees, he goes to his boss and asks for a raise to the equivalent amount, something he most likely would never have done without such knowledge. Still, when the boss responds by saying, "What?! No one here makes anywhere close to that!" the employee quickly settles for far less, taking the employer's word for it rather than pitching his idea to another agency, where he might have secured at least what his colleague was earning, if not more.

Although studies have yet to directly assess the implications of pay transparency for labor mobility, the theory and limited findings outlined here have prompted calls for governments to take action to ensure a more level playing field with regard to the accessibility of pay information. For example, Harris (2018), in the white paper mentioned above, suggested the following pay transparency policy interventions, all aimed at boosting labor mobility in the United States:

- Enact legislation protecting workers who inquire about others' pay or disclose their own pay to others. (For a full discussion of such legislation, see Chapter 1.)
- Require employers with more than some minimal number of employees to annually submit aggregated wage and hours data across job categories, pay bands, and demographic characteristics to EEOC on the basis of an expanded EEO-1 form. (For a full discussion of this policy, initiated by the Obama administration but then halted by the Trump administration in 2017, see Chapter 1.)
- Extend the 1993 "Safe Harbor" requirements specified by the Department of Justice and Federal Trade Commission regarding exchanges of price and cost information between firms to compensation surveys, such that these surveys would only be free from prosecution under antitrust laws if they (a) are managed by a third party, (b) contain data more than 3 months old, (c) include data on at least a minimal number of participating firms, and (d) share data with or make these data accessible to the employees in these firms.
- Make employer requests for prospective workers' wage histories contingent upon the employer's releasing information on average wages for comparable positions within the company. Such reciprocity could partially mitigate at least some of the limitations on labor mobility caused by information asymmetry.

Although such proposed policies (some of which I discuss in greater detail in Chapter 8) might indeed enhance labor mobility, as well as address the gender- or race-based pay disparities discussed earlier, they could have negative consequences for other outcomes. For instance, although regulations mandating pay transparency in Denmark yielded significant reductions in gender pay discrepancies, as reported by Bennedsen et al. (2019), they also generated significant reductions in firm-level productivity (as noted in Chapter 4). And as we next examine, such policies may also have unintended negative consequences with regard to wage distribution and inequality.

Implications for Wage Distribution and Wage Inequality

Wage distribution or dispersion refers to the spread in wages across different kinds of workers, particularly the differential between the pay of those earning the most (e.g., the top 5 percent of wage earners in a firm, sector, or market) and those earning the least. During the past 50 years, wages have become more dispersed in many economies throughout the world. In the United States, for example, in the 40 years between 1980 and 2020, inflation-adjusted hourly wages for those in the lowest 10th percentile rose from $9.75 to $10.07 (i.e., by $0.32). The median hourly wage rose by $2.54 (from $16.79 to $19.33) over this same period. However, for the labor market's highest earners, those in the top 95th percentile, hourly wages rose from $41.15 to $67.14 during this time frame, an increase of $25.99 (Economic Policy Institute, 2020). Put in terms of the change in wage disparities over time, the 95/10 wage ratio—which describes 95th percentile earnings relative to 10th percentile earnings—increased from 4.2 to 6.7. This means that whereas top earners were paid 4.2 times as much in hourly wages as low-paid workers in 1979, they now earn 6.7 times more. Figure 5.1 displays the cumulative percentage change in real hourly wages for men by percentile from 2000 to 2019, showing that the growth in wages for the top 5 percent of male earners was more than three times that of those in the lowest 10th percentile.

Concerns about wage inequality are often heightened when comparisons are made between the pay of CEOs, whose salary typically accounts for just 12 percent of their *total* pay (Hallock, 2012), and the typical low-wage worker. Hallock (2012, p. 17), using data from three combined samples, reports that in the United States, median CEO pay (including salaries, bonuses and other incentives, pensions, stocks and stock options, and "other" pay) was just under $6 million in 2009 (rising to approximately $17 million 10 years later; Mishel & Wolfe, 2019). This figure was approximately 400 times greater than the annual compensation of those workers in the lowest 5th percentile in the United States in 2009. The same comparison would have generated a wage

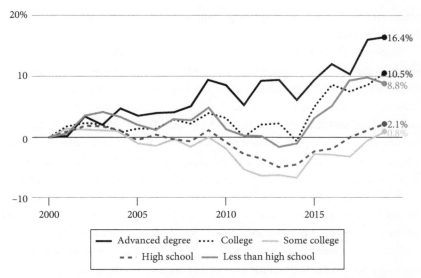

Figure 5.1 Cumulative percentage change in real average hourly wages of men, by education, 2000–2019, showing that wages grew more quickly for men with college or advanced degrees. The xth-percentile wage is the wage at which x% of wage earners earn less and $(100 - x)$% earn more.
Reprinted with permission from Gould (2020).

gap of "just" 140 times in 1979. But what if we compare CEO pay to the pay of a more typical worker? CEO pay was approximately 20 times greater than that of the "median" worker in 1965, increasing to 75 times greater in 1979, 175 times greater in 2009, and 221 times greater in 2019 (Hallock, 2012, p. 18; Mishel & Wolfe, 2019).

It is generally accepted that such gaps have a "major impact on the overall income inequality" in a society (Bapuji et al., 2020, p. 66). However, whether and how pay transparency may mitigate such a problem, and at what cost, are less well understood. As noted in Chapter 1, already in the 1930s, regulators in many countries began turning to transparency reforms to address what many saw to be executive excess at the expense of shareholders. These regulations required publicly traded companies to disclose the compensation of their top-paid executives. But what might be the effect of extending such reforms to cover the entire workforce? That is, what might be the broader labor market implications of some of the pay transparency initiatives suggested in the Brookings Institute white paper (Harris, 2018) noted above, such as allowing employees to inquire about and disclose their own pay information to others or requiring firms to report or even make public pay distribution data?

Studies by Ohlmer and Sasson (2018), Mas (2017), and Wong et al. (2022) suggest that one consequence of such reforms may indeed be a reduction in pay dispersion, or in other words pay compression. Ohlmer and Sasson (2018), exploiting an October 2007 decision of Norway's tax authority to allow all citizens unrestricted access to others' tax records via the internet, examined the impact of a country-wide policy shift in pay outcome transparency on the change in wage dispersion over time (from 2008 to 2012).[3] Their findings indicate that the dispersion of wages in Norway fell by 0.8 percentage points within a year following implementation of the intervention. By 2012, pay dispersion had declined by 1.4 percentage points, equivalent to a total decline of 5.7 percent in national pay dispersion. One explanation for this effect may be that under conditions of greater pay transparency, greater pay inequality (i.e., dispersion) generates a reputational penalty with respect to key stakeholders such as customers and prospective employees (Benedetti & Chen, 2018). With transparency providing stakeholders with a greater awareness of pay disparities within a firm, these individuals may opt to move their business or human capital to competitors deemed more fair (Bapuji et al., 2020).

Although the other two studies point to a similar pay compression effect of pay transparency, they also suggest that transparency-related pay compression may be accompanied by a number of unintended negative consequences. As discussed in Chapter 4, these include the potential loss of difficult-to-replace human capital (Mas, 2017), as well as an increased reliance on less observable rewards such as benefit and developmental idiosyncratic or i-deals (Wong, 2022). Obloj and Zenger (2022) offer further insight into the mechanisms linking pay outcome transparency to both wage compression and the potentially adverse effects that accompany it. Using data on 97,839 distinct individuals employed in 139 colleges and universities across more than a dozen academic fields, Obloj and Zenger (2022) examined the consequences of shifts in pay transparency practices on a variety of market-wide outcomes over time. Included in their data set was information on each scholar's 20-year salary history (1997–2017), academic performance (e.g.,

---

[3] As noted previously, tax records have been public in Norway since the 19th century. Since 2001, Norwegians have been able to access these records online. However, access was still somewhat restricted by various regulations until 2007.

publications, awards, grants, books, and patents), and demographic characteristics (gender, rank, tenure, and discipline). By combining this information with data on changes in pay communication restrictiveness during this same 20-year period in each of the academics' universities, they were able to model the impact of these changes on pay inequality, and specifically dispersion both across levels (vertical dispersion) and within levels (horizontal dispersion), as well as on performance.

First the good news: Obloj and Zenger's findings indicated that pay transparency had "significant and economically sizeable effects in reducing pay inequity, significantly reducing the gender pay gap, as well as more broadly improving the precision with which pay is linked to observable performance metrics and promotion" (pp. 646–655). Specifically, in schools that adopted more transparent pay practices, they observed a shift toward greater concentration of wages around the estimated market wage, and pay variance within departments and universities fell by 20 percent. This is a clear indication of a pay compression effect—or in other words, of the effectiveness of such practices in reducing inequality. Furthermore, they found that whereas prior to a reduction in pay communication restrictiveness women were significantly more likely than men to be paid below the estimated average market wage (as well as significantly less likely to be paid over this market average), these gender-based differences declined significantly (although not entirely) following a transparency shift. Accordingly, Obloj and Zenger conclude that with a shift toward transparency, nonjustifiable demographic factors such as gender play a greatly diminished role in influencing the link between performance metrics and rewards, thus reducing wage inequities.

However, Obloj and Zenger (2022) also found that accompanying the equality-boosting effects of a transparency shift was an unintended and potentially negative consequence, namely that pay became less performance-based. Specifically, they found that following shifts toward greater pay transparency, observable performance (e.g., winning a competitive research grant or publishing higher quality papers) had less of an impact on changes in pay over time. For example, controlling for academic tenure, field, and institution, having star levels of publishing performance (in the 95th percentile) was initially (pre-transparency) associated with an average wage increase of nearly 10 percent. Following a shift toward transparency, this premium of "stardom" fell to just 5.2 percent.

Obloj and Zenger (2022) tested three ways in which pay transparency may reduce the market-wide link between performance and pay. The first possibility they investigated is that under conditions of greater transparency, the pay implications of superior performance relative to one's peers (e.g., winning a grant), or being promoted to a higher position in the organization (e.g., from assistant to associate professor), are diminished. Indeed, the data support such a mechanism. Specifically, in terms of the former, the data show that pay is 37 percent less sensitive to within-rank differences in measurable performance by academics after a shift to greater transparency. In terms of the latter, average pay differences for associate and full professors compared with assistant professors fell from pre-transparency rates of 15 and 32 percent, respectively, to 8 and 23 percent, respectively, post-transparency.

A second possibility investigated by Obloj and Zenger (2022) is that transparency motivates organizations to "equalize" pay by upwardly correcting those earning below average wages, while reducing the pay of those earning above the average, or at least slowing its rate of increase. Evidence is found for this explanation as well. Obloj and Zenger divided their study sample into those who were significantly underpaid and those who were significantly overpaid relative to their institution/department peers earning a median wage. Prior to the adoption of more transparent pay practices, given an average annual base rate increase of 2.4 percent, those in the underpaid group received a yearly base rate increase of 3.8 percent, whereas those in the overpaid group received only 0.8 percent. Following the adoption of pay transparency, those who were overpaid continued to receive the same increase of 0.8 percent, but the underpaid group benefited from a 4.8 percent wage increase (an additional percentage point rise). Accordingly, Obloj and Zenger conclude that with greater pay transparency, organizations strive to achieve greater within-level (horizontal) equality by increasing the magnitude of pay increases for those earning below the median.

One final possibility explored by the investigators is that transparency drives pay equality by stimulating labor mobility—or in other words, by motivating those who view their pay as unfair to leave the organization (as in the demoralization argument discussed in Chapter 4). This effect could be beneficial for the organization if those motivated to leave are poorer performers, as it would represent a form of positive sorting. However, if it is the *best* performers who leave, because they believe their rewards from the organization are not commensurate with their contribution, this would represent negative sorting. Although both effects result in pay being more centered around the median rate (i.e., reduced dispersion and diminished wage inequality), the latter—representing a net outflow of human capital resources—could be harmful to the organization. Evidence of a positive effect was found by Card et al. (2012) in their sample of university staff, whereas Mas (2017) found a negative sorting effect in the municipalities that he studied. Obloj and Zenger (2022) find no support for either a positive or a negative sorting effect in their data.

Overall, Obloj and Zenger's (2022) results suggest that the equality-generating effects of pay transparency operate largely through the first two mechanisms discussed, namely by making pay adjustments less sensitive to differences in measurable performance and by motivating organizations to "correct" pay adjustments at the lower and (sometimes) upper ends of the scale. They also point to a potentially critical trade-off of pay transparency with respect to labor market outcomes. On the one hand, such initiatives appear to mitigate wage inequality and address demographic-based pay disparities (or inequities). On the other hand, they appear to weaken the link between performance and pay, thus potentially reducing the efficiency of reward allocation. Accordingly, Obloj and Zenger suggest that more mid-range pay transparency practices—for example, revealing aggregated pay information by hierarchical rank, or for relevant groups of peers, rather than for individuals—may offer the best of both worlds for organizations and employees alike. As they note, "Such practices may pressure organizations to elevate the fairness and consistency of pay while still maintaining pay for performance" (p. 653).

Until now, we have examined inequality largely in terms of wage differentials within and between levels (i.e., between co-workers doing the same or similar work, and between lower paid and higher paid jobs, respectively). However, inequality may also be considered in terms of how the economic returns of a firm are "split" between the workforce and the employer. One possibility is that transparency boosts returns to workers in the form of higher wages at the expense of executive pay or the employer's profits. This could conceivably occur if lower wage workers observe that they are under-paid and use the visible pay differences to successfully negotiate for higher pay, thus raising mean wages. The resulting increase in labor costs could come at the expense of executive pay and/or shareholder profits, thus potentially reducing inequality in the distribution of income and/or wealth in an economy.

However, in a study referred to in Chapter 4, Cullen and Pakzad-Hurson (2019) present evidence that beyond making wages more equal, pay transparency, rather than raising mean wages, can *reduce* them. How does this

occur and what is the evidence? Simply stated, this occurs because pay transparency can reduce the bargaining power of some workers to renegotiate
(and increase) their pay over time. When pay information is more restricted,
any worker who believes that they deserve more pay can ask their boss for a
raise. If the boss claims that the requested wage would break the top of the
pay range assigned to that job, the worker may either bargain more aggressively or take the employer at their word and settle for some lower wage. But
when workers have immediate access to the wages of their peers (i.e., when
everyone's pay is transparent), they may seek to renegotiate a new, minimum
acceptable wage consistent with that received by the highest paid other. In
response, the employer can (and most likely will) credibly argue that any increase in one worker's pay is likely to drive upward renegotiations with the
others, which could drive the employer out of business. The upshot of this
is that while below equilibrium wage earners may successfully bargain up
their pay to equal that of their peers (thus reducing horizontal inequality, as
noted in Chapter 4), individual workers (and particularly high-performers)
lose bargaining power. In short, transparency gives the employer the ability
to set wages and to do so in a manner reducing total labor costs. Of course,
all of this assumes that wages are not set in stone but rather are dynamic, with
employees able to at least attempt to renegotiate their pay over time (regardless of their access to information about the pay of others). This also assumes
that employees bargain individually and not collectively (i.e., in the context
of a trade union or professional association).

To test their theory, Cullen and Pakzad-Hurson (2019) used data from a
platform linking employers with contract or so-called "gig" workers, namely
TaskRabbit. Most jobs offered on this platform are low-skilled, standardized
jobs for which individual candidates offer themselves at a set wage to the
employer in a private, online negotiation. Once a wage offer is accepted,
the employer cannot renegotiate to lower it. However, the employee is always free to negotiate an increase in the wage before the work is completed.
According to the authors' survey data, workers disclose their wages to one
another in approximately 40 percent of cases (largely when they are in co-
located jobs, facilitating information transfer), thus creating variance in the
degree of pay outcome transparency. So what happens to the final paid wage
under conditions of pay secrecy versus relative pay outcome transparency?
As described in Chapter 4, the first thing Cullen and Pakzad-Hurson observe
is that when—and only when—workers are co-located (allowing for greater
transparency), the bids workers submit *privately* to the platform before the

job begins affect the renegotiation outcomes of their co-workers, resulting in a rise in lower bid wages to the point of near complete wage equality. Second, they observe that employers who disclose the wage assigned to the job when posting the position (i.e., opting for transparency) tend to have fewer resources and offer a lower wage. More important, Cullen and Pakzad-Hurson find that "the very same workers bid hourly wages 7.8 percent lower for work in the same job category when the job description mentions expected wages up front." Finally, and most significantly, they find a market-wide effect of such low-end wage postings in the form of an increasing trend by employers across the market for such jobs to adopt higher levels of pay transparency. Indeed, during the period covered by their study, the proportion of jobs for which a wage was posted along with the job description increased by 1 percent each month.

In a follow-up study, Cullen and Pakzad-Hurson (2019) recruited 365 managers and 964 workers on the MTurk platform. The managers were given a budget and informed that anything left over after their workers completed the assigned task would be theirs as profit. The workers were tasked to negotiate pay for, and then execute, a transcription task taking several hours. The study participants were randomized to transparency and secrecy conditions. In the case of the former, negotiations over wages were conducted in a common chatroom, whereas in the case of secrecy, the negotiations were private. Much as in the TaskRabbit study, pay was equalized 100 percent of the time for those in the transparency condition versus 60 percent of the time for those conducting private negotiations. Moreover, relative to the secrecy condition, managers' profits in the transparency condition were 27 percent higher, and wages were 7.4 percent lower.

These findings raise serious concerns regarding the negative externalities potentially associated with pay transparency's beneficial effects on gender-based wage inequities and inequality more generally. However, several factors may limit their generalizability. First, Cullen and Pakzad-Hurson (2019) examined a very small subset of jobs, namely on-demand labor market jobs filled over the internet. Although such "gig" labor is an increasingly important element of the labor market in the United States, it still remains rather small, accounting for well under 10 percent of the U.S. workforce (Robles & McGee, 2016). Second, the types of jobs examined in both studies are highly standardized (representing labor as a commodity), reducing productivity differences and making whatever differences there are highly observable. But many jobs fail to meet these criteria; and when the nature of the tasks

allows for greater and less observable productivity differences, employee bargaining power is less likely to be diminished by pay outcome transparency,
thus making wages unlikely to settle around a single posted wage. Employers
are likely to find ways of rewarding more productive workers in a less public
manner (e.g., i-deals) in an effort to retain them. Finally, when employees
bargain collectively for wages, the assumed dynamic underlying Cullen
and Pakzad-Hurson's (2019) theory—namely that employers will claim that
acceding to any individual request for higher pay will "break the bank"—is less
likely to apply. As noted in Chapter 1, at least in the United States, employers
may be obligated to open the books to labor representatives when making
such a claim in the context of collective bargaining. Moreover, there is no evidence that the transparency associated with collective bargaining results in
a reduction in worker bargaining power vis-à-vis the employer. Indeed, the
wage agreements emerging from collective bargaining are not only entirely
transparent but also typically associated with a net *gain* rather than loss in
wages—referred to by labor economists as the union wage premium.

Pay Transparency and Employee Happiness
and Well-Being

Thus far, the focus in this chapter has been largely on the market- or society-
wide economic implications of pay transparency. But in the same way that
pay transparency policies were shown in Chapter 3 to impact employee affect
within the firm, it is possible that regulatory efforts to expand pay transparency across organizations or the labor market as a whole may also impact
individual emotions and well-being. As will be recalled, Chapter 3 discussed
equivocal findings regarding employees' affective responses to varying forms
of pay transparency. In particular, SimanTov-Nachlieli and Bamberger
(2021) found that although employees' affective responses to pay *process*
transparency was generally positive, their affective responses to pay *outcome*
transparency depended on their level of pay relative to referent others: those
whose pay was above the median generally reported more positive affective
responses relative to those whose pay was below the median. But are these
referent-contingent affective responses generalizable to the labor market as
a whole?

Findings from a study by Ricardo Perez-Truglia (2020) suggest that they
are. Perez-Truglia argues that by facilitating earnings comparisons, pay

transparency practices make more visible (and less dismissible) income gaps between richer and poorer individuals. Having such information put in front of one's face can generate negative psychological sequelae if one is among the poorer individuals confronted by such information. This is because research suggests that being confronted by one's own relative poverty can lower *self-esteem*, whereas having others observe one's relative poverty can result in the lowering of one's *social* esteem. Opposite effects are posited for those who, when comparisons are facilitated, view themselves or are viewed by others as earning more or being richer. For them, transparency is likely to be associated with enhanced self- and social esteem.

Perez-Truglia (2020) tested this wealth-contingent hypothesis using data from Norway prior and subsequent to that country's decision to make individuals' income tax data accessible to the public via the internet in 2001. Focusing on happiness and life satisfaction, two important indicators of subjective well-being that are highly correlated with objective well-being measures, he reports that the income transparency change led to a 29 percent increase in the association between income and happiness and a 21 percent increase in income's association with life satisfaction. That is, although income had always been positively associated with happiness and life satisfaction, when individuals could easily compare their income with that of others, happiness and life satisfaction became more income-contingent. Moreover, whereas prior to the shift in income transparency there was no year-by-year change in the income–happiness association, there was a distinct change following the adoption of internet accessibility.

However, these transparency-related boosts in the impact of income on emotional well-being were not consistent across all those studied. As shown in Figure 5.2, the transparency reform was associated with a large and sustained increase in the income–happiness gradient only for wealthier individuals (operationalized by higher versus lower levels of internet access). For poorer individuals (those with lower internet access), the impact of income on well-being remained unchanged (i.e., the income–happiness slope remained the same following the 2001 reform). Particularly when considered alongside anecdotal evidence that the new accessibility of tax records was linked with an increase in bullying of kids from poorer households, and that "adults from poorer households felt that they disappointed themselves and others" (Perez-Truglia, 2020, p. 1021), Perez-Truglia's findings suggest that whereas more transparent pay information may improve the emotional well-being of those earning more in a labor market, it offers little

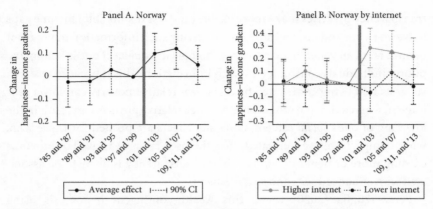

Figure 5.2 Changes in happiness–income gradient in Norway by year.
Reprinted with permission from Perez-Truglia (2020).

psychological benefit (and perhaps even emotional harm) to those earning less. Furthermore, the findings suggest that the pay information made available as a function of pay transparency is evaluated on a relative rather than an absolute basis. Thus, if the available information were to suggest rising incomes for everyone in a given labor market, no change in happiness or satisfaction would be expected. Greater pay transparency gives rise to a positive shift in emotional well-being only for individuals who observe that their income has increased relative to some salient comparison group. Of course, this means that greater happiness for one subset of individuals depends on some other, lower earning subset being disappointed, demoralized, and depressed by the pay information to which they gain access.

What are the implications of all this from a public policy perspective? For the sake of the emotional well-being of those earning less, should policymakers and regulators avoid blanket transparency policies, such as those mandating wide-scale accessibility to individual earnings information as in the Scandinavian countries? Perez-Truglia (2020) suggests that this would mean throwing out the baby with the bathwater. He notes that pay outcome transparency does offer real benefits to the labor market and society, such as those outlined at the start of this chapter. Instead, he suggests that intermediate strategies might be applied. For example, if, as his data suggest, some of the negative effects of pay outcome transparency stem less from the impact on *self*-esteem and more from the impact on *social* esteem (i.e., how one is treated by others), one solution might be to require those seeking others' pay information to do so non-anonymously—as indeed has been the case in Norway since 2014. Such a policy should discourage snooping and bullying without putting barriers in the way of people seeking the information for legitimate reasons, such as to negotiate higher pay, better plan their careers, or identify gender-based pay disparities.[4] Another might be to mandate the release of more aggregated pay information, such as average salaries or salary ranges by organization, occupation, and unit. As Perez-Truglia notes, "These aggregate data can provide most of the information that individuals need while avoiding harmful effects on the well-being of the lowest earners" (p. 1051).

Conclusion

Confused? Given the mixed findings presented above, who wouldn't be? However, while noting that certain pay transparency reforms may exert a nontrivial toll on productivity, overall wages, and even happiness for some, the empirical evidence still points to some important benefits of pay transparency with regard to the reduction of gender-based and other nonjustifiable wage disparities, in addition to the compression of what many view as excessive and unjustifiable pay dispersion. As I have suggested throughout this chapter, from a public policy perspective, there is no shortage of more moderate reforms that have been shown to reduce wage inequalities, and eliminate the most egregious inequities, while generating minimal unintended negative consequences. Some of these reforms may include the expansion of regulations limiting employers' rights to restrict employee disclosures of pay (pay communication transparency), as well as those requiring employers to be open with employees about how pay-related decision are made (pay process transparency). Finally, by instituting policies that make employers accountable to regulatory agencies, such as requiring them to report aggregated pay outcome information (e.g., pay ranges and median pay for each level of pay in the organization, and size of gender and/or racial/ethnic pay disparities), it may be possible to enjoy many of the labor market benefits noted in this chapter while avoiding many of the unintended negative consequences. We return to a discussion of some of these policies in Chapter 8.

---

[4] Perez-Truglia (2020, p. 1029) notes that after tax record searches in Norway became non-anonymous in 2014, any individual could use the tax website to identify who had viewed their records. As a result, the tax agency reported that the number of searches dropped by 88 percent.

6

Employee Pay Disclosure

The bulk of the research we have reviewed thus far has assumed that when it comes to pay transparency and communication, the primary agent is the employer. This is certainly the case when we consider policies and practices involving pay outcome transparency and pay process transparency. After all, except where subject to government regulation and/or specified as part of a collective agreement, these policies and practices are largely determined unilaterally by the employer.

But what about pay communication transparency? Although here too employers can set policies aimed at restricting employee pay disclosure, ultimately this is a matter of employee agency. Employees may opt to disclose their pay to others either directly or indirectly (via some third-party intermediary) even when employers try to restrict such behavior, just as they may opt to refrain from doing so even where such communication is not restricted. Accordingly, when we refer to pay communication transparency, our focus is on the antecedents and consequences of employee pay information exchange.

Pay information exchange has been defined as a domain-specific form of information exchange—specifically, the provision and receiving of reward-related information (Marijn Poortvliet et al., 2007; Smit & Montag-Smit, 2019). This form of exchange has traditionally occurred in the context of person-to-person interactions, with pay information either solicited or shared spontaneously without any explicit request. However, as we discuss below, employee pay information exchange is increasingly taking place indirectly via third-party information intermediaries such as Glassdoor and Payscale. Using such intermediaries, employees can disclose their own information to others and gain access to the pay information supplied by others in return. In this chapter, we explore both forms of employee information exchange, drawing on what little empirical research is available on the topic.

In what follows, after examining the prevalence of employee information exchange, I discuss the more traditional forms of pay information seeking and provision, such as person-to-person pay information exchange and

Exposing Pay. Peter Bamberger, Oxford University Press. © Oxford University Press 2023.
DOI: 10.1093/oso/9780197628164.003.0006

individual pay information searches. Specifically, I examine the psychological forces that might motivate individuals to seek out and/or share pay information, or to refrain from doing so—what Smit and Montag-Smit (2018) refer to as the "disclosure dilemma." Then, focusing on a later study by those researchers, I examine (a) individual and situational predictors of relevant employee attitudes or preferences and (b) how these preferences may help explain actual pay solicitation and sharing behavior. Following this, in the second part of the chapter, I shift to an exploration of internet-mediated pay information exchange. I discuss a research model aimed at explaining the nature and dynamics of such exchange and report the findings from a test of that model using a representative sample of the Australian workforce (Brown et al., 2021). I conclude the chapter with a review of the practical steps that organizations may adopt to manage employee pay information exchange.

Prevalence of Employee Pay Information Exchange

Employee pay disclosure may be defined as an employee behavior in which an individual provides information about their remuneration to others—whether personally (e.g., to family, friends, or work colleagues) or (increasingly) indirectly via internet-based intermediaries. Face-to-face verbal revelations—what most of us imagine when we think about pay disclosures—may be spontaneous, occur in response to another's request for information, or manifest in the context of some broader exchange. Third-party disclosures on the internet are less personal in nature and offer a way of exchanging information with multiple anonymous others.

Although prevalence data on pay information disclosure is sparse, evidence suggests that at least with regard to personal interactions, people tend to consider financial information (including details about their pay) to be nobody's business but their own. At least one British study suggests that people are more willing to talk about their sexual history than about their income: Just 3 percent of 15,000 people surveyed resisted answering questions from a stranger about the former, compared with 20 percent for the latter (Boren, 2015). A more recent study by Cullen and Perez-Truglia (2018b) found a similar hesitancy among employees to directly exchange pay information. In a clever experiment conducted in a Southeast Asian investment bank, these investigators first asked employees about their willingness to inquire about or share pay information with co-workers, compared with information about seniority. Sixty-nine percent rated inquiries about pay as "socially unacceptable," and 89 percent reported that they would feel uncomfortable asking a co-worker about their pay; the comparable figures for seniority were 7 percent and 23 percent. Similarly, only 20 percent said they would feel comfortable sharing their own pay information with peers. The researchers then randomly assigned the participants to two conditions, in which they were given an incentive to share information with five co-workers about their pay (condition 1) or seniority (condition 2). Approximately 40 percent of the participants in the pay condition were unwilling to reveal their salary information to five co-workers even when offered the maximum incentive ($125—the equivalent of a week's pay in the country where the study was conducted). In contrast, only approximately half that proportion were unwilling to share their seniority information with peers when offered the same incentive. No differences between men and women were found for either inquiry or sharing preferences.

Might such findings simply reflect workplace norms traditionally imposed by employers, which discourage or prohibit employees from exchanging pay information? A 2010 survey of 2,700 workers in the United States, already mentioned in Chapter 1, found that less than 35 percent of private companies either made pay information public or explicitly allowed their employees to discuss their pay with colleagues (Institute for Women's Policy Research [IWPR], 2014; Hayes, 2017). At the time of that survey, 41 percent of private companies actively discouraged employees from talking about pay on the job, and another 25 percent formally prohibited such discussions, to the extent that employees "caught discussing wage and salary information could be punished" (Figure 6.1). These findings were surprising even in 2010, in that, as discussed in Chapter 1, such policies have long been illegal in the United States, running counter to Section 7 of the 1935 National Labor Relations Act. But even more surprising is that 10 years after the collection of those data, and despite the passage of explicit regulations in at least 10 U.S. states barring employers from restricting employee exchanges of pay information, the numbers have not changed (Rosenfeld, 2021). Regardless of whether managers are ignorant of the law or are simply willing to risk litigation and relatively weak penalties (IWPR, 2020), there is little doubt that such restrictive workplace policies remain widely prevalent and have the chilling effect desired by employers (O'Connell, 2020).

But the findings outlined above suggest that employer restrictions are not the only factor explaining the low tendency of employees to exchange

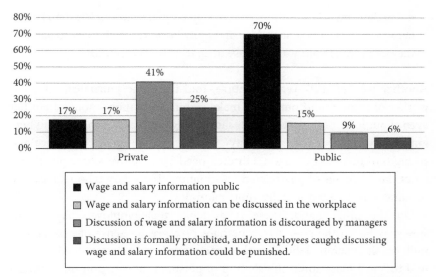

Figure 6.1 Pay secrecy policies by type of employer. Calculations are based on 879 respondents currently employed as wage and salary workers in the private and public sectors and providing answers to the survey item on access to wage information in their workplaces.

Reprinted with permission from IWPR/Rockefeller Survey of Economic Security 2010 as appearing in IWPR No. Q068 (December, 2017). *Private sector workers lack pay transparency: Pay secrecy may reduce women's bargaining power and contribute to gender wage gap.* Retrieved on June 29, 2022, from https://iwpr.org/wp-content/uploads/2020/09/Q068-Pay-Secrecy.pdf.

pay information. Also at play is what some researchers refer to as the "salary taboo"—a strong social norm around pay-related privacy that discourages people from inquiring about or revealing salary information, both inside and outside the workplace (Trachtman, 1999; Edwards, 2005). For some, this taboo may be grounded in a sense that one's pay is highly personal, reflecting a deep-seated self-image about one's value and contribution to society that might be put at risk by open discussion (Cullen & Perez-Truglia, 2018b). For others, this taboo may be based on concerns about gleaning or sharing information that could lead to feelings of envy, resentment, or insecurity (Smit & Montag-Smit, 2018). For example, in an interview with a journalist, a 26-year-old New Yorker working in marketing explained that she is strategic in sharing pay information with others:

> I share my salary with friends who I know make a similar salary, mostly to discuss how they make a budget work with this particular income. I tend

not to share my salary with friends who I know make more or less than I do, because it can be uncomfortable—if they make more, I feel insecure, and if they make less, I don't want to make them feel bad. (Berger, 2017)

Another worker, a 27-year-old nurse, told the same journalist, "If a co-worker of mine found out that I make significantly more money than her even though we both do the exact same thing and she's been working here longer, it will only cause animosity." Overall, the apparent prevalence and strength of this taboo suggest a limited need for employers to explicitly restrict the exchange of pay-related information. The salary taboo appears to be rather effective at doing that quite naturally.

On the other hand, there is evidence that employee pay disclosure may be on the rise, driven perhaps by a greater sense of ease among millennials (usually defined as the generation born between 1981 and the mid to late 1990s) about the sharing of personal information more generally (Milkman, 2017). For example, a 2017 survey conducted by Princeton Survey Research Associates International for *The Cashlorette*, a personal finance website, asked millennials (aged 18–36 years) and baby boomers (aged 53–71 years) whether and with whom they shared salary information. Among the millennials, 63 percent, 48 percent, and 30 percent said they had shared salary information with an immediate family member, friend, and co-worker, respectively. For the baby boomers, the comparable figures were 41 percent, 21 percent, and 8 percent (Berger, 2017). Although some of this difference in generational disclosure preferences may be age based, both theory (Mannheim, 1970) and empirical evidence (Milkman, 2017; Rosenfeld, 2021) suggest that in fact it reflects a sustainable, long-term divergence in world view, one rooted in profoundly distinct historical, sociological, and technological processes.

Generational differences are also apparent with respect to the disclosure of *indirect* pay information to third-party, internet-based intermediaries. For example, the pay information exchange site Glassdoor—which requires users to disclose their own pay in order to access aggregated pay information provided by others—reports more than 60 million unique visits to the website each month, with 50 million salary disclosures from individuals employed by hundreds of thousands of companies worldwide (Brown et al., 2021). Between 2017 and 2020, millennials rose from 36 percent to 42 percent as a proportion of Glassdoor's users (Glassdoor, 2017, 2020). Some of this increase simply reflects the fact that during those years, more millennials entered or advanced in the workforce, but not all of it. Furthermore, studies indicate that employees are increasingly comfortable sharing sensitive information of all sorts online, including information on pay (Trotter et al., 2017).

Although data on the prevalence and distribution of employee pay disclosures across key demographics remain extremely limited, the findings to date suggest two important takeaways. First, as much as employees may appreciate the benefits of pay transparency, when it comes to *directly* disclosing their own personal pay information to others, the salary taboo often dominates. Second, and in contrast, *indirect* forms of pay information exchange are becoming more prevalent, with a greater number of people exchanging their pay information with others via third-party, internet-based intermediaries each year.

The Disclosure Dilemma

The findings presented above suggest that the decision to solicit or share pay information is a difficult one. To better understand the conditions governing such decisions, we need a clear picture of what motivates people to engage (or not) in pay information exchange. In a study examining individuals' pay-related privacy and sharing preferences, Smit and Montag-Smit (2018) identified and explored some of these underlying motivations.

First, in terms of what motivates individuals to solicit and share pay information, Smit and Montag-Smit argue that comparative reward information serves two important purposes: It (a) reduces fairness uncertainty and (b) helps employees decide what, if any, actions they should take to improve their own pay situation. For instance, to the extent that comparative information helps expose unjustifiable pay disparities (based, for example, on gender or race), employees armed with comparative pay information can decide whether to voice their concerns to management or take legal action. Comparative pay information can also help employees make better-informed labor market decisions, such as whether to pursue career advancement within the organization or leave the organization and seek other avenues for advancement.

On the other hand, as already suggested, a number of considerations may motivate employees to keep their pay information to themselves and to avoid soliciting such information from others. First, employees may not be pleased with what they discover when exchanging pay information. Specifically, research on social comparison (e.g., Exline & Lobel, 1999) suggests that learning one is underpaid relative to comparative others may challenge one's self-concept and self-efficacy, potentially triggering distress and feelings of deprivation, anxiety, or even depression (Smith et al., 2012). Second, pay differences between co-workers can grow more salient as they become more visible, generating envy and potentially seeding interpersonal friction and even overt conflict (Bamberger & Belogolovsky, 2017). Note that the experience of envy can be unhealthy for both the envier and the envied. K. Lee et al. (2018) found that a sense of being envied can be unpleasant and anxiety-provoking, with negative implications for the envied individual's work engagement and job performance—especially if the employee fears that envious co-workers may approach the employer over the pay discrepancy, thus potentially threatening future pay increases for the envied individual. Finally, these destructive and unhealthy outcomes may arise regardless of who the higher and lower earners are in any exchange (i.e., the person who initially shares or initially receives the information) and whether or not the information is initially solicited or shared spontaneously. Interpersonal relationships can also suffer if one person spontaneously shares pay information and the other fails to reciprocate. Accordingly, individuals may be motivated to abstain from exchanging any pay information simply in order to avoid rocking the boat.

To understand how these various motivations ultimately influence employee behavior, Smit and Montag-Smit (2018) collected survey data on pay disclosure preferences from several samples of MTurk workers (with each sample containing more than 100 online participants). Their findings indicate that across these samples, a roughly equivalent proportion of participants were willing (37 percent) and not willing (39 percent) to seek out pay information from others. The proportions were roughly the same for willingness to share personal pay information: 38 percent and 37 percent, respectively. Moreover, the findings offer some insight into how individual differences with regard to the positive and negative motivations noted above may influence such preferences. Specifically, Smit and Montag-Smit found that a preference for soliciting pay information is more prevalent among individuals who report experiencing more uncertainty and unfairness at work, particularly among those who are generally more sensitive to equity and uncertainty concerns (Huseman et al., 1987). This is not surprising in that, as Smit and Montag-Smit note, "acquiring pay information reduces uncertainty and verifies pay fairness, which simultaneously

alleviates risks associated with a lack of information, and offers instrumental benefits to employees" (p. 540).

In contrast, Smit and Montag-Smit's (2018) findings indicate a robust inverse association between pay information sharing and three variables: need
to belong, a desire to avoid behavior that might harm others, and wishing
to maintain a positive reputation among work colleagues. According to the
study authors, these findings suggest that a reluctance to share pay information largely reflect a motivation to maintain one's public appearance rather
than a concern with interpersonal relationships more generally. Indeed,
consistent with the work of others (e.g., Schall et al., 2016), the greater
participants' emphasis on the importance of maintaining their reputation at
work (i.e., wanting to be seen positively), the stronger their preference for
pay privacy and the desire to conceal their own personal pay information
from others.

Finally, in addition to these individual difference characteristics associated with sharing preferences, Smit and Montag-Smit (2018) also found an
inverted-U (i.e., curvilinear) relationship between perceptions of one's own
pay relative to others and individuals' willingness to share their pay information. Specifically, willingness to share was lowest among those perceiving
themselves as paid either much less or much more than colleagues (Figure
6.2). These findings suggest that in addition to concerns with protecting one's
public appearance, privacy preferences are also heightened by concerns with
protecting one's self-image.

Employee-to-Employee Disclosure

With this understanding of the motivations driving (or repressing)
employees' seeking and sharing of pay information, we turn to the forms of
pay information exchange. We begin with direct employee-to-employee disclosure. Although such disclosures are discouraged or even expressly prohibited in many organizations, if employees really want to compare their pay,
they will likely do so. One executive of an information technology company,
interviewed by a member of my research team, put it this way: Despite contractual provisions forbidding such behavior in her company, "when people
wanted to find out their peers' salary, they actually went with their paystub
and compared. This wasn't allowed but people still did it." This executive
also mentioned that certain subgroups within the unit she managed would

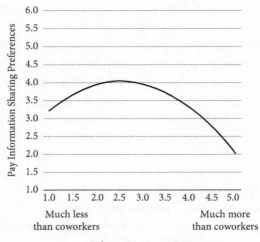

Figure 6.2 Relationship between perceptions of pay relative to others and pay information sharing preferences.
Source: Smit and Montag-Smit (2019).

frequently talk about and compare their pay, whether by showing their paystubs to one another or through informal conversation.

Such disclosures need not necessarily be direct. For example, employee A may disclose the salary of employee B to employee C on the basis of "water-cooler talk" or gossip (Brady et al., 2017). Smit and Montag-Smit's (2019) findings from a study of self-reported disclosures among members of an MTurk sample of working adults, and a separate sample composed largely of individuals employed by a public university, shed light on both indirect (e.g., gossip-based) and direct pay information solicitation and sharing.

Participants in both samples were asked to respond to four items capturing pay information exchange behaviors: two items covering the solicitation of pay information from co-workers ("At work, I have asked co-workers about their (a) salary information, (b) pay raise information," answered on a 7-point agreement scale) and two items capturing the sharing of their own pay information with other employees ("At work, I have disclosed my (a) salary information, (b) pay raise information to . . .," answered on a 5-point scale, where 0 = no one and 4 = everyone). These results were then compared with information exchange preferences collected as part of separate research 1 or 2 years earlier. Even when taking into account such possible confounds as income, age, pay fairness or distributive justice perceptions, and pay level satisfaction, Smit and Montag-Smit (2019) found that pay information exchange preferences collected at an earlier point in time were significant predictors of behaviors reported 1 and even 2 years later. In terms of gossip, results from the MTurk sample indicated that information-seeking preferences were positively but weakly associated with co-worker gossip, with the association explaining 7–9 percent of the variance in such self-reported gossip-based disclosure behavior. With respect to sharing behavior, in both samples, approximately 16 percent of the variance in this outcome was explained on the basis of the earlier measures of sharing preferences. However, seeking preferences were less strongly predictive of subsequent direct efforts to solicit others' pay information, with no significant effect found in the sample of university employees (perhaps because the university already made pay information quite accessible to employees) and only a weak positive effect in the MTurk sample, explaining just 9 percent of the variance in direct pay information seeking.

Smit and Montag-Smit's (2019) findings are no less interesting in terms of what they *fail* to show. Specifically, the relatively small effect sizes for information-seeking preferences suggest that other factors aside from individual differences, such as organizational policies and practices, may play a more robust direct or indirect role in determining whether employees actually seek pay information from co-workers. This makes intuitive sense, in that people who are motivated to ask others about their pay have less reason to do so (in formal terms, such behavior has less perceived utility) if the organization is transparent about pay-related matters, meaning the desired information is already accessible. With respect to information-sharing preferences, although these explain a more significant proportion of the variance in actual pay sharing behavior, here too organizational practices or other factors may account for the lion's share of the variance. For example, regardless of individual preferences, pay sharing may rise or fall depending on whether doing so is explicitly protected by law or on whether the surrounding culture is more individualistic or more collectivist (such that social comparison is not only more acceptable but also may even be implicitly encouraged; Buunk & Gibbons, 2007; Bamberger & Belogolovsky, 2017). We explore some of these factors next as we turn to research on internet-mediated forms of pay information exchange.

Internet-Mediated Pay Information Disclosure

As noted earlier, the seeking and sharing of pay information via internet-mediated pay information exchange services such as Glassdoor and Payscale is becoming increasingly widespread (Figure 6.3). This type of pay information exchange is in many ways similar to person-to-person exchange. First, in both cases, pay disclosures are rarely unsolicited. Rather, as in the case of direct pay information disclosure, internet-mediated pay disclosure is also driven by the principles of information exchange (Smit & Montag-Smit, 2019), with employees typically being asked to disclose their pay information as a condition for gaining access to the pay information provided by others. For example, Glassdoor states that to gain full access to its database, "We ask that you provide your salary information. . . . Everything you add helps others find a job and company they'll love" (Glassdoor, 2020). Second, although internet-mediated pay disclosures are significantly more discrete than person-to-person exchanges, and the exchange sites assure users that their identity will

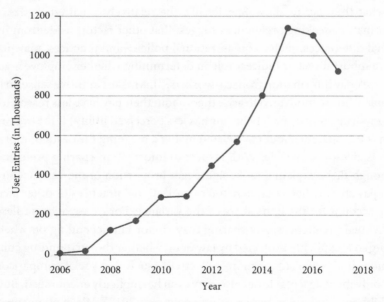

Figure 6.3 User entries in Glassdoor. Number of new user entries in website between 2006 and 2017. Entries are reported in thousands.

Reprinted with permission from Karabarbounis and Pinto (2018).

remain strictly confidential, users must nonetheless accept a disclaimer that disclosures in violation of organizational policies may expose them to dismissal and legal action and are at the user's own risk. Finally, both forms of disclosure offer reasonable levels of information quality. In peer-to-peer disclosures, which are by definition non-anonymous, accountability and reputational concerns ensure that the information exchanged is of high quality (i.e., largely accurate). In the case of internet-mediated pay information exchange services, the sheer amount of information received on any particular position strengthens the quality of the information available. Information service providers also have an interest in vetting the information submitted so as to ensure the reputation of their service (Rosenfeld, 2017; Karabarbounis & Pinto, 2018).

In theory, information gleaned through internet-mediated pay information exchange services should reduce employee–employer information asymmetry. This, in turn, could motivate employees to voice concerns about pay discrepancies (i.e., ask for a raise) and enable them to secure better employment terms by enhancing their bargaining power. No study that I am aware of has examined whether and how employees make use of the data gleaned from exchange services in this way. However, there is a good deal of anecdotal evidence suggesting that they can and do (much of it, not surprisingly, appearing on the websites of the exchange services themselves). In my own work, I, too, have encountered individuals who reported leveraging such internet-sourced data in their own personal wage negotiations. For instance, a customer service manager recounted that she turned to Glassdoor when her gut was telling her that others in similar positions in both her company and competing firms were earning more than her. She explained that she first approached some fellow managers in her company, but all those to whom she turned refused to offer even a broad indication of their pay or stock options. She said, "That's when I checked on Glassdoor and saw from there that they were indeed getting paid more than me." Despite concerns over the precision of what was revealed to her online, she was emboldened by the data and ultimately brought her concerns—along with the Glassdoor data—to her supervisor.

Missing from this manager's account was reference to the fact that in order to secure information on her colleague's pay, she first had to enter her own pay information into the system. To what degree are individuals willing to do so when, as seen in the findings of Smit and Montag-Smit (2019) discussed earlier, general attitudes regarding pay disclosures are, at best, mixed? What factors explain employees' actual disclosures of pay information to such internet-mediated services?

Building on uncertainty management theory (UMT; see Chapter 2), Brown et al. (2021) suggested that internet-mediated employee pay disclosure is governed by three basic principles (Figure 6.4). First, they proposed that the perceived utility of information offered for exchange by an internet-mediated pay information service induces a willingness to disclose one's own pay, but this perceived utility is heavily influenced by the amount and quality of "taster" information supplied by the service provider when offering the exchange. Second, they proposed that perceived utility mainly affects willingness to disclose among individuals for whom fairness uncertainty is *less* salient, on the grounds that those who are more perturbed by the possible unfairness of their compensation will readily do what is needed to obtain information without engaging in a deliberate, detailed utility calculation. Third, they proposed that even when the individual works in an enterprise that prohibits pay disclosure, a high willingness to share pay information will be predictive of actual sharing later on. However, this effect of willingness to share on actual sharing is predicted to be weaker under two conditions, namely when the individual is employed in a context in which pay communication is subject to employer restrictions and when the individual is encouraged to more carefully consider the possible implications of disclosure before actually sharing any information.

With respect to the first principle, Brown et al. (2021) conjectured that despite being motivated to reduce uncertainty in general, and fairness uncertainty in particular, individuals are likely to be cautious when engaging in pay-related information exchange. This is because use of an internet-mediated pay information service carries its own potential costs and risks. For example, individuals may fear that if they are identified (e.g., through a data breach) as having shared pay information on the site, they may expose themselves to embarrassment, become the target of others' envy or ill-will, or even be sanctioned by the employer for breaking implicit norms or explicit rules of pay communication secrecy (Exline et al., 2004; Colella et al., 2007; Smit & Montag-Smit, 2019). Consistent with the principle of utility maximization, UMT suggests that individuals will only be willing to disclose their pay to an exchange service if they perceive the expected benefits of doing so as outweighing the potential interpersonal or normative costs. However, these utility calculations must also take into account questions about the value of the information to be received in exchange. Given that users must

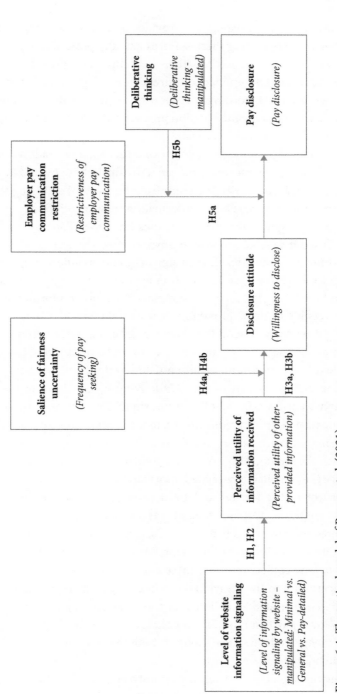

Figure 6.4 Theoretical model of Brown et al. (2021).
Source: Brown et al. (2021).

input their own data before seeing data provided by others, they may well ask, first, whether those operating these services actually possess the data they promise to provide and, second, whether the information provided will be sufficiently relevant or fine-grained to address the user's personal pay-related fairness uncertainties. Accordingly, risks with respect to the accessibility, quality, and relevance of the information promised are likely to influence the individual's overall utility calculations.

Internet-mediated pay information services often attempt to address these risks when soliciting pay information from individuals, both by (a) stressing their emphasis on data security and confidentiality and (b) signaling to potential contributors the value of the information they are offering as part of the exchange, highlighting the quality and breadth of their database and how others have used it to secure a raise or advance their career (Chamberlain, 2015). In its most minimal form, such signaling may manifest simply as an exhortation to share one's pay information for the common good; or it can be more explicit, taking the form of a sample of the kind of information that becomes accessible to those providing their own pay details. That sample, in turn, might be fairly general (e.g., mean rates of job satisfaction or voluntary turnover in a given organization) or more tailored to the profile of the individual (e.g., minimum, maximum, and average pay for their occupation and level of work experience). Underlying such actions on the part of third-party websites is the implicit proposition that a priori provision of employment-related information will enhance the utility perceptions of potential information contributors, and these utility perceptions are likely to be greatest when the provided information is similar to that requested as part of the exchange (i.e., detailed pay-related information).

With respect to the second and third principles, Brown et al. (2021) argued that employee attitudes toward internet-mediated pay disclosures serve as a precursor to actual behavioral disclosure, with willingness to disclose motivated by an interest in reducing fairness uncertainty. However, as noted above, they conjectured that these effects depend on the salience of fairness uncertainty to the individual (an individual difference factor) and two transparency-related situational factors, namely (a) the restrictiveness of employer pay communication policies and (b) the degree to which employees engage in deliberative thought about the possible implications of disclosure in light of these policies.

Regarding the salience of fairness uncertainty, extensive research indicates that some individuals are more fairness-sensitive than others (Huseman et al., 1987). Likewise, as noted by van den Bos and Lind (2002, p. 47), trait-based individual differences, such as the value people attach to comparative information (Gibbons & Buunk, 1999), make some people more sensitive to fairness uncertainty than others. For those individuals, a sense of not being sure that they are being treated fairly, and not being taken advantage of or exploited, leads to anxiety and other psychologically aversive emotional states. Logically, then, those for whom fairness uncertainty is more salient will likely be predisposed to favor actions aimed at resolving this unpleasant situation regardless of any specific utility considerations, whereas those less sensitive to fairness uncertainty may only be motivated to disclose their pay if they attribute high utility to the information they expect to receive in return.

Finally, in terms of situational factors potentially conditioning the impact of *willingness* to disclose on *actual* disclosure, Brown et al. (2021) highlighted two possible moderators: the restrictiveness of employer pay communication policies and the degree to which employees engage in deliberative thinking about these policies. Drawing from UMT, Brown et al. posited that in the absence of deliberative thinking about the potential implications of pay information sharing, the effect of pay communication context is likely to be automatic, driven by heuristic processes. Specifically, they conjectured that lacking information about the fairness of effort–reward outcomes, individuals will substitute information regarding the fairness of reward practices (van den Bos & Lind, 2002). Given that a restrictive pay communication policy is likely to serve as a source of negative inferences regarding the fairness of reward outcomes, employees may quite automatically assume that they are being unfairly rewarded. This is because, as noted by Belogolovsky and Bamberger (2014), "individuals uncertain about their social standing in groups and organizations tend to pay more attention to information supportive of a stance of distrust than of trust, thus leading them to be suspicious regarding others' motives and intentions"—or what Kramer (1998, 2001) refers to as "sinister attributions." Indeed, Montag-Smit and Smit (2021) showed that employer restrictions on pay communication are positively associated with employee perceptions that management is seeking to exploit them.

Given all this, and building on the fair process effect element of UMT—the tendency of individuals to adopt more resistant behavior in reaction to negative fairness judgments (Folger et al., 1979)—Brown et al. (2021) argue that restrictive pay communication policies may prompt precisely the behavior that these policies seek to prevent. Specifically, a feeling that one is being treated unfairly may give rise to a sense of psychological license (D. T. Miller & Efron, 2010) justifying acts of implicit protest (Vermunt et al., 1996). As noted by van den Bos (2005),

> People who experience unfair treatment are more likely to leave their jobs (Alexander & Ruderman, 1987), are less likely to cooperate (Lind, 2001), show lower levels of morale and higher levels of work stress and overt and covert disobedience (Huo et al., 1996), are more likely to initiate lawsuits (Lind et al., 2000), and may even start behaving in antisocial ways. (p. 276)

Accordingly, to the degree that more restrictive pay communication policies make employees suspicious about the fairness of their pay, the fair process effect may weaken compliance with such restrictions (Lind et al., 1993).

On the other hand, where employees engage in deliberative thought about the benefits and costs of exchanging their personal pay information, the result may be an attenuation of the otherwise positive association between willingness to disclose one's pay and the probability of actual disclosure. This is because deliberative thinking challenges people's natural tendency to favor viscerally attractive (hedonic) options (Derfler-Rozin et al., 2016)—in this case, reducing fairness uncertainty and/or reasserting control by exchanging pay information. Indeed, manipulations aimed at making people exert mental effort to contrast viscerally attractive options with others that are less immediately enticing have been associated with less deception (Shalvi et al., 2012), more ethical behavior (Gunia et al., 2012), and reduced organizational rule-breaking (Derfler-Rozin et al., 2016).

Brown et al. (2021) tested these principles, and the model they suggest (shown in Figure 6.4) in an experimental field study using a representative sample of 642 Australian workers. The researchers designed a realistic third-party pay information website expressly for the study. All participants were informed that they were to contribute to the development of a new national pay website, with potential benefits for all users. All participants also completed a survey soliciting information about their pay, job satisfaction, frequency of pay information seeking, perceived utility of information provided by others, willingness to disclose pay information, perceptions of employer pay communication policies, and other measures. Participants were randomly assigned to one of three information provision conditions and either a neutral or a deliberative thought condition.

The study first manipulated information provision by the website. In the first (control) condition, participants were given only the general description of the website but no employment-related information. In the second condition ("general information"), participants were also provided with mean and comparative rates of employee job satisfaction for those in their occupation. In the third condition ("detailed pay information"), participants were given occupation-specific pay information, including the actual minimum, maximum, and average pay for employees in their occupation and with their level of experience. In both the second and third conditions, participants were told that the data were "collected from employees like yourself."

For the second manipulation, participants were randomly assigned to either a deliberative thinking or a neutral condition. All participants were asked to report their willingness to disclose their pay to others. To prompt deliberative thinking, those in the intervention condition were then asked to complete an instrument designed to make them think about the possible costs (5 items) and benefits (5 items) of pay disclosure (e.g., "Disclosure could make me feel embarrassed"; "Disclosure could help me improve my own pay level"). After completing this, they were asked to disclose their own pay. For those assigned to the neutral condition, the "willingness to disclose" item was immediately followed by the next section of the survey, in which they were asked to disclose their pay.

Analyzing the results, Brown et al. (2021) found broad support for the proposed model. First, they found that the perceived utility of using the website was marginally higher under the general information condition compared to the control, and it was significantly higher under the detailed pay information condition compared to the control (t value = 2.67, p = 0.008). In addition, the greater the perceived utility of the information provided by the new website, the more willing the participant was to disclose their own pay information (t value = 3.34, $p < 0.01$). Moreover, perceived utility was found to mediate the link between the nature of the information provided (minimal or general information versus pay-related information) and willingness to disclose.

With respect to fairness uncertainty, Brown et al. (2021) argued that the salience of this construct is best assessed on the basis of a behavioral proxy. They therefore used the frequency with which individuals solicit pay information from others for this purpose. Accordingly, they posited that the association between the perceived utility of the information provided by an internet-mediated pay information service and willingness to disclose one's own pay information to it is moderated by the frequency of pay information seeking, such that this relationship is amplified under conditions of less frequent information seeking (i.e., lower fairness uncertainty) and attenuated under conditions of more frequent information seeking (higher fairness uncertainty). As proposed, they found a significant interaction (t value= −2.45, $p < 0.01$) between the frequency of pay information seeking and the perceived utility of other-provided information in predicting willingness to disclose. The form of the interaction is shown in Figure 6.5. As can be seen in that figure, individuals who report frequently seeking pay information express high willingness to disclose their pay regardless of the perceived utility of the information provided by others (slope coefficient = −0.03, not significant). In contrast, among individuals reporting less information seeking, there was a

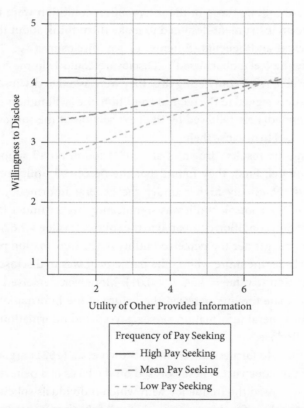

Figure 6.5 Utility of other-provided information on willingness to disclose, moderated by frequency of pay seeking.
Source: Brown et al. (2021).

significant positive relationship between the utility of other-provided information and willingness to disclose (slope coefficient = 0.22, $p < 0.01$).

Finally, after demonstrating a robust main effect between willingness to disclose pay information and actual pay disclosures, the researchers tested the sensitivity of this association to both employer pay communication policy and deliberative thinking about the possible repercussions of disclosure. As shown in Figure 6.6, the findings indicate a three-way interaction effect between disclosure willingness, employer pay communication restrictiveness, and deliberative thinking. In the neutral condition (Figure 6.6A), the relationship between willingness to disclose and actual disclosure is unaffected by the level of employer pay communication restrictiveness. Specifically, among participants *not* primed to engage in deliberative thinking about the possible consequences of pay disclosure, there was no significant interaction between willingness to disclose and participant perceptions of the restrictiveness of employer pay communication policy; regardless of the restrictiveness level, higher willingness was associated with higher actual disclosure. In contrast, under the deliberative thinking condition (Figure 6.6B), the relationship between willingness to disclose and actual disclosure is, as hypothesized, weaker (stronger) when participants perceive employer pay communication policy as more (less) restrictive. In other words, when participants were primed to think about the possible positive and negative repercussions of disclosure under conditions of employer pay communication restrictiveness, the positive association between disclosure willingness and actual disclosure was weaker.

Overall, the study by Brown et al. (2021) offers a number of important insights with regard to the growing prominence of internet-mediated pay information services. First, it suggests that employee disclosures to these services are largely motivated by an interest in reducing the individual's own fairness uncertainty. In particular, employees who are more sensitive to such uncertainty are natural consumers for pay information services that can offer—or at least claim to offer—accurate and specific pay data, even if this means that users have to disclose their own pay information. Second, employers with more restrictive pay communication policies should not expect automatic compliance with those policies, especially among employees who are particularly troubled by fairness concerns and who are comfortable with their pay information being in the open. Indeed, Brown et al.'s findings suggest that such policies have no significant impact with respect to either dissuading or encouraging pay disclosures. It is only when employees

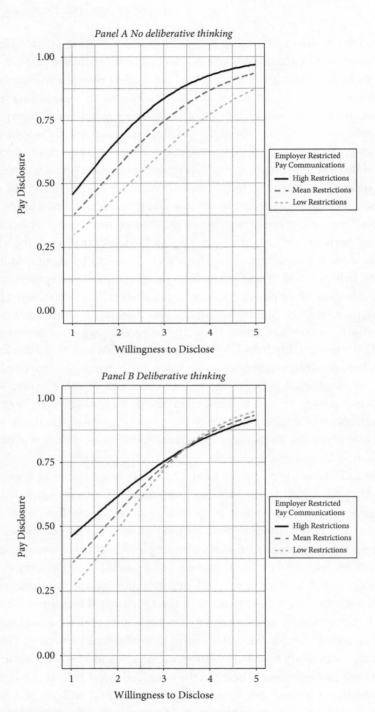

Figure 6.6 Willingness to disclose: three-way interaction.

Source: Brown et al. (2021).

consciously consider the possible ramifications of their actions that restrictive pay communication policies have their intended effect. Essentially,
employers' best means of making restrictive pay communication policies
work is to encourage employees to think hard about the consequences of
ignoring them. However, with employers' enforcement of such restrictive
policies increasingly limited by transparency regulations, their options for
encouraging employee compliance are likewise shrinking—thus raising
questions about the overall utility of such policies as a disclosure deterrent
in the first place.

Conclusion

Employee pay disclosure represents an important form of pay communication and one that, due to the internet, is likely to only grow in signif-
icance. Fairness uncertainty, or more precisely a desire to mitigate the
tensions and anxiety associated with it, likely serves as the primary motivation for employees to share their personal pay information, with employees
recognizing that one has to give to receive (figuratively, through reciprocity,
in the case of person-to-person exchanges, or literally in the case of internet-
mediated services). However, empirical evidence suggests that preferences
for privacy are about as prevalent as preferences for sharing, making spontaneous employee pay disclosures relatively rare even in the absence of employer restrictions on employee pay communication. For many, the perceived
psychological costs of disclosure appear to outweigh the psychological and
instrumental benefits of soliciting and sharing such information.

Where does this leave employers? First, the evidence suggests that
restrictions on employee pay communication are likely to be of limited value.
In the absence of constant enforcement (designed to, at minimum, make
employees carefully consider the consequences of flouting the rules), these
policies appear to have no significant effect, and enforcement is likely to be
problematic in and of itself, particularly in jurisdictions where such policies
have been made illegal or where the courts have found them to be inconsistent with laws governing labor relations or equal rights.

Second, because fairness uncertainty serves as a primary motivator for
employees to share pay information, employers may be able to mitigate
both face-to-face and internet-mediated employee information exchange
by offering employees more information to begin with. This might involve

increasing transparency around the processes underlying pay practices and decisions. For instance, as noted by Cornell University's Linda Barrington (as cited in Henneman, 2015), "Companies could be transparent about how a particular performance score translates into a particular merit increase." Rutgers University's Ingrid Fulmer (as cited in O'Connell, 2020) agrees, suggesting that employers consider

> giving people information about how their pay is determined, how they can earn a raise, and how their bonus is computed, among other compensation-related information. This is the least controversial strategy, because . . . it takes away some of the mystery surrounding how their pay is determined.

Employers can also directly address employee fairness uncertainty concerns through efforts aimed at boosting pay outcome transparency. For example, they might give employees access to explicit information on aggregate pay allocations (e.g., level-specific ranges and median rates of pay within ranges). Indeed, some companies now include pay ranges and median pay rates as part of their job descriptions for positions listed on online sites (Maurer, 2018). Research suggests that providing detailed benefits information also facilitates recruitment. For instance, a 2017 study by Appcast, a maker of job advertising software, capturing 50 million job ad clicks by 3.7 million applicants indicated a direct association between the number of benefits (e.g., dental insurance and paid time off) mentioned in the job ad and the application rate. According to Rob Green, the vice president of marketing for Appcast, "Organizations that listed at least four noncash benefits found a 20 percent-plus improvement in the effectiveness of their online recruitment advertising" (as cited in Maurer, 2018).

Finally, enterprises may consider conducting periodic pay equity audits— an internal analysis of the organization's compensation system aimed at identifying pay differences between employees that cannot be explained due to job-related factors—and making the results of such audits available to their employees. Several U.S. states encourage firms to conduct such self-audits by offering safe harbor protections in the event of an equal pay claim. For example, in Massachusetts, a provision in state law ensures that

> an employer . . . who, within the previous three years and prior to the commencement of the action, has both completed a self-evaluation of its pay practices in good faith and can demonstrate that reasonable progress has

been made towards eliminating wage differentials based on gender for comparable work . . . shall have an affirmative defense to liability.

Furthermore, research suggests that to the degree that employees are able or encouraged to participate in and contribute to such audits, such efforts may be particularly useful in boosting perceptions of procedural justice, and thereby reducing fairness uncertainty (Greenberg & Folger, 1983). We discuss some of these practical steps taken by organizations throughout the world in Chapter 7.

7

Tales from the Trenches

Three Companies—Three Approaches
to Pay Transparency

With the internet providing employees with greater access to pay informa-tion than ever before, and governments throughout the world increasingly adopting pro-transparency legislation, employers are under increasing pres-sure to make pay policies and practices more transparent. Yet, given the mixed implications of pay transparency for employers and employees alike, it comes as no surprise that organizations are experimenting with a wide range of pay communication strategies rather than adopting a single pay transparency template. In this chapter, my aim is to take a deep look at three approaches adopted by three different firms: one that maintains full and com-plete pay transparency; a second that offers substantial, but not full, transpar-ency; and a third applying a more guarded approach that although far less secretive than the classic approach of the past, still offers only select and par-tial information. I begin with Cogent, a privately held Australian informa-tion technology (IT) consultancy with approximately 70 employees, which has made a name for itself as following a policy of complete pay transparency since its establishment. I then move on to Whole Foods, an American multi-national supermarket chain recently acquired by Amazon. Although its pay practices are less comprehensively transparent than those of Cogent, it serves as a classic example of how a large organization can leverage pay transpar-ency as a basis of competitive advantage. Finally, the third case focuses on Stratasys, a publicly held (NASDAQ: SSYS) developer and manufacturer of three-dimensional (3D) printers that employs approximately 2,600 people throughout the world. During the past 5 years, Stratasys has taken a number of steps aimed at making certain aspects of its remuneration more trans-parent and increasing employees' understanding of reward mechanisms.

In addition to differing by age, location, and size, these three companies represent a range of industries (IT, retail, and industrial machinery) and employ very different workforces. Each one offers a unique profile of pay

Exposing Pay. Peter Bamberger, Oxford University Press. © Oxford University Press 2023.
DOI: 10.1093/oso/9780197628164.003.0007

communication practices, driven by its own unique history. In each case, I first describe that profile and delineate the factors leading up to the adoption of the pay communication practices currently in place. Then, for each company, I also outline some of the challenges experienced by managers living with those practices, and where relevant, I describe ways in which those responsible for rewards management in these enterprises are thinking about changing their company's current approach.

Cogent: Total Transparency

Cogent was founded in 2007 with a strong focus on transparency as one of its core values. Transparent pay, as the most obvious and actionable element of transparency, was adopted early on as a clear manifestation of this core value in action. At the end of its initial year of operation, when the company still had only a handful of employees, the founders applied the principle of pay transparency by calling all employees together for a conversation about pay and asking, "Who wants a pay raise and why?" Marty Andrews, one of the founders, recalled that at first there was silence. "Then, one person spoke up, saying that they would like a raise as they recently had a kid. We made it clear that this was not a compelling approach." With no one else speaking up, the two co-founders wrote some numbers on the board, and according to Andrews, "everyone immediately agreed." "With just a few people, most of them with pre-existing relationships, there was a lot of trust, making a transparent process easy."

By 2010, with 25 employees, the enterprise had grown beyond the size where it could retain such an informal approach to pay determination. According to Andrews, "By 2010, we had learned that there would be unequal pay among those in the company and that we had to be able to defend that inequality in an objective and measurable way." Accordingly, the company adopted what is best described as a competency-based pay system, with each individual assessed on three factors: skill, responsibilities, and potential impact. Based on these three parameters, Cogent established a 29-level salary table (Tables 7.1 and 7.2), with all employees at a given level earning the same salary. Pay rates at each level are adjusted to stay competitive in the three labor markets from which Cogent draws talent (developers, designers, and product managers), and any pay increase beyond that market adjustment is contingent on an employee's ability to demonstrate a meaningful positive

Table 7.1 Selected Cogent Salary Level Descriptions

Role	Radius	Level	People	Experience	Impact	Skills	Responsibilities
Graduate	Individual Has an impact primarily on themself. Focused on growing their skills.	1				Just starting out with learning basic delivery skills.	Self responsible.
						Unit testing, class design, basic patterns, etc.	Completes expected work. Seeks out clarity when needed on task at hand or further work. Communicates progress. Can be relied on to get the job done.
		2			Contributed to the team's work under supervision.	Has created production-ready output regularly. Still under guidance.	
					Others within the team were aware of what was being worked on by you.	Possibly guidance through pairing, pull requests with close attention, etc.	

Associate	Team contributor			
Contributes to their delivery team.				
4	Parham	Contributed to team decision-making.	Skills forming across languages. Examples are Ruby, Javascript, Objective C, Swift, Java, Scala, Clojure etc.	Works effectively in a lean/agile model, including: managing their own work on stories through card walls source control management in git, including pull requests and reviews continuous build/deployment management for their own work.
			Has shown ability to work comfortably across developer's tools and techniques. Includes editors, testing, git, CI, deployment.	
5	Jason	Worked unsupervised on small, well-defined tasks (the how).	Has implemented components of work (feature areas) with occasional guidance, using key concepts. Supported for more challenging pieces of work.	Liaises with customers in an effective fashion.

(continued)

Table 7.1 Continued

Role	Radius	Level	People	Experience	Impact	Skills	Responsibilities
Consultant	Team influencer Influences their delivery team.	7	Anwesha Matt Rebekka		Influenced team decision-making.	Good working knowledge of software design patterns and their applicability to implementation.	
		8	Adam Brendon Rabea		Has influenced team decision-making on multiple occasions.	Has been on multiple projects and is able to contribute effectively in multiple areas of delivery. Able to pair with designers to implement simple design concepts in real time.	Gets actively involved in design workshops (sketches, pin-up feedback)
		11	Brett David Petar		Contributed effectively to all aspects of the team's product delivery (what the team delivered is better).	Has been involved in one or more projects end to end, and contributed to all aspects.	Leads focused conversations in relevant areas of expertise, including with customers.

| Senior | 15 | Team leader | Is an informal leader within their delivery team. | Improved the team's delivery capability. Stakeholders are aware of the team's objectives, work, and status. | Has been involved in multiple successful deliveries, including being instrumental for key aspects. | Dean Jen John Lonnie Patrik Rebecca | Delivery leader. | Has led whole delivery team—outside domain expertise—from day one. Influences whole team, communicates with all levels of stakeholders, has successfully held full responsibility for delivery of desired key outcomes, and has done this on multiple projects. |

(*continued*)

Table 7.1 Continued

Role	Radius	Level	People	Experience	Impact	Skills	Responsibilities
Lead	Company influencer	18	Ben	Has driven through many projects end to end.	The team has objectives to work towards.	1. Communicates with Influence and Empathy	Leads communicate professionally, within projects and with team members, with a transparent approach that conveys influence, gravitas, and empathy to achieve alignment and clarity.
	Is responsible for lead roles within teams.				Team members understand their personal development options and how they will be supported in achieving those (within their area of expertise).	2. Drives for Results	Leads continually focus on achieving positive, concrete results contributing to Cogent's success and Cogent's people. They provide leadership to the customer and across the delivery team, influencing and shaping customer objectives and have been critical to achieving successful outcomes across many projects.
	Has influence on company activities as well.				Issues are resolved early.	3. Develops Customers and Our Brand	Leads ensure the customer's perspective is the driving force behind decisions within projects. Their interpersonal skills, communication methods, and understanding of the customer's goals help them gain trust and build positive momentum and connections with values-aligned customers. They positively identify and act upon business and brand-building opportunities. They are starting to represent Cogent within the Melbourne digital community.
					The team's work is of a high quality.		
					The team delivers predictably against their objectives.		

19	Dominic Kathryn	Improved team dynamics and morale. Improved productivity of multiple teams. Contributes to the Cogent employer brand.	**4. Makes Balanced Decisions** Leads balance a longer term view with immediate requirements to make the best decisions on projects. They analyze factual information and tests assumptions; taking into consideration opportunities, risks, resources, constraints, and Cogent's values. **5. Gets the Job Done** Leads achieve timely and exceptional outcomes for clients. They take action, organize, communicate, enable, prototype, and try things in a timely manner. They're a master of follow-through and don't drop the ball. They contribute to areas of the business outside of their primary delivery discipline (i.e., people management, recruitment, finance).
20	Andrew Cameron Craig Erin	Ownership of objectives. Effective balance of short- vs. long-term team objectives with those of stakeholders.	**6. Develops and Empowers Others** Leads enhance the engagement, capabilities, and performance of team members through effective coaching, primarily through mentoring more junior team members while on projects. They develop and set up others for success within projects. They create ownership and accountability within projects. They understand that deliberate attention to learning, both inside and outside of projects, will improve Cogent's capability overall.

(*continued*)

Table 7.1 Continued

Role	Radius	Level	People	Experience	Impact	Skills	Responsibilities
					Stakeholders understand and agree with the team's decisions.	7. Builds and Leads Teams	Leads develop and motivate their agile teams to attain successful shared objectives on projects. They set clear goals for themselves and others, assigning responsibility, measuring performance, and seeking and delivering feedback to achieve quality, timely results. They actively work to improve team dynamics and the team's morale, by explicitly undertaking activities that improve them (i.e., organizing team get-togethers, team building activities, etc.). They understand that diverse teams are more effective, and strive for inclusivity of varying backgrounds and skills in their team.
					Smooth operation of decision group processes.		
					Facilitates and drives team decision-making.		
					Influences and shapes pillar objectives.		
					Team risks and issues identified and quantified.		
		21	Adam Murray			8. Manages Conflict and Negotiation Calmly	
			Kath Cashion				Leads handle situations that are antagonistic at project level. They use appropriate interpersonal techniques to reduce tension or emotion and achieve a practical and satisfactory outcome. They consider the personal well-being of everyone involved.
			Navin Keswani				

Table 7.2 Cogent Salary Table[a]

Level	Development Amount (+ Allowances + Super)	Development Contractor Day Rate (inc. Super)	Design Amount (+ Allowances + Super)	Design Contractor Day Rate (inc. Super)	Product Amount (+ Allowances + Super)	Product Contractor Day Rate (inc. Super)
−1	$54,911		$53,834		$56,000	
0	$59,213		$58,052		$60,388	
1	$63,516		$62,271		$64,777	
2	$67,820		$66,490		$69,165	
3	$72,194	$420	$70,779	$420	$73,627	$437
4	$76,502	$453	$75,002	$453	$78,020	$471
5	$81,346	$492	$79,751	$492	$82,959	$512
6	$87,222	$537	$85,511	$537	$88,952	$559
7	$92,122	$576	$90,316	$576	$93,951	$600
8	$97,024	$616	$95,122	$616	$98,949	$641
9	$102,478	$660	$100,468	$660	$104,511	$688
10	$107,932	$705	$105,816	$705	$110,074	$733
11	$113,386	$750	$111,163	$750	$115,635	$780
12	$118,840	$794	$116,510	$794	$122,035	$832
13	$123,741	$834	$121,315	$834	$127,069	$873
14	$128,642	$873	$126,120	$873	$132,101	$915
15	$133,544	$913	$130,925	$913	$137,134	$956
16	$138,444	$952	$135,730	$952	$142,167	$998
17	$142,804	$986	$140,004	$986	$146,643	$1,032
18	$147,163	$1,020	$144,278	$1,020	$150,082	$1,061
19	$151,521	$1,054	$148,550	$1,054	$154,528	$1,096
20	$156,418	$1,088	$153,351	$1,088	$159,521	$1,132
21	$161,319	$1,122	$158,156	$1,122	$164,519	$1,168
22	$166,221	$1,157	$162,961	$1,157	$169,517	$1,203
23	$178,000	$1,191	$178,000	$1,191	$178,000	$1,239
24	$178,000	$1,225	$178,000	$1,225	$178,000	$1,274
25	$181,545	$1,259	$177,985	$1,259	$185,147	$1,310
26	$186,757	$1,294	$183,095	$1,294	$190,462	$1,345
27	$191,968		$188,204		$195,777	
28	$197,180		$193,314		$201,093	

[a]All salaries are in Australian dollars (AUD).

shift across those three criteria. In addition, beyond the salary specified in the salary table, all employees (including executives) receive a grant for work-related expenses (approximately Australian dollars [AUD] 5,000), as well as a profit-based bonus. The size of this bonus pool is equivalent to half of the firm's profits (the other half goes to shareholders). This pool is divided using three mechanisms. First, senior management is allocated up to 7 percent of the pool. Another 10 percent of the pool is allocated to a discretionary bonus fund, with the proceeds awarded to employees nominated by their peers as having made contributions that do not easily fit the criteria defined in the salary table, such as helping a colleague. The remaining funds are split evenly among all of Cogent's employees regardless of base pay. According to Mark Wells, Cogent's CEO, that typically means an annual bonus of between AUD 10,000 and 15,000.

Salary levels are assigned as part of the hiring process, with the hiring team assessing the candidate and then discussing with the candidate the salary table and the individual's place on it (see Table 7.1). Depending on their education and experience, newly hired developers are typically slotted anywhere up to level 26. Newly hired designers typically fall in at around level 10 and upwards on the salary table, whereas project managers usually start at levels 12–14 and upwards. For existing employees, salaries are adjusted annually, in a month-long process that starts with a 2-week window for confidential, online peer feedback. (Simultaneously, upper managers assess the external competitiveness of the salary table and make aggregate changes to ensure that Cogent's levels are, according to one manager, "right above the market.") All employees can input feedback on anyone else and recommend a salary level change for them. Senior managers then review the peer feedback, solicit additional feedback (including, where relevant, from customers), and then adjust individuals' salary level if there is justification for doing so. In an average year, 30–40 percent remain at their current level, 20–30 percent move up one level, and the rest move up more than one level. Feedback is shared with employees, who are given the opportunity to challenge the review and the outcome, but according to Wells, in an average year the firm sees only one or two challenges, with the usual result being a decision to "stick with the determination but to reevaluate again in 6 months." According to Wells, the system is not flawless: "We make mistakes, but because we're transparent, after a few months, errors are corrected." Such corrections (some involving a two- or three-level adjustment) are often initiated by peers who believe that a colleague's assigned salary level is inappropriate given their responsibilities, skills, and impact. Interestingly,

Wells noted that "if we find ourselves having slotted an individual too high, we never lower their level. Rather, we wait for them to catch up."

Wells acknowledged that individuals who are shyer and less comfortable talking about pay—whether new hires or current employees who believe they may have been shortchanged in the review process—may suffer relative to those who are better at advocating for themselves. However, he also pointed out that given the nature of the business and the need for staff to advocate for their coding or design, those who are hesitant about arguing their position are less likely to be hired in the first place. Wells also highlighted the firm's salary review system, described above, whereby errors in assigning an employee's pay level are usually recognized by the individual and/or peers and then addressed (with a raise) within a few months.

Cogent employees noted that for newcomers, the idea of full transparency can take some getting used to. Matt, a lead designer at Cogent for nearly 8 years ("by far the longest I've stayed at a job"), noted that Cogent's breaking of the pay disclosure taboo and its overall transparent approach were what got him interested in the company, signaling for him that something at the firm would be different. Still, he noted that "it takes people about 6 months to start to feel comfortable with the whole thing. People with a corporate background take a while to adjust." Dan, a manager in development, added,

> I've had a couple candidates that didn't quite understand how open and trusting we need people to be. If someone is very guarded, we'll see that early on in the interviewing phase. It's only happened once or twice, but candidates tend not to make it through the values interview if they don't understand that it's important to be open and honest.

Notably, given Cogent's full-transparency policy, all employees have full access to the firm's strategy decisions, as well as all salary and corporate financial data. Still, interestingly, Wells noted that although everyone has 24/7 accessibility, "people don't pay much attention to the data. People just trust that we're managing this stuff right."

Transparency as a Draw for (the Right Kind of) Talent

Cogent conducts an employee engagement survey every 6 months using a popular assessment app called Culture Amp, which allows Cogent to benchmark itself against other tech firms. Recent scores placed Cogent within the top 8 percent of tech enterprises in Australia with regard to general employment conditions, and in the top 1 percent with regard to "fair pay." In addition, the company's Glassdoor ratings have consistently been 5 out of 5 on its primary evaluation parameters, namely culture, work–life balance, senior management, compensation and benefits, and career opportunities.

Although there is no evidence that pay transparency reduces talent loss, Cogent's turnover rate is also exceptionally low for the industry. Nevertheless, as Mark Wells noted, Cogent still loses talent on occasion:

> The salary table doesn't solve all problems. Cogent may still lose talent because we don't necessarily match the market when an employee is offered a higher rate by a labor market competitor. For example, female developers are rare in our industry, so we were not surprised when one of our competitors poached one of ours. They simply needed to boost the number of females in that role in their firms and offered her a premium Cogent could not match without breaking our salary table. We had no choice but to see her go.

Scott, a product manager, noted that although there may be cases in which employees leave Cogent to take a position with a better package, it is rare for staff to leave because of pay transparency or factors related to it. Indeed, Scott observed that "if they end up leaving due to envy or some other transparency-related factor, that's okay. Our whole selection process biases away from people that are financially driven." Similarly, Wells noted that individuals who have a problem with pay transparency tend not to work for Cogent in the first place, and if they apply for a position, they will be unlikely to make it past the initial interview stages. "Our system may not appeal to everyone. Some cultures put a premium on privacy and when it comes to those with such values, we may lose out on their talent." Still, he insists that the company's transparent approach ultimately serves its employees well, particularly those who often experience pay disparities due to their gender or ethnic background. According to Wells, transparency largely prevents such disparities. "There can be bias in assessing individuals, but it does not stick for very long. The system won't allow it."

Finally, when it comes to attracting talent, Wells believes that the advantages of transparency far outweigh the disadvantages. In his view, pay transparency serves as an important "differentiator" in the labor market, helping Cogent stand out and thus facilitating recruitment. As he states, "It offers external evidence that we stand by our values; something that helps us attract precisely the kind of people that we're looking for; people that fit well in our culture."

Challenges: Where to from Here?

As noted in earlier chapters, researchers and practitioners have identified a variety of challenges posed by pay transparency. First, the intersection of pay transparency with a focus on *relative* contribution as a basis for salary increases may lead to impression management behaviors or, worse, to envy, which in turn can drive employees to withhold resources or information that might make other workers look better than themselves, or even to sabotage the efforts of their colleagues. Asked if these problems could emerge at Cogent, Mark Wells responded by arguing that behavior is not simply a function of incentives; culture matters as well. As he stated,

> Transparency is a cultural generator. It signals that something is a bit different here, and it attracts people that want to have clear, ethical ways of working. People observe that the way to behave and to get ahead here is to be fair because it's the dominant thesis of being at Cogent. One of the things it generates, counter to what most people believe, is trust, and trust breeds altruism, not competition. Competition tends to emerge only when resources are limited. So we don't say to anyone ever that we only allow x number of people at level 15, and with that level all filled up, we can't slot you in there. We never say that. Some companies say we already have four line managers, you have to wait, but we don't do that. If you demonstrate the necessary attributes, we will find a spot for you. In our business there's no scarcity of supply (of pay resources) because we bill our customers for the higher rate. If someone moves up a level, I charge my customer more for them. And our customers don't care as they know that the more you pay for someone, the higher value you get. The customers prefer to pay more and get higher talent. In fact, I get minimal resistance to senior people and more resistance to junior people. As we play in the IT industry, the velocity of the business is more important than the use of capital.

Matt, the design manager, agreed, adding that transparency tends to discourage envy because it drives others to try to help those who may not have moved up a level, and it is difficult to be envious of those trying to help you. He recalled a recent case in which everyone on a particular team moved up a level except for a particular designer. Due to the firm's transparent practices, this was clear to everyone on the team. As soon as the staff levels were published, the others on the team immediately came to Matt with offers to help their lagging colleague:

> The response I got from the team was, how can I help? What can we do to help them? Can we offer mentoring? Can they shadow me on some stuff, or can I coach them? This all comes from a place of something is not right, so how can we help? I guess some people may not like being the target of such helping . . . it can be a confronting experience for some people. But I haven't had anyone say no to it.

A second potential challenge of pay transparency is the possibility that managers, feeling pressured by employees, might opt toward compressing pay differentials such that few employees fall outside the central pay levels. Wells acknowledged that, in all companies, people always think they are worth more than they are being paid. However, he disagrees with the compression thesis: "I would argue that our transparency generates a counter-pressure on pay compression. Employees contemplating a push for a raise are likely to look at those above them and realize that, "Shoot, I have more to learn.'" Indeed, in our conversations, none of the Cogent managers expressed any such sense of pressure to compress pay. Indeed, they highlighted how the transparent salary table reshapes performance reviews, turning them more into learning-focused coaching. For example, one manager noted that with transparency, his people "know how much they want to move up and turn to me for help in figuring out what they need to do to get there." Another noted that "as a manager, the transparent salary review process allows one to better understand someone's edge. When the subordinate feels like you really understand, it allows you as the manager to create the best environment for them to grow."

A third concern regards the impact of transparency on poaching, particularly whether competitors might use a company's pay information opportunistically to steal top talent. Wells dismissed this concern as well, responding that Cogent's pay is sufficiently competitive to make such poaching extremely rare.

A fourth challenge relates to the diversity-related implications of a transparent approach to pay, particularly the possibility that gender- or race-based differences in how employees advocate for themselves in pay negotiations may lead to some employees losing out, even if they have the attributes required to move to a higher level. In particular, it is often argued that women may be socialized to less intensively advocate for themselves, meaning the approach adopted at Cogent could operate to women's disadvantage (although, as discussed in earlier chapters, there is evidence that pay transparency reduces the gender pay gap). Here, too, Wells had an answer:

> The way we used to run our systems was that you are generally expected to make your own case. We've changed that over the years so that we now seek out and get feedback on everyone and make the case ourselves. There will always be the people that are more aggressive, but now we are trying to help the ones that aren't. In any case, I think transparency works most of this all out. The men in the company are particularly sensitive to judging women and want pay to be equal. But we don't leave it to that. Rather, we actively try to balance it. For instance, our gender balance was very poor, but it's moved to be much better now, with women accounting for 30% of our workforce, which for our industry is really good.

Wells and his managers identified several other challenges, the most important one having to do with the scalability of pay transparency. Three scalability problems stand out. The first concerns the annual review process, which is becoming increasingly demanding and time-consuming as the firm's numbers grow. As one manager stated,

> Having grown as we have, the salary adjustment process consumes the leadership of the company for a couple months. It's an issue we're trying to work through so that we can spread it out in a way that's less impactful on the business.

He noted that the problem is with the discretionary aspects of assessing an employee's level:

> The level-specific criteria are pretty well within the ballpark, but there is still a subjective part to it. While this gives managers some flexibility, it's an increasingly significant weakness in the model as the company grows

in that figuring out and validating that discretionary part now involves around six to eight people.

Tied to this first scalability challenge is a second one having to do with familiarity and trust. As Wells noted,

> Transparency works well where everyone knows everyone else. But as the numbers grow, it's hard to judge people. The whole model might break at that point. We're trying to deal with that. We're assuming that we'll get to 100–120 people and then stop. That's my working assumption right now.

Finally, a third scalability challenge stems from the diversity of careers emerging within Cogent as the company grows. According to one manager, although the salary table is based on a linear, silo-oriented pattern of career and salary growth, as Cogent has developed, the company is witnessing "a divergence from the way that careers have developed in the past." The manager noted that this is a challenge that the firm has yet to master:

> We have some designers with no graphics skills but with great stakeholder skills, but our salary model doesn't allow for that. How do we equalize that and pay these people fairly? The table has yet to offer a solution for these kinds of hybrid career profiles.

Whole Foods: Pay Transparency as an Element of "Conscious Capitalism"

In the 1980s, natural food stores were still considered "fringe," but John Mackey and Renee Lawson Hardy wanted to make healthy, organic food available to the public. Accordingly, in 1980, Mackey and Hardy, owners of the recently established SaferWay health food store, combined forces with Craig Weller and Mark Skiles, owners of Clarksville Grocery store, both in Austin, Texas. Selling meat, beer, and wine in addition to high-quality natural foods, the new supermarket was a hit with the counterculture, hippie market in Austin. But just 8 months after Whole Foods' opening, Austin was hit by its worst flooding in nearly 100 years, putting the store under 8 feet of water. Lacking flood insurance, Whole Foods nearly went out of business. What saved the nascent firm was the help offered by its customers and employees, who volunteered to get the store back up and running. As Mackey notes in his book *Conscious Capitalism* (Mackey & Sisodia, 2014),

> All the major stakeholders—customers, team members, suppliers and investors—pitched in after the flood to make sure Whole Foods Market didn't die and that we were able to reopen. And reopen we did, a mere 28 days after the flood. (p. 6)

According to him, this experience "drew the young company together. It demonstrated to us that all our stakeholders have the potential to form close relationships with us, to care and to commit intensely."

That experience also taught Mackey that it was critical to expand as a way of spreading the risk, and in 1988, he sold 34 percent of the business to venture capitalists at an $8.5 million valuation. Needing more cash for further expansion, Whole Foods raised an additional $28 million in 1992, with a valuation of $100 million. With the cash raised, Whole Foods acquired dozens of other natural food grocery stores throughout the United States. By 2016, it was operating 460 stores in North America and the United Kingdom, employing 87,000 people and racking up $16 billion in annual sales (Clifford, 2017).

Conscious Compensation and the Role of Pay Transparency

Mackey opens his book *Conscious Capitalism* (Mackey & Sisodia, 2014) by recalling the flood story, referring to it as the driving force behind his "awakening" to a realization that "business can be a wonderful vehicle for both personal and organization learning and growth," particularly if one's creative impulses are "channeled toward fulfilling higher purposes and helping the world to a better place," what he refers to as "conscious business." According to Mackey and Sisodia (2014, p. 35), conscious business is driven by four basic tenets: a higher purpose, stakeholder integration, conscious leadership, and a conscious culture. All require a deep commitment to such core values as trust, accountability, and transparency.

Mackey acted on these principles early on in the development of Whole Foods. Within just 6 years of its establishment, Whole Foods established a policy of pay transparency, giving employees the ability to view one another's rates of pay. In a 1996 interview (Fishman, 1996), Mackey commented that he put the policy into place because "I kept hearing from people who thought I was making so much money. Finally, I just said, 'Here's what I'm making; here's what [co-founder] Craig Weller is making—heck, here's what everybody's making.'"

However, the motivation to institute pay transparency may have also been grounded in the overarching principles on which Whole Foods was established. In comments remarkably similar to those of Cogent's Mark Wells, Mackey notes in his book (Mackey & Sisodia, 2014), "No matter what an organization says about its values and purpose, how it compensates is a form of 'walking the talk'" (p. 92). Accordingly, Whole Foods implemented an approach to pay that not only reflected its core values but also put it into real terms. For example, its focus on integrating and empowering employees through team-based work, and building stores that were team-centric, was reinforced by incorporating gain sharing (a form of team-based pay that implicitly encourages some degree of inter-store competition) into its compensation package. Its focus on conscious leadership, and the notion that leaders need to care more about "the purpose and the people of the company than they do about their own power or personal enrichment" (p. 94), led the company to adopt an internal equity policy whereby benefits were equivalent for all employees regardless of position, and total cash compensation (including salaries and bonuses, although not equity awards and similar incentives) was capped for all employees (including executives) at 19 times the average pay of all Whole Foods employees. To put this in perspective, Hallock (2012) reported levels of pay dispersion many times greater than this for companies of equivalent size. Similarly, following the principles of efficiency wage theory (Akerlof & Yellen, 1986), Whole Foods adopted a practice of paying above-market wages. Already in 2016, the average hourly wage at Whole Foods was $20.15, whereas comparable supermarkets were typically paying the federal minimum wage of $7.25 (Alvarez et al., 2017). Such practices paid off in a variety of ways, including an average annual employee turnover rate of just 9 percent, relative to 50 percent or higher at its competitors (Quicklet, 2019).

These practices were put in place not only in order to align with the company's ethical underpinnings but also because Mackey and his team believed that they would be good for business. As Mackey and Sisodia (2014) explain it, "Nothing saps motivation as quickly as the *perception* [italics added] that the compensation system is unfair and rigged" (p. 92). I highlighted the word "perception" in this statement because as much as Whole Foods' approach to compensation was structured around fairness and equity, the company recognized that pay communication practices were key to ensuring that employees would *perceive* them as such. Transparency in both pay and team financial performance was adopted as a means to drive such perceptions and to reinforce the core value of trust.

With respect to pay transparency, the company not only permitted any employee to view the remuneration of any other team member (including executives) but also made it easy for them to access that information. This practice went beyond the somewhat more commonplace disclosure of ranges and salary midpoints by level. According to Fishman (1996), already in the mid-1990s, every Whole Foods store had a book listing the salary and bonus earned the previous year by all employees of the firm (then numbering approximately 6,500), by name.

In addition, Whole Foods shared a substantial amount of the company's performance and financial data with its employees. For example, according to an article in *Fast Company* (Fishman, 1996), Whole Foods' managers were required to post detailed sales reports on a daily and weekly basis. Also, store profitability data were disclosed to all store team members each month. Such open financial disclosure practices were aimed at fostering a stronger sense among team members of how their behaviors and decisions impacted the organization. Interestingly, with 93 percent of stock options going to non-executives (the norm being 75 percent to executives in comparable companies; Mackey & Sisodia, 2014, p. 107), this practice of disclosing information to employees before it was made public resulted in the company's employees being designated "insiders" by the U.S. Securities and Exchange Commission (SEC). (Restricted stock units [RSUs] were available at Whole Foods to employees with at least 3 years of full-time employment, and a large proportion of employees owned such RSUs.)

In their book, Mackey and Sisodia (2014) explain how these two transparency practices reinforced one another in helping Whole Foods grow. First, making pay and financial information transparent boosted a sense of trust and shared fate among the company's employees. Employees were able to see real evidence of where the company was performing well and how this performance was reflected in rewards. As Mackey stated, "If you're trying to create a high-trust organization, an organization where people are all-for-one and one-for-all, you can't have secrets" (as cited in Fishman, 1996, p. 103).

Second, it encouraged conversations among employees and promoted a *positive* sense of competition (Griswold, 2014). Mackey differentiates such positive competition, in which high performers are rewarded for their contributions, from the kind of negative competition implemented in other companies (he uses Jack Welch's practices at General Electric as an example), where competition is framed around avoiding termination. Mackey emphasizes that although performance-based pay is the norm in most companies, encouraging conversations about pay differences is highly unusual. Transparency allows employees to better understand what the pay differences are and why particular pay decisions are made. In the process, he explains, they gain an enhanced understanding of what type of achievements and performance ratings allowed others to earn more money, something which he believes boosts motivation and success.

Finally, as Mackey and Sisodia (2014) note, "Because it is transparent, team members can give feedback on what they find to be unfair, giving the company an opportunity to change and evolve" (p. 92). In an interview with *Fast Company*'s Fishman in 1996, Mackey was asked if the open pay policy motivated employees to challenge him on salaries. He responded,

> I'm challenged on salaries all the time . . . [like] "how come you are paying this regional president this much, and I'm only making this much?" I have to say, "because that person is more valuable. If you accomplish what this person has accomplished, I'll pay you that, too." It leads to deeper conversations than you'd have otherwise. (p. 103)

In this way, transparency encouraged conversations that served as a basis for identifying and addressing inequities (building trust), as well as for reinforcing the company's core values and offering constructive, learning-oriented feedback.

On a day-to-day basis, the (largely anecdotal) evidence is mixed as to how transparency impacts employee behavior at Whole Foods. Similar to the situation at Cogent, Fishman (1996) notes,

> By most accounts, rank-and-file team members don't spend much time consulting the salary book. Once the novelty wears off, and people discover that the cashier in the next aisle (or city) makes roughly what they make, they focus on team goals and job satisfaction. (p. 103)

But Fishman (1996) also notes that this may not be the case at higher levels. He quotes one manager as saying that "store leaders 'tend to be more interested' in the salary book, 'looking at their earnings potential if they go to this store or take that job.'" (p. 103). Moreover, other evidence suggests that Whole Foods employees at all levels hold more passionate attitudes—both positive and negative—regarding the company's policy of pay transparency. Twitter feeds indicate that there is a good deal of employee appreciation for the approach, with comments including "Wish this management practice that Whole Foods has about salary was actually law" and "Sharing salary info is beneficial to productivity and growth." On the other hand, *Business Insider* commentators have posted remarks such as "Totally abhorrent policy," "I'm sorry, but the idea of transparency has gone a little too far," and "I don't think knowing everyone's salaries makes for a rosier culture or happier employees" (Peterson, 2014).

Amazon's Acquisition of Whole Foods

In 2017, facing increasing challenges from Trader Joe's and other retailers, Whole Foods was sold to Amazon for $13.7 billion. Addressing concerns that Whole Foods' operations were not cost-competitive and that its goods were overpriced (indeed, the store was increasingly becoming known as "Whole Paycheck"), Amazon made significant adjustments to the company's culture and operational practices. Although these changes have led to higher store profitability, they have not necessarily been well-received by employees. Indeed, even before the acquisition, experts in the field predicted that the two cultures, so fundamentally different, would quickly clash. Specifically, whereas Whole Foods valued employee engagement, creativity, and collaboration, Amazon is characterized by a strong customer focus and by operational efficiency, frugality, and highly challenging norms of output and productivity (Alvarez et al., 2017). In a 2017 interview with *Fast Company*, Mackey largely concurred with the idea that Amazon's acquisition would bring culture change (Weissman, 2017). He noted,

> One of the things they do better than us, they are more customer-centric than we are. They really are. And one of my takeaways is that, by God, we're gonna become as customer-centric as Amazon. We're gonna import their passion about that. Because I think, sometimes, our company's gone a little bit too much team-member focus at the expense of our customers. And that's one definite evolution that's gonna happen.

Among the operational shifts enacted as part of the acquisition have been changes to Whole Foods' employment and remuneration practices. Although Whole Foods has retained its policy of pay transparency, Amazon reduced store headcounts while capping employee hours, thus creating a situation in which employees fill expanded jobs for lower weekly pay. Furthermore, whereas—as noted earlier—non-executive employees had received a substantial portion of RSUs in the past, some media accounts indicate that under Amazon's control, the retailer has largely stopped giving out those stock options to non-executive staff (PYMNTS, 2018). And whereas prior to the acquisition, Whole Foods prided itself on its high rate of employee retention, according to an article in *Grub Street*, Amazon's policies are now impacting employee turnover, "either causing firings, or making people so fed up that they quit" (Rainey, 2018). Higher rates of employee turnover pose multiple threats to a retailer such as Whole Foods in that the hiring and training of new employees is costly, and employee experience is key to quality customer service.

Mackey, who served as the CEO of Whole Foods until September, 2022, insists that pay transparency still serves as an important means by which the company drives retention and maintains its traditionally low rate of churn. As he noted in a 2020 interview (Clifford, 2020),

> It gives people something to strive for, leading employees to think: "Wow, I had no idea that a coordinator could get paid that much. I want to be a coordinator." Or, "I really want to be a store team leader, because I had no idea that including their RSUs—the restricted stock units they get from Amazon—I mean, they may be making well over $100,000." And if you don't have a college degree, that's something to aspire to.

Stratasys: Partial Transparency

Founded in 1989, Stratasys, Ltd., is a publicly traded (NASDAQ) manufacturer of 3D printers and 3D production systems for office-based rapid prototyping and direct digital manufacturing solutions. Stratasys' development operations are based largely in Israel as a result of its 2012 merger with an Israeli manufacturer of 3D printers, Objet. Its manufacturing operations are based in Israel and Minnesota, where it produces in-office prototyping and direct digital manufacturing systems for automotive, aerospace, industrial, recreational, electronic, medical, and consumer product original equipment manufacturers.

Stratasys' pay communication practices have undergone significant change during the past 5 years, in part due to the arrival of Stacey Katz, the company's Global Vice President of Compensation, Benefits & HR Operations. As she put it, "Because they felt that the employees did not understand their compensation or appreciate what they were receiving, when they hired me, it was made clear to me that a top priority was going to be pay communication." Accordingly, Katz initiated her efforts at pay communication by meeting with employees and managers to hear from them what they understood and failed to understand about pay at Stratasys:

> It was clear that the bonus program was not well communicated. No one understood how it worked. The sales incentive was changing every quarter, quotas were changed, draws were given. Even though it was in favor of the employee, it represented too much change and it resulted in a lack of trust and stability. While it offered a reasonable foundation on which to build, it was also not effective, serving as a recipe for disengagement and not delivering the results intended. Furthermore, a series of mergers and acquisitions resulted in a collection of pay levels that were never really integrated into the company. As a result, there were lots of titles at different levels and the structure was a mess. Benefits were also very poorly understood, both who's getting what and why some leaders get some benefits, but not others.

After embarking on a series of changes to address these concerns, Katz made pay communication a priority, doing a global roadshow, the intent of which was to present the company's compensation philosophy, clarify the different components of pay at Stratasys, and ensure employees had a good sense of how each component worked. Katz also posted the mechanisms underlying the pay system on the company intranet and sent a personal email to each employee (thousands of them) clarifying the factors underlying their personal remuneration package. Since that time, Stratasys' compensation and benefits team annually sends a personalized communication titled "My Compensation Overview" to each employee. This document details the components of the employee's remuneration over the course of the year (e.g., base pay, variable compensation, employee recognition program awards, equity, benefits, and gifts) and how each one works. In addition, each employee receives a summary of their individual objectives, their unit's key performance indicators, and company targets so they can understand how these align and contribute to the company's success.

One thing that changed little was pay communication transparency, or in other words the company's policy regarding employee pay disclosures. Although the company does not restrict employees' ability to discuss pay with one another, management encourages the workforce to keep their individual pay—for example, base salary and equity awards—confidential. Katz explained that employees generally comply with this request:

> Honestly, we have had very few instances with someone disclosing pay to others. And usually, when pay is disclosed, it's misinformed and not accurate. Usually it stems from something being sent by mistake. Then employees ask me questions and I just explain how it all works.

Similarly, Stratasys does not disclose either individual or average rates of base pay. Katz explained that doing so could create "retention risks," particularly in those years when, for competitive reasons, the company may pay below market salaries for particular roles. In such situations, she explained that it is critical to retain flexibility; something that is lost when pay rates are made transparent. As she stated,

> There are certain roles for which I can't really compete. People will leave us for those companies paying more. Furthermore, lots of employees believe that they have to leave in order to get a significant pay increase. Not always can I increase rates across the board to prevent this. So I need to have the flexibility. Obviously, if we start making a lot of exceptions, we'll develop a trust issue. But the minute pay rates are transparent, I lose my flexibility. So I want to keep all the tools in my shed in order to be able to take care of people that I want to keep.

In contrast, during the past several years, the company has made the processes by which pay and bonus decisions are made, as well as the philosophy underlying these rewards, largely transparent. In addition, the company has made its business-level financials transparent to the workforce. As Katz noted,

> We share results at business unit levels (after first meeting SEC requirements as a public company), highlighting what are the unit's objectives and—every

quarter—how we stack up to those goals. Employees don't know everything all the time, but they certainly know what they need to do in order to estimate their bonus. Everyone has a clear understanding of their own compensation, how it works, and its elements.

Nowhere is this now more the case than with respect to employee bonuses and merit pay increases. With regard to bonuses, managers are given a budget from which they can allocate individual bonuses to their employees based on the employee's performance, within specified ranges. According to Katz, the ranges for bonus awards are communicated to everyone. However, these ranges are quite wide, with the aim of leaving managers substantial discretion, and the focus is on making the manager accountable for using this budget in the most effective way. As she stated,

> If you're exceptional, you're here [pointing high]. If you're good, you're here [pointing lower]. Everyone can see that. A manager can't pay a person that is exceptional and [one that is] average the same amount. It may be confidential, but we know employees talk. If one is working hard, and the other isn't, and they discover that they're making the same bonus, the former will have no reason to continue to work as hard, and the latter won't improve. So the managers have discretion but it comes with accountability. Managers can't weasel their way out of it and say this person's base salary is low so I'm going to give them more bonus to make up for it. So there's flexibility, but there is structure as well.

As for communication relating to merit pay increases, the company shares limited information regarding pay ranges only with managers, typically sharing no more than the median rate of pay for a given pay level. Katz explained that were managers able to see the full range of pay, many would end up "taking it to the right" (i.e., awarding increases that would place many of their employees above that specified median). Instead, managers are given guidelines to help them make fair and appropriate pay decisions, taking into account the individual's compa-ratio (i.e., position within the pay range for their level), performance, and salary trends in the market. Relating to the same manager-focused approach as used for bonuses, she stated,

> We don't want the managers to be lazy. We want them to know their people. So if an employee's compa-ratio is low and they're exceptional, you as a

manager will see a guideline for a high merit increase—but the manager has to make the call. I don't like anything prepopulated, but I don't mind giving a recommendation.

Katz noted that Stratasys is in the process of transforming the way it assesses employee performance, moving away from annual ratings following a forced distribution framework (scores ranging from 1 to 5, with managers constrained in the proportion of subordinates that can fall under any particular rating) and toward a more continuous and less formal performance "conversation." When asked how such assessments will translate into bonuses and merit-based increases in base pay, she responded,

> We won't have a behind-the-scenes rating system that the employees don't know about. Rather, we may use some kind of narrative-based scorecard, but it will be shared. We want it to be transparent. Regardless, the bonus budget won't change, so I'm not concerned about pay compression. Managers that compress pay in their units will have a rough time. They won't have the budget to back it up, and they know it. I'm not predicting a lot of "exceptional" performers—it'll likely remain under the 5% that we had with fixed distribution. But we may see a greater number of "excellents," and if that's the case, these will all get relatively small bonus awards. This is something the managers will have to deal with.

Finally, Stratasys conducts an annual pay audit aimed at assessing diversity-based pay discrepancies. Recent findings show that at least from a gender perspective, the company is doing well, and women at Stratasys are paid fairly during compensation processes (bonus distributions and merit increases). As Katz stated, in the 5 years that the company has been running pay audits, "we've seen very few instances where the females' pay was unexplainably lower. When I see that, I dig deeper and try to determine why that is. We're asking the questions." Meanwhile, discussions are underway as to how to release these findings to the wider workforce. Katz believes it is important to release the findings in order to educate Stratasys' managers on how rewards are distributed. On the other hand, she notes significant challenges in going public with the findings:

> First, the audit is still less than comprehensive. There is more that needs to be done. Second, if we go public, we need to be able to show what we're

doing to address any identified problems. Diversity and inclusion is something that we're paying attention to right now, but this should've been a priority earlier.

Conclusion

These "tales from the trenches" offer important insights into the practical experience of different types of enterprises in addressing the challenges posed by pay communication. To a large extent, the observations shared by managers at these three companies reflect the mixed findings from the scholarly research on pay communication. Whereas the experience of pay transparency has been largely positive for some, for others it is seen as presenting a mixed bag of opportunities and threats. Taken together with the equivocal findings presented in earlier chapters, the thoughts and insights shared here suggest that practitioners and policymakers need to exercise caution when considering whether and how to adjust existing pay communication policies and practices.

8

Policy Implications and
Research Challenges

Pay transparency has been a contentious issue for more than a century. On the one hand, proponents argue that greater transparency is both more consistent with the ethical underpinnings of liberal, humanistic societies and likely to benefit employees, employers, and/or society at large. On the other hand, opponents highlight the ethical challenges that transparency may pose to personal privacy rights, as well as its potential social, psychological, and economic risks for (you guessed it) employees, employers, and/or society at large. Advocates for both positions have, at least until recently, held something in common: They had little empirical evidence on which to base their arguments. During the past decade, however, there has been a burst of empirical research, offering us the first bits of evidence to support—or challenge—the conjectures of both sides. Research in economics, psychology, and management suggests that pay transparency does make a difference, impacting individuals and groups, as well as the organizations in which they work and, more broadly, the societies in which they live, and often doing so in rather surprising ways. In this book, I have sought to bring these empirical findings to bear, allowing us to move beyond speculation and offer a more evidence-based answer to the question posed in the Preface: Is pay transparency a good thing or a bad thing?

Unfortunately, as should be obvious from the research results shared in the preceding chapters, the question has no definitive answer. Although there are clear and consistent findings regarding the implications of pay transparency on *specific* outcomes, across the *range* of outcomes and criteria examined, the evidence remains equivocal. That is, whereas the adoption of more transparent pay practices is likely to benefit the interests of a particular set of stakeholders (e.g., workers, employers, women, and minorities) along some set of parameters of particular concern to them, the same practices are likely to have adverse effects with respect to a *different*

Exposing Pay. Peter Bamberger, Oxford University Press. © Oxford University Press 2023.
DOI: 10.1093/oso/9780197628164.003.0008

set of parameters of primary concern to *other* stakeholders. Nevertheless, there may be some transparency-related practices or policy shifts that most stakeholders are likely to welcome, or at least accept. There are also transparency-oriented reforms whose benefits are likely to outweigh particularistic stakeholder costs and thus, from a public policy perspective, to offer meaningful utility.

In the first two sections of this chapter, I review implications for the workplace and for public policy. Specifically, I consider the practical next steps that—based on the empirical results presented in this book—have the highest probability of being accepted by both labor and management. I also present some more controversial policy reforms that—again, based on the empirical results presented in the preceding chapters—policymakers might want to consider more carefully. Following this, I outline implications for future research into pay communication, identifying issues and questions that remain unresolved and highlighting the challenges scholars face when trying to address them. I conclude this chapter (and the book) with a discussion of implications for practice—steps that *practitioners* might want to consider if they are interested in enhancing their employees' pay knowledge.

Implications for the Workplace

Throughout this book, we have worked on the assumption that pay transparency is best examined in terms of three related but distinct pay communication elements: (a) the accessibility of information about organizational pay processes and practices (pay process transparency), (b) employees' ability to disclose their own pay information to others or discuss organizational pay practices with others (pay communication transparency), and (c) organizational disclosure of actual personal or aggregated pay information (pay outcome transparency). The literature and findings reviewed throughout this book suggest that organizations may have more to gain than lose by adopting practices that offer employees greater information about how their pay is determined (i.e., greater pay process transparency) and lifting restrictions on employees' ability to talk about their pay (i.e., greater pay communication transparency). However, the situation is more complex with regard to the implications of pay outcome transparency. Let's review each in turn.

Pay Process Transparency

As will be recalled, the adoption of more transparent pay processes typically means giving employees more extensive information about the how organizational decision-makers determine levels of base pay, benefits, pay raises, and incentive pay. Although this form of transparency has been the focus of only limited empirical investigation, the existing findings suggest that pay process transparency is typically deemed beneficial by both labor and management, with few, if any, unintended negative consequences reported. For example, SimanTov-Nachlieli and Bamberger (2021) found pay process transparency to be positively associated with employee perceptions of both procedural and distributive justice. Meta-analytic evidence indicates that fairness perceptions such as these are strongly associated with job satisfaction, trust, organizational commitment (central to employee retention), organizational citizenship behavior, and job performance (Colquitt, 2001).

Furthermore, because more transparent pay determination processes are subject to public scrutiny, they are likely to incentivize a greater sense of accountability among those charged with formulating these procedures. This, in turn, should motivate decision-makers to more carefully validate their design decisions and to ensure that pay practices are justified, yield the intended outcomes, and are free from any unintended consequences (e.g., the reinforcement of existing gender or racial pay discrepancies). Similarly, transparent pay processes appear to limit managerial opportunism and populism (Wong et al., 2022). Managers may complain that transparency forces them to adhere rigidly to the rules when making pay-related decisions, thereby restricting their autonomy and agility in responding to singular or uncommon situations. However, the upside of such transparency is that it limits the ability of managers to be "cognitive misers" (Tetlock, 1985), forcing them to work harder to ensure pay determination criteria are justifiable and applied consistently, both of which are central to perceptions of fairness.

Not surprisingly, therefore, organizations are becoming increasingly receptive to reducing restrictions on pay process information. For example, in their 2017 study of more than 500 human resources (HR) professionals in Switzerland, Arnold and associates (2018) found that 69 percent of the firms (public, private, and nongovernmental organizations) informed employees about how benefits were determined; 50 percent provided similar information about base pay, pay raises, and team/organization-level variable pay;

and 40 percent provided information on the determination of individual-level variable pay.

Pay Communication Transparency

Pay communication transparency refers to the extent to which employers refrain from imposing restrictions—whether normative or penalty-based—on employees' freedom to discuss pay-related matters. As discussed in Chapter 1, under the National Labor Relations Act (NLRA), it has long been illegal for employers in the United States to impose restrictions on employee pay communications, much less to take retaliatory action against employees who violate such restrictions. Nevertheless, as noted earlier, two-thirds of the private sector employees surveyed as part of the 2010 IWPR/Rockefeller Survey of Economic Security reported that pay-related discussions with co-workers and others were either discouraged or formally prohibited by their employer (Institute for Women's Policy Research, 2014; Rosenfeld, 2017). Furthermore, few organizations that are formally agnostic to employee pay disclosures actually appear to encourage them. Remember Erika Baker, the Google employee who in 2015 sent around a pay spreadsheet to her peers? Many of her colleagues expressed their gratitude by allocating to her a $150 peer bonus. At Google, such bonuses customarily receive more or less automatic supervisory approval. But Baker never saw a penny of the bonus money awarded to her by her peers; every single peer bonus nomination was declined by Baker's supervisor (Le Beau, 2019).

Since then, however, a lot has changed. First, in addition to consistent court rulings defending employees' right to discuss their pay under the NLRA, since 2010 more than a dozen U.S. states have passed supplementary legislation extending the protection afforded to employee pay-related communication and making it explicitly illegal for employers to retaliate against employees engaging in such communication. Second, as discussed in Chapter 6, the internet has greatly facilitated the (largely anonymous) exchange of pay information, with tens of thousands of employees disclosing and sharing their personal pay information with co-workers, potential and actual job candidates, and other employers on a daily basis. Finally, the findings of Brown et al. (2021), discussed in the same chapter, indicate that formal employer restrictions on employee pay communication may have very little efficacy in any event, particularly when employees believe that by sharing their own information they may gain useful information from others. Accordingly, especially in light of the widespread (indeed, nearly universal) social taboo against discussing one's finances with others, one has to wonder what benefit employers may gain from imposing (often illegal) pay communication restrictions on employees, no less enforcing them. Managers may certainly "claim a wide-ranging right to secrecy on the basis of the privacy of the 'private' companies they run" (Caulfield, 2021, p. 3). However, even advocates of pay secrecy acknowledge that the issue is not so much about denying individuals access to information that may help them make better employment decisions ("often a good thing," according to Caulfield) but, rather, the morality of making it "an obligation on the part of firms to disclose pay" (Caulfield, 2021, p. 3). Given that pay communication transparency places no disclosure obligation on the firm, ethically there appears little basis for restricting employee pay information exchange.

Pay Outcome Transparency

Pay outcome transparency, which refers to employer disclosure of actual pay levels, is the most controversial of all three forms of pay transparency. The more detailed and extensive the pay information disclosed, the more complex the issue becomes. On the one hand, as discussed in Chapter 3, making individual pay levels accessible to the public facilitates social comparison and social monitoring. Studies indicate that such individual-level pay outcome transparency may have beneficial implications with respect to employee motivation, task performance, and the retention of superior performers (Bamberger & Belogolovsky, 2010; Belogolovsky & Bamberger, 2014; Cullen & Perez-Truglia, 2018a). Furthermore, as noted in Chapters 5 and 6, the social monitoring afforded by pay outcome disclosure allows women and minorities to more easily track any unjustifiable pay discrepancies. In turn, this is likely to motivate managers to, at the very least, pay greater attention to whether their pay-related decisions are based on validated criteria and whether they generate or reinforce gender- or race-based pay discrepancies.

On the other hand, the social comparison facilitated by the disclosure of individual pay information has been associated with a number of problematic outcomes, such as increased envy and reduced collaborative behavior (Bamberger & Belogolovsky, 2017), as well as increased counterproductive work behavior (SimanTov-Nachlieli & Bamberger, 2021). In addition, employer disclosure of individuals' pay raises significant privacy concerns, particularly because, as noted by Montag-Smit and Smit (2021), many employees—especially those at the higher or lower ends of a pay scale—may prefer not to have their personal pay information shared with others. Finally, as highlighted in Chapter 6, economists have shown that at both organizational and societal levels, disclosure of individual-level rates of pay can have negative implications for various outcomes, including overall rates of job satisfaction and retention intentions (Card et al., 2012), pay dispersion (Mas, 2017; Wong et al., 2022), the sensitivity of pay to individual differences in productivity (Obloj & Zenger, 2022), and—at least for gig employment—even workers' bargaining power and wage levels (Cullen & Pakzad-Hurson, 2019).

Some of these disadvantageous consequences of disclosing individuals' pay levels—particularly those relating to individual privacy concerns, envy, and contextual work behaviors (helping and counterproductive work behavior)—may be avoided or at least diminished by limiting pay outcome transparency to the disclosure of *aggregated* information, in the form of the mean, median, and/or range for salaries and any merit-based increases or bonuses for a given pay grade or level. Such aggregate information might even be broken down further—for example, by gender or race; or data on performance-based pay (e.g., merit increases) could be linked to performance rating and/or relative position in a pay range. In theory, such approaches should be able to reduce the negative ramifications of pay outcome transparency while retaining the beneficial motivational effects noted above. Furthermore, such approaches should retain most of the pay equity benefits associated with the disclosure of individual pay levels, in that they would still facilitate a high degree of social monitoring. Yet questions remain as to the ethical basis of obligating employers to disclose such information when a reasonable case can be made that they are not responsible for broader social conventions underlying gender- or race-based pay discrepancies (Caulfield, 2021) and also when the release of such "proprietary information" or "trade secrets" may adversely affect their ability to compete effectively (Estlund, 2014, p. 792; see also Bierman & Gely, 2004).

As described in Chapter 7, there are some excellent models for how firms may navigate the advantages and disadvantages of pay outcome transparency, with an increasing number of firms either exploring the issue or opting to disclose certain forms of aggregate pay information. Indeed, in its "2020 Compensation Best Practices Report," Payscale (2020b) reported that although only 19 percent of the 5,000 North American enterprises in its survey stated they share *full* pay range data with their employees, more than 35 percent of enterprises share *level-specific* pay range data (the range of pay for a given pay level or grade)—and for firms with more than 5,000 employees, that proportion is closer to 45 percent. Together, these data indicate that more than half the enterprises in that sample share some pay range data with their employees. Moreover, Payscale's findings indicate that a substantial portion of responding firms that have not yet adopted such aggregated forms of pay outcome transparency are considering doing so. Similarly, Arnold et al. (2018) report that 40 and 30 percent of the Swiss enterprises they surveyed disclosed, respectively, aggregate and exact individual-level base pay information to their employees; and 37 and 23 percent, respectively, disclosed aggregate and individual-level information on performance-based pay. Moreover, due to policy shifts in many jurisdictions (i.e., states and countries; e.g., New York City), employers are increasingly obligated by law to implement some aggregate form of pay outcome transparency. For example, as shown in Table 1.2, many medium-sized and large enterprises in the European Union are (or will soon be) required to submit to government authorities periodic audits of gender/ethnic/racial pay gaps by job or pay level, as well as to make such reports accessible to employee representatives and—in certain situations—even to individual employees.

Public Policy Implications

A key objective of any public policy initiative on pay communication should be to enhance competition in the labor market. Labor market competition is generally deemed beneficial for two reasons. First, it ensures that human capital assets are more efficiently deployed where they are likely to be the most productive. Those employing these assets less productively will simply be unable to offer pay at levels offered by those able to employ these assets more productively. Second, heightened labor market competition is likely to drive excess liquidity to workers, as opposed to asset markets. This itself has two advantages: It (a) incentivizes employers to adopt productivity-boosting innovations (e.g., McDonald's self-service kiosks) and (b) raises income levels among people with a higher marginal propensity to consume (i.e., low-income workers), thus increasing aggregate demand and boosting economic activity (Card & Kreuger, 2015).

Policy initiatives aimed at enhancing pay transparency and increasing employees' understanding of relative rates of remuneration should boost labor market competition in several ways. First, pay transparency should make workers more aware of better paying alternatives in the labor market. Second, it should give them enhanced insight into what they might be sacrificing (or gaining) with respect to their earnings by moving to some other employer as opposed to remaining with their current employer. Third, it should give them a greater understanding of the underlying fairness of organizational remuneration practices, as well as of the relative probabilities of increasing their income through advancement within the organization (versus with a different employer). Finally, as noted in Chapter 1, this enhanced pay knowledge has the potential to significantly boost employees' leverage when negotiating with employers over pay-related matters.

These effects, although potentially redistributing a greater share of income to workers, are not necessarily to the disadvantage of employers. As noted above, increased labor market competition typically drives employers to adopt more productive work practices. No less important, in theory, it should force employers to pay greater attention to their pay models and to establish pay systems and structures that maximally leverage their pay resources. Of course, as described in Chapter 4, there is evidence that pay outcome transparency does precisely the opposite, motivating managers to allocate pay in a more "populist" manner by compressing pay dispersion. These dysfunctional consequences can be readily addressed at the level of the firm by (a) requiring managers to show that performance-based pay is *justifiable* and driven by evidence-based differences in individual contributions and (b) linking managers' *own* performance-based pay to how effectively they leverage the pay resources allocated to them. Nevertheless, given that pay outcome transparency—even in its more aggregate forms—can lead to such problems, several lower risk policy initiatives may be more likely to win legislative support. As shown in Table 8.1, these include policy interventions or laws that do the following:

- Protect employee pay-related communication: As noted in Chapter 1, the past decade has seen substantial legislative progress in North America and Europe with regard to protecting workers from employer retaliation for either discussing their wages or refusing employer demands that they waive their right to disclose their pay to others. Despite these advances, even in countries in which contractual provisions prohibiting

Table 8.1 Public Policy Initiatives Addressing Pay Information Asymmetry

Policy Initiative	Status
Protect employee pay-related communication	Regulations in place in the European Union, United States, and other states and territories
Prohibit employers from requiring applicants to disclose pay history	Regulations in place in 28 U.S. states
Mandate pay audits	Various forms of pay audit regulations enacted in the European Union, with enforcement varying by country Federal regulations pending in the United States, with several states enacting regulations requiring periodic audits
Enact safe harbor protection for employers disclosing pay outcomes to their employees	Yet to be adopted

pay disclosures are not legally enforceable, these provisions remain in many firms, reinforcing social conventions by which people keep their pay to themselves. Accordingly, even in countries such as the United States, in which employer retaliation for employee wage disclosures is illegal, policymakers might consider requiring employers to inform job applicants and employees about their pay communication rights. Similar employer information mandates are already in place in the United States with regard to other federal employment laws, such as laws covering equal employment opportunities.

• Prohibit employers from demanding that applicants disclose their pay history: As of 2020, in 28 states and territories in the United States, it was illegal for employers to ask candidates for their pay history (although in most cases, employers may still ask candidates about their pay expectations). The motivation behind such legislation is the recognition that (a) employers clearly have leverage when requesting this information from job applicants; (b) for employers to possess candidates' pay history further exacerbates pay information asymmetries in favor of the employer; and (c) as a result, such information can further entrench or exacerbate gender- or race-based pay discrepancies. Indeed, a recent Payscale survey of visitors to the site found that 43 percent of participants had been asked about their salary history when applying for a job, with only 25 percent of these refusing to answer. Interestingly, refusal to answer was associated with a 1.8 percent lower rate of pay for women, as opposed to a 1.2 percent increase for men (Payscale, 2017). A study by Barach and Horton (2021) found that restricting employers from accessing wage histories boosted initial wage offers for candidates who chose to bargain by 9 percent more than in a control group where employers were permitted to ask about candidates' wage histories.

Despite the apparent positive effects overall of restrictions on employers' ability to inquire about candidates' salary history, Harris (2018) points to a number of drawbacks. First, prior wages can give an indication as to candidates' productivity, which is something employers legitimately have an interest in knowing. Second, such information is often used by employers to tailor a more *attractive* offer. Accordingly, Harris (2018) proposes a policy alternative aimed at maximizing the information available to both parties (employers and job applicants), namely allowing employers to ask candidates for their prior pay history on condition that they furnish the candidate with information on the average or median pay of comparable workers in comparable positions in their enterprise. That is, as Harris notes, laws regarding discussions of a candidate's wage history should make such discussions contingent on reciprocity. In this way, "firms could choose between either forgoing any discussion of prior pay levels (for both the firm and prospective worker) or fully disclosing pay of comparable workers" (p. 13).

- Mandate pay audits: Equal pay and civil rights legislation in the United States and other countries make pay disparities based on ascribed characteristics such as gender or race illegal. However, as recognized by the European Union (see Chapter 1), enforcement of such legislation can be weak and haphazard. Unless employees are aware of these disparities and file suit, employers are unlikely to be held accountable. Moreover, in many cases, employers may themselves be unaware that their pay practices (unintentionally) discriminate against one or more protected groups. In a well-publicized White House event in the summer of 2016, a number of U.S. companies, including Accenture, Cisco, and Salesforce, pledged to conduct internal pay audits aimed at identifying and addressing pay inequities (Merluzzi, 2016). Paralleling this corporate initiative, as noted in Chapter 1, in January 2016 the Obama administration announced that enterprises employing more than 100 workers would be required to submit to the Equal Employment Opportunity Commission an annual report covering aggregated wage and hours data across job categories, pay bands, and demographic characteristics. Such audit and reporting requirements are now in place in a number of European countries (see Table 1.2). Although the Trump administration issued a stay against the implementation of this order in 2017 in the United States (just weeks before it was to go into effect), individual states (e.g., Illinois) are adopting such requirements, and indications are that audit and reporting requirements may be reinstated by the Biden administration.

This type of policy initiative offers a number of significant advantages. First, it provides an incentive for enterprises to proactively identify and address pay inequities. This can put employers in a strong position when recruiting talent in increasingly competitive labor markets and help firms' pursuit of social responsibility goals (Estlund, 2014). Second, it will allow agencies responsible for enforcing equal pay legislation to screen enterprises for possible pay discrimination without requiring them to publicly disclose proprietary pay information. Finally, in the same way that equal employment regulations changed the culture of employee recruitment and selection, forcing employers to validate their selection tools (something of obvious benefit to the employers themselves), mandatory pay audits may also change the culture of pay communication, motivating employers to more carefully examine the efficacy of pay administration policies and practices implemented more on the basis of norms and "tradition" than economic efficiency.

- Provide safe harbor protections for employers who make pay outcomes transparent: As noted earlier, a strong ethical argument can be (and has been) made against public policies that obligate employers to publicly disclose their employees' pay, in that such disclosures put firms in a weaker bargaining position when negotiating pay—all in order to address a societal problem (a gender- or race-based pay gap) that these firms may neither endorse nor have intentionally contributed to (Caulfield, 2021). Mindful of these concerns, Ramachandran (2012) suggests that a "safe harbor" policy would balance such considerations against the fact that regardless of who is at fault, "employers are profiting from the past and [from] societal discrimination" (p. 1061).

Safe harbors are a legal tool that frees individuals or legal bodies from prosecution when alleged to have engaged in rule-breaking conduct, so long as they meet specified requirements. Although various pay transparency safe harbor arrangements have been proposed (e.g., see

Ramachandran, 2012; Harris, 2018), they all have two basic components in common. First, in order to qualify for a safe harbor defense, employers must demonstrate evidence of (a) disclosure of pay outcomes to their employees (e.g., job- or level-specific rates of base and variable pay, or any employer-commissioned salary survey data) and (b) employees' failure to voice concerns over possible pay discrimination within a reasonable amount of time (e.g., 180 days) following such disclosure. Second, they all offer employers an attractive "carrot," namely that by meeting safe harbor requirements, the employer receives a guarantee that any pay discrimination claim made against them will be automatically dismissed.

Policy analysts suggest that such safe harbor provisions offer two important advantages. First, from an ethical standpoint, under these provisions employers need not make pay outcomes transparent unless they deem it in their best interests to do so. As noted by Ramachandran (2012), such provisions incentivize pay transparency "by targeting employers whose own self-assessment indicates higher risk of liability for pay discrimination and lower costs of pay transparency" (p. 1048), thereby transforming pay transparency into a potential source of competitive advantage. Second, by encouraging employers to implement transparent pay practices, these provisions give employees the information they need in order to monitor their employer's pay systems, and thereby shift some of the social responsibility for pay discrimination onto labor. Should they fail to demand (either individually or collectively) resolution of any observed pay discrepancies, workers are left with only one option, namely to seek new employment.

Various stakeholders may take (or advocate) more aggressive steps to promote pay transparency, address pay disparities, or boost employees' pay knowledge. However, research on pay communication is still in its infancy. We still have much to learn about how individuals and groups respond to the removal of restrictions on pay communication and greater access to pay information, in addition to the longer term implications (including unintended negative consequences) of some of the more basic initiatives already implemented. Indeed, although the idea of transparency may appeal to those who subscribe to the norms of progressive neoliberalism (e.g., Harari, 2016, 2018), we have seen in this book—particularly in the empirical findings described in Chapters 3–6—that in many contexts, certain forms of pay transparency can be a double-edged sword. Until we learn more about the mechanisms underlying the potentially adverse consequences of pay transparency, as well as the conditions governing them, it may be best to follow a path of caution, adopting innovative interventions slowly, and with systems in place to carefully and systematically monitor and evaluate their effects. With that in mind, let us turn to the research that might be useful to guide executives, labor leaders, and policymakers in the future.

Implications for Research

In her 2014 law review article, Cynthia Estlund identifies a number of "distinctive questions" raised by pay transparency. The research discussed in this book at least begins to answer some of these questions. For example, among the questions posed by Estlund is whether employers might respond to pay secrecy by compressing the wage scale. As noted in Chapter 4, a small but growing body of research consistently suggests that the answer to that question is "yes." But just how that compression occurs (reducing the wages of those at the top or raising the wages of those at the bottom), whether such compression is a short-term (versus permanent) response to pay transparency, and how organizations may respond to the problems potentially introduced by transparency-driven compression remain largely unanswered. Indeed, beyond the questions posed by Estlund that have yet to be answered are numerous other questions generated by studies offering at least partial answers to her questions. Although it is not possible to present a list of all of the questions associated with pay transparency, I encourage research on a number of issues (listed in Table 8.2) that are either pressing from a public policy perspective or likely to be most impactful from a theoretical perspective.

From a public policy perspective, further research is needed to understand the wage and employment implications of pay transparency. In particular, we need to better understand how policies mandating or encouraging any of the three forms of pay transparency examined in this book—pay process, communication, and outcome transparency—affect wages. Under what conditions might they indeed spur labor market competition, or at least improve employer compliance with mandated employment standards such as minimum wage and overtime payments? In contrast, are there situations or contexts in which pay transparency might facilitate implicit

Table 8.2 Pay Communication Topics Awaiting Further Study

Research Question	Independent Variables	Possible Dependent Variables
What are the wage and employment implications of pay transparency?	Communication transparency Process transparency Outcome transparency	Employer compliance with basic labor standards Labor mobility Wage rates Pay compression Employer investment in productivity-enhancing initiatives
What are the implications of pay transparency on organizational effectiveness?	Communication transparency Process transparency Outcome transparency	Firm performance Return on investment Competitive advantage Human capital resources
What are the implications of pay transparency on employee health and well-being?	Communication transparency Process transparency Outcome transparency	Stress Burnout Depression Metabolic syndrome
What are the implications of pay transparency on cognitive function and information processing?	Communication transparency Process transparency Outcome transparency	Working memory Attention to detail Processing speed Cognitive flexibility
What are the drivers of enterprise-level pay transparency?	Workforce characteristics Leader characteristics Labor market factors Institutional factors	Communication transparency Process transparency Outcome transparency

labor market collusion by employers (i.e., reinforcement of monopsony) or—as suggested by Cullen and Pakzad-Hurson (2019)—restrict workers' bargaining power, both of which might in fact *reduce* labor market competition? Research examining these questions is important in that if pay transparency in fact reduces labor market competition and/or reduces worker bargaining power, the implications on inequality, labor mobility, and the entrenchment of social class divisions could be significant (Bapuji et al., 2020). Furthermore, to the degree that pay transparency results in a compression of pay disparities by raising the wages of those at the lower ends of corporate pay scales, might this motivate employers—particularly in more labor-intensive sectors—to adopt productivity-boosting innovations that reduce their demand for labor?

Studies are also needed to examine the net effects of various forms of pay transparency on the performance of work units or firms. As we have seen in this volume, although there is growing evidence for how various forms of pay transparency affect outcomes theoretically linked to firm performance (e.g., individual task performance, employee turnover, collaborative behavior, and counterproductive work behavior), these findings present a mixed bag, with some suggesting beneficial effects and others largely detrimental effects. Unfortunately, we have yet to see research examining the total, *net* effect. Complicating this question is a lack of research on how pay transparency might affect other outcomes that are also likely to influence firm performance. For example, although a handful of studies suggest that certain forms of pay transparency may boost particular justice perceptions and trust in the organization, what are the conditions governing transparency's impact on organizational climate or culture at the more macro level? And what about the implications of pay transparency for overall enterprise competitiveness? Might more accessible pay information weaken an organization's position by facilitating competitive intelligence gathering on the part of a competitor or by enabling competitors to more easily target and poach key talent? Although, as discussed in Chapters 3 and 4, we have some understanding of how and when varying forms of pay transparency may impact employee turnover, we know little about its impact on the acquisition or retention of key talent or on the composition of a firm's human capital assets more generally. Does pay transparency facilitate the recruitment of high-quality candidates? And once talent is acquired, do certain forms of pay transparency have more of an impact on the firm's ability to retain that talent than other forms? Does that hold true across all organizational levels? Once we have a better picture of the organizational processes and metrics potentially impacted by pay transparency, research is needed on developing what might be considered a grand or unified theory of pay transparency's impact on the firm. Such a model would specify the primary means by which varying forms of pay transparency have the most robust effects on firm performance.

In addition, research is needed to examine how pay transparency at the societal level may impact broader social issues such as those relating to education, taxation, and migration. For example, although scholars have long debated the benefits and costs of merit pay among teachers (Pham et al., 2021), I am unaware of any research exploring the potential moderating effects of pay transparency on merit pay's impact on educational outcomes (e.g., students' standardized test scores). Research suggests that pay for performance, when combined with wider pay dispersion and more open pay communication, facilitates the attraction and retention of higher performers (Shaw & Gupta, 2007). To the degree that this applies in education, might these benefits compensate for some of the known disadvantages of merit pay for teachers? Similarly, researchers might examine the degree to which transparency-related regulatory interventions (e.g., those implemented in Norway), by dis-incentivizing tax evasion, facilitate more equitable and effective taxation. Finally, pay transparency's implications on human capital flight (i.e., brain drain) from developing countries are largely unknown. On the one hand, to the degree that more transparent pay in developed countries might strengthen the motivation of highly educated and/or skilled professionals to leave their home countries, it could adversely impact efforts to boost developing economies and thus exacerbate a global migration crisis. On the other hand, policy initiatives aimed at encouraging pay transparency in developing countries might address the wide pay disparities and economic inequality that can debilitate economic development and motivate emigration (Bapuji et al., 2020).

At the micro or individual level of analysis, little is known regarding how pay transparency or pay information more generally impact the health and well-being of workers. Perez-Truglia (2019) offers important insights into how access to pay information impacts the gap between rich and poor with regard to happiness and life satisfaction. But we also know that variable pay has important (largely adverse) health consequences for employees (Dahl & Pierce, 2020). How might greater access to pay information and the likely uptick in social comparison impact the actual physical or mental health of those at the upper or lower ranges of a pay scale? On the one hand, any increase in social comparison might exacerbate the detrimental implications on workers' mental health identified by Dahl and Pierce (2020). On the other hand, the decrease in unfairness uncertainty might have beneficial implications.

Further understanding of the cognitive implications of pay transparency and pay information is also needed. Much of the research reviewed in this volume is grounded in the proposition that pay information has implications for automatic processing, potentially biasing individuals' perceptions or impacting the relative weights people place on different perceptions. Two interesting areas that deserve attention are (a) how pay information might impact the expression of (i.e., activate) underlying personality traits and (b) how such information may impact human cognitive processing. In terms of the former, Fulmer and Shaw's (2018) compensation activation theory offers a comprehensive and systematic framework for understanding how pay information might impact employee behavior via the activation of otherwise latent behavioral tendencies. However, this theory has not yet been subject to empirical testing. In terms of pay transparency's impact on human cognitive processing, research suggests that affective stimuli have robust effects on individuals' executive function, impacting working memory, processing speed, attention to detail, and cognitive flexibility (Riskin et al., 2020). Based on research examining how pay transparency can provoke envy (Bamberger & Belogolovsky, 2017), we already know that pay information serves as an important, emotion-laden stimulus when that information provides insight into one's remuneration relative to (higher earning) comparison others. Accordingly, it is reasonable to conjecture that these mechanisms may also impact employees' cognitive functioning, including basic processes at the core of task performance. What we do not know is the nature, magnitude, and temporal latency of such effects. How exactly does learning that one is paid less than a comparison peer affect cognitive function, and for how long? What about pay information that generally elicits positive affect—for example, learning that one is paid *more* than a comparison peer?

Finally, we know little about the drivers of pay communication policies and practices at the enterprise level. Macro-level studies such as those by Alterman et al. (2021) and Wong et al. (2022) show that there is significant variation in the extent (and nature) of firms' pay transparency practices. Yet we have little understanding as to the factors underlying firms' differing decisions on pay transparency. Can they be explained by the nature of the workforce employed by these enterprises, the characteristics of their leaders, or various labor market factors? Answering these questions is important in that a deeper understanding of the factors driving pay transparency may enable policymakers to rely more on incentives and less on regulatory mandates to motivate firms' adoption of transparency-related policies and practices.

With all these open questions, why is it that there is still relatively little research on pay transparency? One reason may be that compensation more broadly, as noted by Gupta and Shaw (2014), is "the neglected area of HRM research" (p. 1). But another reason may be that conducting research on pay transparency is difficult! Field experiments, although ideal in their ability to demonstrate causal linkages in real-life situations (Eden, 2017), are typically nonstarters in terms of pay transparency, for the simple reason that managers are rarely interested in having scholars "play" with their pay systems or do anything that brings attention to pay more than is absolutely necessary. Although managers may be less opposed to field surveys in which investigators collect

data on employee perceptions of pay administration, as well as on other, potentially co-varying parameters (e.g., job satisfaction and turnover intentions),
such surveys still raise concerns simply because they bring to the fore issues,
including pay transparency, that managers would in most cases prefer to remain as non-issues. Accordingly, most research on pay communication to
date has involved simulations and natural experiments. Although studies of
these sorts have made significant contributions to our understanding of pay
communication, both are somewhat limited. The problem with the former is
that they often lack the mundane realism that allows for generalizability to the
real world. The problem with the latter is that they are typically limited by the
uniqueness of the situations studied (hence limiting external validity), the archival nature of their data, and the often less-than-ideal measures available.

How might these research challenges be addressed in the future? One option is to collaborate with organizations intending to implement some form
of pay transparency and then work with these organizations to integrate an
experiment into that implementation. Although it may not be possible to
impose a traditional experimental design, a quasi-experimental approach
(with limited randomization and controlled manipulation) may still provide significant insight into causal effects while also minimizing any equity or ethical dilemmas that could be associated with research of this kind
(Grant & Wall, 2009). Studies of this sort by Castilla (2015) and Cullen and
Perez-Truglia (2018a, 2018b) have generated important findings, as noted
in previous chapters of this book. A second option, particularly suitable for
more macro or policy-oriented research, might be to follow the model of
Bennedsen et al. (2019) and use a "difference-in-differences" approach. This
approach leverages the fact that most pay transparency policy interventions
are imposed only on enterprises meeting a certain size threshold. By
comparing enterprises just below that threshold (and therefore exempt from
the regulation) with those above it, and controlling for possible confounds or
covariates, it may be possible to generate reasonably strong causal inferences.
Propensity score analysis might offer an alternative means to similarly compare "treated" with "untreated" organizations (Li, 2013).

Implications for Practitioners

Despite the problems and concerns associated with heightened levels of
transparency in pay communication, the business case for moving toward

greater transparency in pay-related matters may be compelling for many organizations. As noted in Chapter 1 and elsewhere in this book, many national and regional governments have already adopted regulatory frameworks that limit firms' ability to restrict employee pay communication and require employers to make more pay information available to employees. Furthermore, the increased availability of pay information via the internet has raised employee expectations regarding more open pay communication. Indeed, a report by the HR consulting firm Mercer (An & Rahman, 2020) noted that "companies who don't actively engage in a dialogue on pay transparency could risk losing the trust of their employees, candidates and even their customers" (p. 3). Finally, the widespread availability of pay information, combined with institutional demands that organizations conduct periodic pay equity audits, also places greater pressure on firms to communicate pay structures, ranges, practices, and opportunities as a means to improve pay equity.

Despite this, as highlighted by some of the mini-case studies presented in Chapter 7, the transition to more transparent pay communication can be difficult for firms. According to Mercer (An & Rahman, 2020), complicating this transition are typically three main obstacles that should be addressed prior to adopting more transparent pay policies and practices. The first obstacle stems from the fact that in many firms, ranges in practice deviate considerably from espoused and/or ideal ranges (i.e., ranges in theory). Accordingly, prior to communicating pay ranges, employers should ensure that the pay structure has been designed to balance labor market demands (external competitiveness) with the demands of the business model and enterprise-specific fairness norms and also that there are no unjustifiable pay differences based on gender or other demographic factors. To the extent that management believes such a salary structure is in place, validation of this structure via a pay audit may be helpful. Employers should then enforce policies aimed at protecting that structure—for example, by preventing managers from offering excessive packages in an effort to attract or retain human capital resources.

The second obstacle concerns the assumption that the communication of pay information directs employees' attention to issues around pay and so leads them to become suspicious of pay inequities. There are two reasons why this obstacle should be easy to address in most organizations. First, the assumption is largely false. Both theory (e.g., uncertainty management theory) and empirical evidence suggest that avoiding discussions of pay does not make employees less concerned about pay equity. If any-thing, it *raises* suspicions. Second, given contemporary regulatory trends and the increasing availability of accurate pay information on the internet, avoidance is likely to be an increasingly less viable strategy. Accordingly, once management has ensured that the organization's pay structure is in fact balanced and fair, the Mercer report recommends that firms do the following: (a) develop a compelling explanation of the organization's ap-proach to pay, (b) disclose certain forms of aggregate pay information (e.g., salary ranges for specific positions) as a means to strengthen that explana-tion, and (c) train managers to effectively communicate such pay informa-tion to their team's members.

Finally, employers are often concerned that even if pay structures are eq-uitable and logically grounded in the market and the firm's business model, communication of pay-related information may itself drive employee perceptions of unfairness. According to the Mercer report (c p. 5), this con-cern is justified on the basis of a key finding from WorldatWork–Mercer's (2020) pay transparency study, namely that "61% of managers are not trained to effectively communicate pay information to their employees." Of course, the solution does not lie in restricting pay communication but, rather, as the Mercer report states, in "enabling managers to explain pay with empathy and logic" (An & Rahman, 2020, p. 5).

In addition to addressing these obstacles, employers interested in improving the pay-related knowledge of candidates and employees might consider making pay more transparent by adopting the following sequen-tial steps:

1. Treat current employees and internal candidates the same as external candidates with regard to the communication of pay information. WorldatWork–Mercer (2020) data suggest that organizations typically offer substantially more pay information to external candidates than to internal candidates (i.e., current employees). As shown in Figure 8.1, the difference is stark with respect to provision of salary range data before an offer is made, in either the job posting or at the inter-view stage: 41 percent of internal candidates are presented with salary range data by the time of the interview versus 52 percent of external candidates. Furthermore, as shown in Table 8.3, whereas only 2 per-cent of respondents in the WorldatWork sample reported sharing in-formation about long-term incentives with current employees, more

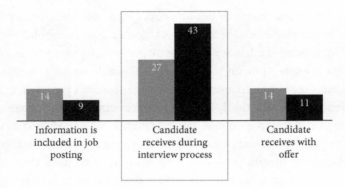

Results shown are percentages. Not all companies provide pay range information to internal or external candidates.

● Internal   ● External

Figure 8.1 Percentage of organizations providing pay range information to internal and external candidates at different stages of the hiring process.
Source: WorldatWork–Mercer (2020). Reprinted with permission from WorldatWork.

than 20 percent reported sharing such information with candidates during the selection process. Such an unbalanced pay communication policy is likely to be risky, particularly to the extent that external candidates are actually hired and may disclose this knowledge to their new workplace peers. Assuming that equitable salary structures have been developed and validated through an equity audit, the benefits of communicating salary range information to current employees as well as external candidates are likely to far outweigh any risks.

2. Ensure that the enterprise has put in place the basic transparency practices that are either currently required by regulatory agencies or likely to be required in the future. This might include ensuring that (a) employees are provided with complete information regarding their own personal remuneration on an annual basis; (b) those involved in the hiring process refrain from inquiring into candidates' salary history; (c) employment agreements do not infringe on employees' right to disclose their pay to others; and (d) periodic pay equity audits are conducted, with their results made available to the organization's workforce.

3. Using Box 8.1 as a guide, start thinking strategically as to how the adoption of additional transparency-related policies and practices

Table 8.3 Percentage of organizations providing specific forms of pay information to existing employees versus job candidates

	Existing employees have access to this information for all roles	Information is included in internal job posting	Candidate receives during interview process	Candidate receives with offer of promotion	Candidate receives during negotiation (if appl.)	Candidate receives with congratulatory letter	Information is not made available prior to promotion date	Not applicable
Hiring pay range	5%	14%	27%	14%	6%	1%	18%	14%
Salary range	11%	13%	19%	5%	5%	1%	28%	18%
Bonus/short-term incentive target	8%	6%	30%	27%	6%	3%	6%	13%
Long-term incentive target	2%	2%	21%	21%	5%	4%	9%	38%

Source: WorldatWork–Mercer (2020). Reprinted with permission from WorldatWork.

may offer the organization a source of competitive advantage in attracting, engaging, and retaining key talent. Although the model of full pay transparency adopted by Cogent (described in Chapter 7; shown at the bottom of Figure 8.1) may go too far for many firms, consider what forms of pay transparency and levels of employee pay knowledge may—particularly when considered alongside other

---

Box 8.1 Increasing Levels of Transparency in Pay Communication

---

Basic: Regulatory Compliance Level/Pay Communication Transparency

- Every employee knows their own salary.
- No restriction of employee rights to disclose pay information to others.

Low: Basic Pay Process Transparency

- Employees can review internal policies that describe how pay is calculated.
- Employees can review the company's understanding of what the market pays and how the company tries to compensate based on that.

Moderate: Partial Aggregate Pay Outcome Transparency

- Applicants can see salaries or salary ranges for open positions.
- Employees know salary ranges or grades for their role.
- Employees know salary ranges or grades for their role and other roles and discuss salary during reviews.

High: Partial Detailed Pay Outcome Transparency

- Employees know anonymized salary numbers for their role.

Extensive: Detailed Pay Outcome Transparency

- Employees know the salaries of all other employees within their discipline (all developers, all designers, etc.).
- All employees can see the salaries of all employees.

core organizational values—reinforce both these core values and the desired employee attitudes and behaviors these values are aimed at driving. With this level of transparency identified, consider what unintended negative consequences could potentially emerge as the organization transitions to such an approach and how such negative consequences might be mitigated. Given the risks of pay transparency noted elsewhere in this book, after taking steps to mitigate any negative consequences, transition toward those ultimate pay communication objectives incrementally, gathering employee feedback at each phase of the rollout.

4. Have metrics in place to assess the potential effects (positive and negative) of more transparent pay policies and practices on employees, teams, and the organization as a whole. As the organization transitions incrementally toward the objective established in Step 3, use these metrics to assess the impact of each newly adopted policy and practice on key outcomes.

5. Develop training modules for managers, current employees, and new hires. Training for managers should aim at ensuring that they feel comfortable explaining the firm's overall pay structure, how pay-related decisions are made, why individual employees are remunerated as they are, and how individual remuneration may be increased. Depending on the level of transparency adopted, consider training employees (particularly newcomers) in advocating for themselves and others when they believe that pay adjustments are warranted, as well as in understanding the parameters influencing pay decisions, such as current job market rates and trends, organizational finances, and individual, team, and unit performance.

Conclusion

Whether pay and pay systems should be more or less transparent is a question that employers, labor leaders, policymakers, and researchers have been debating for decades. Based on the literature reviewed in this volume, it should be apparent that the past 10 years have seen a burst of empirical research on the topic. This collective body of new knowledge, much of it from countries other than the United States, offers some of the first evidence regarding the real-life implications of different policy interventions at both organizational and societal levels. It cannot be ignored. Nevertheless, there is much more that we need to know. I hope that this book will motivate others to meet the research challenges noted above and continue the search for new knowledge on pay administration in general and pay communication in particular.

References

Adams, J. S. (1963). Toward an understanding of inequity. *Journal of Abnormal and Social Psychology*, *67*, 422–436.

Adler, L. (2021). *From the job's worth to the person's price: The transformation of US pay-setting practices since 1950* [Working paper]. Harvard University.

Akerlof, G. A. (1970). The market for "lemons": Quality uncertainty and the market mechanism. *Quarterly Journal of Economics*, *84*(3), 488–500. https://doi.org/10.2307/1879431

Akerlof, G. A., & Yellen, J. L. (1986). *Efficiency wage models of the labor market.* Cambridge University Press.

Akerlof, G. A., & Yellen, J. L. (1990). The fair wage-effort hypothesis and unemployment. *Quarterly Journal of Economics*, *105*(2), 255–283. https://doi.org/10.2307/2937787

Alexander, S., & Ruderman, M. (1987). The role of procedural and distributive justice in organizational behavior. *Social Justice Research*, *1*(2), 177–198.

Alterman, V., Bamberger, P. A., Wang, M., Koopmann, J., Belogolovsky, E., & Shi, J. (2021). Best not to know: Pay secrecy, employee voluntary turnover, and the conditioning effect of distributive justice. *Academy of Management Journal*, *64*(2), 1–27. https://doi.org/10.5465/amj.2019.0231

Alvarez, J. B., Lane, D., & Coughlin, J. (2017). Amazon buys whole foods (Case 9-518-056). Harvard Business School, Harvard University.

Ambrose, M. L. (2002). Contemporary justice research: A new look at familiar questions. *Organizational Behavior and Human Decision Processes*, *89*(1), 803–812. https://doi.org/10.1016/S0749-5978(02)00030-4

Amernic, J. H. (1988). Accounting disclosure and industrial relations: A review article. *British Accounting Review*, *20*(2), 141–157.

Ames, M. (2014, March 22). Revealed: Apple and Google's wage-fixing cartel involved dozens more companies, over one million employees. *Pando.* https://pando.com/2014/03/22/revealed-apple-and-googles-wage-fixing-cartel-involved-dozens-more-companies-over-one-million-employees

An, C., & Rahman, T. (2020). *The case for pay transparency* (Report 6010695-CR). Mercer. Retrieved March 26, 2021, from https://www.mercer.us/our-thinking/career/the-case-for-pay-transparency.html

Arnold, A., Fulmer, I. S., Sender. A., Allen, D. G., & Staffelbach, B. (2018). *Compensation and pay transparency practices in Switzerland: Survey report 2018.* Center for Human Resource Management, University of Lucerne. https://www.unilu.ch/fileadmin/fakultaeten/wf/institute/hrm/dok/Forschung/PayTransparency_CH_SurveyReport_2018_.pdf

Arrowsmith, J., & Marginson, P. (2011). Variable pay and collective bargaining in British retail banking. *British Journal of Industrial Relations*, *49*(1), 54–79. https://doi.org/10.1111/j.1467-8543.2009.00768.x

Baker, G., Gibbons, R., & Murphy, K. J. (1994). Subjective performance measures in optimal incentive contracts. *Quarterly Journal of Economics, 109*(4), 1125–1156. https://doi.org/10.2307/2118358

Baker, G., Gibbons, R., & Murphy, K. J. (2002). Relational contracts and the theory of the firm. *Quarterly Journal of Economics, 117*(1), 39–84. https://doi.org/10.1162/003355302753399445

Baker, J. C. (1939). Executive compensation payments by large and small industrial companies. *Quarterly Journal of Economics, 53*(3), 404–434. https://doi.org/10.2307/1884415

Baker, M., Halberstam, Y., Kroft, K., Mas, A., & Messacar, D. (2019). *Pay transparency and the gender gap* [Working paper No. 25834]. National Bureau of Economic Research.

Balderston, C. (1935). *Executive guidance of industrial relations.* University of Pennsylvania Press.

Bamberger, P. A., & Belogolovsky, E. (2010). The impact of pay secrecy on individual task performance. *Personnel Psychology, 63*(4), 965–996. https://doi.org/10.1111/j.1744-6570.2010.01194.x

Bamberger, P. A., & Belogolovsky, E. (2017). The dark side of transparency: How and when pay administration practices affect employee helping. *Journal of Applied Psychology, 102*(4), 658–671.

Bamberger, P. A., Biron, M., & Meshoulam, I. (2014). *Human resource strategy: Formulation, implementation and impact.* Routledge.

Bamberger, P. A., & Levi, R. (2009). Team-based reward allocation structures and the helping behaviors of outcome-interdependent team members. *Journal of Managerial Psychology, 24*(4), 300–327. https://doi.org/10.1108/02683940910952705

Bapuji, H., Ertug, G., & Shaw, J. D. (2020). Organization and societal economic inequality: A review and way forward. *Academy of Management Annals, 14*, 60–91. https://doi.org/10.5465/annals.2018.0029

Barach, M. A., & Horton, J. J. (2021). How do employers use compensation history? Evidence from a field experiment. *Journal of Labor Economics, 39*(1), 193–218.

Barankay, I. (2012). *Evidence from a randomized workplace experiment.* https://repository.upenn.edu/cgi/viewcontent.cgi?article=1074&context=bepp_papers

Barker, S. L. (2019, June 6). *Can pay transparency improve company culture? Cultural Magazine.* https://medium.com/culturati/can-pay-transparency-improve-company-culture-461af5715555

Barney, J. B. (2001). Resource-based theories of competitive advantage: A ten-year retrospective on the resource-based view. *Journal of Management, 27*(6), 643–650. https://doi.org/10.1016/S0149-2063(01)00115-5

Barroso, A., & Brown, A. (2021, May 25). *Gender pay gap in U.S. held steady in 2020.* Pew Research Center. https://www.pewresearch.org/fact-tank/2019/03/22/gender-pay-gap-facts

Bartol, K. M., & Martin, D. C. (1989). Effects of dependence, dependency threats, and pay secrecy on managerial pay allocations. *Journal of Applied Psychology, 74*(1), 105–113. https://doi.org/10.1037/0021-9010.74.1.105

Becker, G. S. (2002). The age of human capital. In E. P. Lazear (Ed.), *Education in the twenty-first century* (pp. 3–8). Hoover Institution Press.

Belcher, D. W. (1955). *Wage and salary administration.* Prentice-Hall.

Bellace, J. R., & Gospel, H. F. (1983). Disclosure of information to trade unions: Comparative perspective. *International Labour Review, 122*(1), 57–74.

Belogolovsky, E., & Bamberger, P. A. (2014). Signaling in secret: Pay for performance and the incentive and sorting effects of pay secrecy. *Academy of Management Journal, 57,* 1706–1733. https://doi.org/10.5465/amj.2012.0937

Belogolovsky, E., & Bamberger, P. A. (2015). Panacea or Pandora's box? The role of fairness perceptions and interpersonal competitiveness in determining how pay secrecy affects individual task performance. In A. Ortenblad (Ed.), Handbook of *research* on *management ideas* and *panaceas*: Adaptation and *context* (pp. 77–95). Elgar.

Belogolovsky, E., Bamberger, P., Alterman, V., & Wagner, D. T. (2016). Looking for assistance in the dark: Pay secrecy, expertise perceptions, and efficacious help seeking among members of newly formed virtual work groups. *Journal of Business and Psychology, 31*(4), 459–477. https://doi.org/10.1007/s10869-015-9427-4

Benedetti, A. H., & Chen, S. (2018). High CEO-to-worker pay ratios negatively impact consumer and employee perceptions of companies. *Journal of Experimental Social Psychology, 79,* 378–393. https://doi.org/10.1016/j.jesp.2018.09.003

Bennedsen, M., Simintzi, E., Tsoutsoura, M., & Wolfenzon, D. (2019). *Do firms respond to gender pay gap transparency?* [Working paper]. National Bureau of Economic Research. https://doi.org/10.3386/w25435

Berger, S. (2017, October 18). *Salary secrets spilled: Millennials are piping up about their paychecks.* Bankrate. https://www.bankrate.com/personal-finance/smart-money/who-shares-salary-information

Bernstein, E. S. (2017). Making transparency transparent: The evolution of observation in management theory. *Academy of Management Annals, 11*(1), 217–266.

Bierman, L., & Gely, R. (2004). "Love, sex and politics? Sure. Salary? No way": Workplace social norms and the law. *Berkeley Journal of Employment and Labor Law, 25*(1), 167–191.

Blanes, I., Vidal, J. B., & Nossol, M. (2011). Tournaments without prizes: Evidence from personnel records. *Management Science, 57*(10), 1721–1736. https://doi.org/10.1287/mnsc.1110.1383

Blau, P. M. (1964). Justice in social exchange. *Sociological Inquiry, 34*(2), 193–206.

Bloomfield, D. (1923). *Financial incentives for employees and executives.* H. W. Wilson, Modern Executive's Library.

Bölingen, F. (2021). The effectiveness of pay transparency laws. LMU-Munich School of Management.

Boren, Z. B. (2015, September 19). Talking about money is Britain's last taboo. Independent. https://www.independent.co.uk/news/science/talking-about-money-is-britain-s-last-taboo-10508902.html

Borman, W. C., & Motowidlo, S. J. (1997). Task performance and contextual performance: The meaning for personnel selection research. *Human Performance, 10*(2), 99–109. https://doi.org/10.1207/s15327043hup1002_3

Brady, D. L., Brown, D. J., & Liang, L. H. (2017). Moving beyond assumptions of deviance: The reconceptualization and measurement of workplace gossip. *Journal of Applied Psychology, 102*(1), 1–25. https://doi.org/10.1037/apl0000164

Breza, E., Kaur, S., & Shamdasani, Y. (2018). The morale effects of pay inequality. *Quarterly Journal of Economics, 133*(2), 611–663. https://doi.org/10.1093/qje/qjx041

Brown, M., Bamberger, P., Shields, J., & Bliese, P. (2021). *Fairness uncertainty and pay information exchange: Insights from a field experiment on employee pay disclosure to pay information websites* [Working paper]. University of Melbourne.

Bruner, R. (2022). N.Y. will soon require businesses to post salaries in job listings. Here's what happened when Colorado did it. *Time.* Retrieved June 29, 2022, from https://time.com/6179485/pay-transparency-law

Buunk, A. P., & Gibbons, F. X. (2007). Social comparison: The end of a theory and the emergence of a field. *Organizational Behavior and Human Decision Processes, 102,* 3–21. https://doi.org/10.1016/j.obhdp.2006.09.007

Cable, D. M., & Judge, T. A. (1994). Pay preferences and job search decisions: A person–organization fit perspective. *Personnel Psychology, 47*(2), 317–348. https://doi.org/10.1111/j.1744-6570.1994.tb01727.x

California legislative information. (n.d.). https://leginfo.legislature.ca.gov/faces/home.xhtml

Call, M. L., Nyberg, A. J., & Thatcher, S. M. B. (2015). Stargazing: An integrative conceptual review, theoretical reconciliation, and extension for star employee research. *Journal of Applied Psychology, 100*(3), 623–640.

Campbell, W. K., Bonacci, A. M., Shelton, J., Exline, J. J., & Bushman, B. J. (2004). Psychological entitlement: Interpersonal consequences and validation of a self-report measure. *Journal of Personality Assessment, 83*(1), 29–45. https://doi.org/10.1207/s1532 7752jpa8301_04

Canadian Legal Information Institute. (2021, August 31). *Pay Equity Act.* https://www.canlii.org/en/ca/laws/stat/sc-2018-c-27-s-416/latest/sc-2018-c-27-s-416.html

Card, D., & Krueger, A. B. (2015). *Myth and measurement: The new economics of the minimum wage: Twentieth-anniversary edition.* Princeton University Press.

Card, D., Mas, A., Moretti, E., & Saez, E. (2012). Inequality at work: The effect of peer salaries on job satisfaction. *American Economic Review, 102*(6), 2981–3003. https://doi.org/10.1257/aer.102.6.2981

Castilla, E. J. (2015). Accounting for the gap: A firm study manipulating organizational accountability and transparency in pay decisions. *Organization Science, 26*(2), 311–333. https://doi.org/10.1287/orsc.2014.0950

Caulfield, M. (2021). Pay secrecy, discrimination, and autonomy. *Journal of Business Ethics, 171,* 399–420. https://doi.org/10.1007/s10551-020-04455-y

Chalupsky, A. B. (1964). Incentive practices as viewed by scientists and managers of pharmaceutical laboratories. *Personnel Psychology, 17,* 385–401. https://doi.org/10.1111/j.1744-6570.1964.tb00075

Chamberlain, A. (2015). *Is Salary Transparency more than a trend?* Research Report Issue. https://www.glassdoor.com/research/

Chamberlain, A., Stansell, A., & Zhao, D. (2019, November 12). Is salary transparency more than a trend? Lessons from economic research. Glassdoor Economic Research. https://www.glassdoor.com/research/is-salary-transparency-more-than-a-trend

Chamberlain, A., Zhao, D., & Stansell, A. (2020). *Progress on the gender pay gap: 2019.* Glassdoor Economic Research. https://www.glassdoor.com/research/gender-pay-gap-2019

Clifford, C. (2017). *How a college dropout grew Whole Foods into the company Amazon just bought for $13.7 billion.* Retrieved April 10, 2021, from https://www.cnbc.com/2017/08/28/how-a-college-dropout-grew-whole-foods-into-the-company-amazon-just-bought-for-13-point-7-billion.html

Clifford, C. (2020, November 25). Whole Foods CEO John Mackey: Store managers could be *making "well over $100,000," without a college degree.* CNBC. https://www.cnbc.com/2020/11/05/ceo-john-mackey-on-how-much-you-can-make-working-at-whole-foods.html

Cohn, A., Fehr, E., Herrmann, B., & Schneider, F. (2014). Social comparison and effort provision: Evidence from a field experiment. *Journal of the European Economic Association, 12*(4), 877–898. https://doi.org/10.1111/jeea.12079

Colella, A., Paetzold, R. L., Zardkoohi, A., & Wesson, M. J. (2007). Exposing pay secrecy. *Academy of Management Review, 32*(1), 55–71. https://doi.org/10.5465/AMR.2007.23463701

Colquitt, J. A. (2001). On the dimensionality of organizational justice: A construct validation of a measure. *Journal of Applied Psychology, 86*(3), 386–400. https://doi.org/10.1037//0021-9010.86.3.386

Comartin, M. (2018, January 24). *Ontario finalizes Pay Transparency Act, 2018, targeting large employers.* Ogletree Deakins. https://ogletree.com/insights/ontario-finalizes-pay-transparency-act-2018-targeting-large-employers

Commons, J. (1919). *Industrial goodwill.* McGraw-Hill.

Connelly, B. L., Certo, S. T., Ireland, R. D., & Reutzel, C. R. (2011). Signaling theory: A review and assessment. *Journal of Management, 37*(1), 39–67. https://doi.org/10.1177/0149206310388419

Cornfield, D. B. (1986). Declining union membership in the post-World War II era: The United Furniture Workers of America, 1939–1982. *American Journal of Sociology, 91*(5), 1112–1153.

Cowherd, D. M., & Levine, D. I. (1992). Product quality and pay equity between lower-level employees and top management: An investigation of distributive justice theory. *Administrative Science Quarterly, 37*(2), 302–320. https://doi.org/10.2307/2393226

Cox, A., & Dunlop, J. T. (1950). Regulation of collective bargaining by the National Labor Relations Board. *Harvard Law Review, 63*(3), 389–432.

Cullen, Z. B., & Pakzad-Hurson, B. (2019). *Equilibrium effects of pay transparency in a simple labor market* [Working paper].

Cullen, Z. B., & Perez-Truglia, R. (2018a). *How much does your boss make? The effects of salary comparisons* (No. w24841). National Bureau of Economic Research.

Cullen, Z. B., & Perez-Truglia, R. (2018b). *The salary taboo: Privacy norms and the diffusion of information* (No. w25145). National Bureau of Economic Research.

Dahl, M. S., & Pierce, L. (2020). Pay-for-performance and employee mental health: Large sample evidence using employee prescription drug usage. *Academy of Management Discoveries, 6*(1), 12–38. https://doi.org/10.5465/amd.2018.0007

Dalal, R. S., Lam, H., Weiss, H. M., Welch, E. R., & Hulin, C. L. (2009). A within-person approach to work behavior and performance: Concurrent and lagged citizenship counterproductivity associations, and dynamic relationships with affect and overall job performance. *Academy of Management Journal, 52*(5), 1051–1066.

Demand Pay Transparency. (2021). *4 countries who have introduced pay transparency.* https://www.demandpaytransparency.org.nz/4_countries_who_have_introduced_pay_transparency

Derfler-Rozin, R., Moore, C., & Staats, B. R. (2016). Reducing organizational rule breaking through task variety: How task design supports deliberative thinking. *Organization Science, 27*(6), 1361–1379.

Deutsch, M. (1949). A theory of co-operation and competition. *Human Relations, 2*(2), 129–152.

De Vaan, M., Elbers, B., & DiPrete, T. A. (2019). Obscured transparency? Compensation benchmarking and the biasing of executive pay. *Management Science, 65*(9), 4299–4317.

Dobbin, F., & Kalev, A. (2016, July–August). Why diversity programs fail. *Harvard Business Review,* 52–60.

Doolittle, R. (2021, May 17). *Sunshine lists have helped narrow the gender pay gap, but Ottawa won't commit to one.* https://www.theglobeandmail.com/canada/article-sunsh ine-lists-have-helped-narrow-the-gender-pay-gap-but-ottawa-wont

Duffy, M. K., Scott, K. L., Shaw, J. D., Tepper, B. J., & Aquino, K. (2012). A social context model of envy and social undermining. *Academy of Management Journal, 55*(3), 643–666.

Duffy, M. K., & Shaw, J. D. (2000). The Salieri syndrome consequences of envy in groups. *Small Group Research, 31*(1), 3–23.

Economic Policy Institute. (2020). *State of working America wages 2019.* https://files.epi. org/pdf/183498.pdf

Eden, D. (2017). Field experiments in organizations. *Annual Review of Organizational Psychology and Organizational Behavior, 4,* 91–122. https://doi.org/10.1146/annurev-orgpsych-041015-062400

Edwards, M. A. (2005). The law and social norms of pay secrecy. *Berkley Journal of Employment and Labor Law, 26,* 41–63.

Eisenhardt, K. M. (1989). Agency theory: An assessment and review. *Academy of Management Review, 14*(1), 57–74.

Equal Employment Opportunity Commission. (2020). *Dell sued by EEOC for violation of equal pay laws.* https://www.eeoc.gov/es/node/133537

Estlund, C. L. (2011). Just the facts: The case for workplace transparency. *Stanford Law Review, 63*(2), 351–407.

Estlund, C. L. (2014). Extending the case for workplace transparency to information about pay. *UC Irvine Law Review, 4,* 781–799.

European Commission. (2021). *Directive of the European Parliament and of the Council to strengthen the application of the principle of equal pay for equal work or work of equal value between men and women through pay transparency and enforcement mechanisms.* https://ec.europa.eu/info/sites/default/files/aid_development_cooperation_fundame ntal_rights/com-2021-93_en_0.pdf

Eurostat. (2021). *Gender pay gap statistics.* Retrieved February 23, 2021, from https:// ec.europa.eu/eurostat/statistics-explained/index.php/Gender_pay_gap_statistics

Exline, J. J., & Lobel, M. (1999). The perils of outperformance: Sensitivity about being the target of a threatening upward comparison. *Psychological Bulletin, 125*(3), 307–337. https://doi.org/10.1037/0033-2909.125.3.307

Exline, J., Single, P., Lobel, M., & Geyer, A. L. (2004). Glowing praise and the envious gaze: Social dilemmas surrounding the public recognition of achievement. *Basic and Applied Social Psychology, 26*(2-3), 119–130.

Fahn, M., & Zanarone, G. (2020). *Accountability versus social comparisons: A theory of pay secrecy (and transparency) in organizations* [Presented paper]. 2020 Meeting of the Society for Industrial and Organizational Economics. Cambridge, MA: MIT.

Ferrante, C. J., & Rousseau, D. M. (2001). Bringing open-book management into the academic line of sight: Sharing the firm's financial information with workers. In C. L. Cooper & D. M. Rousseau (Eds.), Trends in organizational behavior (Vol. 8, pp. 97–116). Wiley.

Festinger, L. (1954). A theory of social comparison processes, *Human Relations, 7,* 117–140.

Festinger, L. (1957). *A theory of cognitive dissonance.* Row, Peterson.

Fishman, C. (1996). Whole Foods is all teams. *Fast Company, 2,* 103. https://www.fast company.com/26671/whole-foods-all-teams

Fiske, S. T., & Goodwin, S. A. (1994). Introduction: Social cognition research and small group research, a *West Side Story* or . . .? *Small Group Research*, 25(2), 147–171.

Fiske, S. T., & Taylor, S. E. (1991). *Social cognition*. McGraw-Hill.

Folger, R., Rosenfield, D., Grove, J., & Corkran, L. (1979). Effects of "voice" and peer opinions on responses to inequity. *Journal of Personality and Social Psychology*, 37(12), 2253–2261.

Frank, R. H. (1985). The demand for unobservable and other non-positional goods. *American Economic Review*, 75(1), 101–116.

Fulmer, I. S., & Chen, Y. (2014). How communication affects employee knowledge of and reactions to compensation systems. In V. D. Miller & M. E. Gordon (Eds.), Meeting the challenge of human resource management: A communication perspective (pp. 167–178). Routledge.

Fulmer, I. S., & Shaw, J. D. (2018). Person-based differences in pay reactions: A compensation-activation theory and integrative conceptual review. *Journal of Applied Psychology*, 103(9), 939–958.

Futrell, C. M., & Jenkins, O. C. (1978). Pay secrecy versus pay disclosure for salesman: A longitudinal study. *Journal of Marketing Research*, 15(2), 214–219. https://doi.org/10.1177/002224377801500204

Gibbons, F. X., & Buunk, B. P. (1999). Individual differences in social comparison: Development of a scale of social comparison orientation. *Journal of Personality and Social Psychology*, 76(1), 129–142.

Gittleman, M., & Pierce, B. (2015). Pay for performance and compensation inequality: Evidence from the ECEC. *Industrial & Labor Relations Review*, 68(1), 28–52. https://doi.org/10.1177/0019793914556241

Glassdoor. (2017). *50 HR and recruiting statistics for 2017*. https://resources.glassdoor.com/rs/899-LOT-464/images/50hr-recruiting-and-statistics-2017.pdf

Glassdoor. (2018, June 4). 18 companies that aren't afraid to reveal what they pay. https://www.glassdoor.com/blog/companies-salary-estimates

Glassdoor. (2020, October 14). HR and recruiting stats for 2020. https://www.glassdoor.com/employers/resources/hr-and-recruiting-stats/#reasons-to-use-glassdoor

Glassdoor Economic Research. (2020). *Progress on the gender pay gap: 2019*. https://www.glassdoor.com/research/app/uploads/sites/2/2019/03/Gender-Pay-Gap-2019-Research-Report-1.pdf

Gobel, L. K., Weller, I., & Nyberg, A. (2020). How employers and employees react to rising pay transparency expectations: An exploratory study. *Academy of Management Proceedings*, 2020(1). https://doi.org/10.5465/AMBPP.2020.130

Goethals, G. R., & Klein, W. M. (2000). Interpreting and inventing social reality. In J. Suls & L. Wheeler (Eds.), Handbook of *social comparison* (pp. 23–44). Springer.

Goethals, G. R., Messick, D. M., & Allison, S. T. (1991). The uniqueness bias: Studies of constructive social comparison. In J. Suls & T. A. Wills (Eds.), *Social comparison: Contemporary theory and research* (pp. 149–176). Erlbaum.

Golman, R., & Bhatia, S. (2012). Performance evaluation inflation and compression. *Accounting, Organizations and Society*, 37(8), 534–543.

Gould, E. (2020). *State of working America wages 2019: A story of slow, uneven, and unequal wage growth over the last 40 years*. Economic Policy Institute. https://files.epi.org/pdf/183498.pdf

Grant, A. M. (2013). *Give and take: A revolutionary approach to success*. Penguin.

Grant, A. M., & Wall, T. D. (2009). The neglected science and art of quasi-experimentation. *Organizational Research Methods, 12*(4), 653–686. https://doi.org/10.1177/109442810 8320737

Greenberg, J. (1990). Organizational justice: Yesterday, today, and tomorrow. *Journal of Management, 16*, 399–432. https://doi.org/10.1177/014920639001600208

Greenberg, J. (1993). Stealing in the name of justice: Informational and interpersonal moderators of theft reactions to underpayment inequity. *Organizational Behavior and Human Decision Processes, 54*(1), 81–103. https://doi.org/10.1006/obhd.1993.1004

Greenberg, J. (2003). Creating unfairness by mandating fair procedures: The hidden hazards of a pay-for-performance plan. *Human Resource Management Review, 13*, 41–57.

Greenberg, J., & Folger, R. (1983). Procedural justice, participation, and the fair process effect in groups and organizations. In P. Paulus (Ed.), *Basic group processes* (pp. 235–256). Springer.

Griswold, A. (2014). Here's why Whole Foods lets employees look up each other's salaries. *Business Insider.* https://www.businessinsider.com/whole-foods-employees-have-open-salaries-2014-3?international=true&r=US&IR=T

Gruys, M. L., & Sackett, P. R. (2003). Investigating the dimensionality of counterproductive work behavior. *International Journal of Selection and Assessment, 11*(1), 30–42. https://doi.org/10.1111/1468-2389.00224

Gumbrell-McCormick, R., & Hyman, R. (2019). Democracy in trade unions, democracy through trade unions? *Economic and Industrial Democracy, 40*(1), 91–110.

Gunia, B. C., Wang, L., Huang, L., Wang, J., & Murnighan, J. K. (2012). Contemplation and conversation: Subtle influences on moral decision making. *Academy of Management Journal, 55*(1), 13–33.

Gupta, N., & Shaw, J. D. (2014). Employee compensation: The neglected area of HRM research. *Human Resource Management Review, 24*(1), 1–4. https://doi.org/10.1016/j.hrmr.2013.08.007

Hallock, K. F. (2012). *Pay: Why people earn what they earn and what you can do now to make more.* Cambridge University Press.

Harari, Y. N. (2016). *Homo deus: A brief history of tomorrow.* Random House.

Harari, Y. N. (2018). *21 lessons for the 21st century.* Random House.

Harris, B. (2018). *Information is power: Fostering labor market competition through transparent wages.* Hamilton Project, Brookings Institution.

Hayes, J. (2017). *Private sector workers lack pay transparency: Pay secrecy may reduce women's bargaining power and contribute to gender wage gap.* Institute for Women's Policy Research. https://iwpr.org/publications/private-sector-pay-secrecy

Hegewisch, A., & Mefferd, E. (2021, September). *Lost jobs, stalled progress: The impact of the "she-cession" on equal pay.* Institute for Women's Policy Research. https://iwpr.org/wp-content/uploads/2021/09/Gender-Wage-Gap-in-2020-Fact-Sheet_FINAL.pdf

Hegewisch, A., Williams, C., & Drago, R. (2011). Pay secrecy and wage discrimination [Fact sheet No. C382]. Institute for Women's Policy Research.

Heneman, R. L., Greenberger, D. B., & Strasser, S. (1988). The relationship between pay-for-performance perceptions and pay satisfaction. *Personnel Psychology, 41*(4), 745–759. https://doi.org/10.1111/j.1744-6570.1988.tb00651.x

Henneman, T. (2015). Pay transparency: Paid in full disclosure. Workforce. https://www.workforce.com/news/pay-transparency-paid-in-full-disclosure

Hermalin, B., & Weisbach, M. (2013). Information disclosure and corporate governance. *Journal of Finance*, *67*, 195–233.

Hirschman, A. O. (1970). *Exit, voice, and loyalty: Responses to decline in firms, organizations, and states* (Vol. 25). Harvard University Press.

Hornung, S., Rousseau, D. M., & Glaser, J. (2008). Creating flexible work arrangements through idiosyncratic deals. *Journal of Applied Psychology*, *93*(3), 655–664. https://doi.org/10.1037/0021-9010.93.3.655

Hornung, S., Rousseau, D. M., & Glaser, J. (2009). Why supervisors make idiosyncratic deals: Antecedents and outcomes of i-deals from a managerial perspective. *Journal of Managerial Psychology*, *24*(8), 738–764.

Houston, J. M., Farese, D. M., & La Du, T. J. (1992). Assessing competitiveness: A validation study of the competitiveness index. *Personality and Individual Differences*, *13*(10), 1153–1156. https://doi.org/10.1016/0191-8869(92)90030-S

Huet-Vaughn, E. (2013). *Striving for status: A field experiment on relative earnings and labor supply* [Job market paper]. University of California, Berkeley.

Huet-Vaughn, E. (2014, April 8). c. *Atlantic Monthly*.

Huo, Y. J., Smith, H. J., Tyler, T. R., & Lind, E. A. (1996). Superordinate identification, subgroup identification, and justice concerns: Is separatism the problem; Is assimilation the answer? *Psychological Science*, *7*(1), 40–45.

Huseman, R. C., Hatfield, J. D., & Miles, E. W. (1987). A new perspective on equity theory: The equity sensitivity construct. *Academy of Management Review*, *12*(2), 222–234. https://doi.org/10.2307/258531

Institute for Women's Policy Research. (2014). *Pay secrecy and wage discrimination* [Fact sheet No. C382].

Institute for Women's Policy Research. (2020, November 2). Out in the open: Stopping work retaliation against salary sharing. https://iwpr.org/media/in-the-lead/out-in-the-open-stopping-work-retaliation-against-salary-sharing

Isen, A. M. (1984). Toward understanding the role of affect in cognition. In R. S. Wyer, Jr., & T. K. Srull (Eds.), *Handbook of social cognition* (Vol. 3, pp. 179–236). Erlbaum.

Johnson, L. D. (2012). History lessons: Understanding the decline in manufacturing. *MinnPost*. Retrieved January 17, 2020, from https://www.minnpost.com/macro-micro-minnesota/2012/02/history-lessons-understanding-decline-manufacturing

Jones, E. E., & Harris, V. A. (1967). The attribution of attitudes. *Journal of Experimental Social Psychology*, *3*(1), 1–24.

Jost, J. T. (1995). Negative illusions: Conceptual clarification and psychological evidence concerning false conscientiousness. *Political Psychology*, *16*(2), 397–424. https://doi.org/10.2307/3791837

Kahneman, D. (2011). *Thinking, fast and slow*. Lane.

Kahneman, D., & Frederick, S. (2004). Attribute substitution in intuitive judgment. In M. Augier & J. G. March (Eds.), *Models of a man: Essays in memory of Herbert A. Simon* (pp. 411–432). MIT Press.

Kahneman, D., & Tversky, A. (1979). Prospect theory: An analysis of decision under risk. *Econometrica*, *47*(2), 263–292.

Kanfer, R. (1990). Motivation theory and industrial/organizational psychology. In M. D. Dunnette & L. Hough (Eds.), *Handbook of industrial and organizational psychology* (Vol. 1, pp. 75–170). Consulting Psychologists Press.

Karabarbounis, M., & Pinto, S. (2018). What can we learn from online wage postings? Evidence from Glassdoor. *Economic Quarterly*, *104*(4), 173–189.

Kaufman, B. E. (2001). The theory and practice of strategic HRM and participative management: Antecedents in early industrial relations. *Human Resource Management Review, 11*(4), 505–533.

Kelley, H. H., & Thibaut, J. W. (1978). *Interpersonal relations: A theory of interdependence.* Wiley.

Kidwai, A. (2020, March 18). 3 employers share their approaches to pay transparency. *HRDive.* https://www.hrdive.com/news/3-employers-share-their-approaches-to-pay-transparency/574398

Kleiner, M. M., & Bouillon, M. L. (1988). Providing business information to production workers: Correlates of compensation and profitability. *Industrial and Labor Relations Review, 41*(4), 605–617. https://doi.org/10.1177/001979398804100409

Kochan, T. (2000). Building a new social contract at work: A call to action. *Perspectives on Work, 4*(1), 3–12.

Kramer, R. M. (1998). Paranoid cognition in social systems: Thinking and acting in the shadow of doubt. *Personality and Social Psychology Review, 2*(4), 251–275.

Kramer, R. M. (2001). Organizational paranoia: Origins and dynamics. *Research in Organizational Behavior, 23,* 1–42.

Kristal, T., Cohen, Y., & Navot, E. (2020). Workplace compensation practices and the rise in benefit inequality. *American Sociological Review, 85*(2), 271–297. https://doi.org/10.1177/0003122420912505

Krueger, A. B., & Mas, A. (2004). Strikes, scabs, and tread separations: Labor strife and the production of defective Bridgestone/Firestone tires. *Journal of Political Economy, 112*(2), 253–289. https://doi.org/10.1086/381479

Kruger, J. (1999). Lake Wobegon be gone! The "below-average effect" and the egocentric nature of comparative ability judgments. *Journal of Personality and Social Psychology, 77*(2), 221. https://doi.org/10.1037/0022-3514.77.2.221

LaViers, L. (2019). *The effect of pay transparency on narcissists: Can personality type predict reciprocity?* ProQuest.

Lawler, E. E. (1965). Managers' perceptions of their subordinates' pay and of their superiors' pay. *Personnel Psychology, 18*(4), 413.

Lawler, E. E. (1966). The mythology of management compensation. *California Management Review, 9,* 11–22. https://doi.org/10.2307/41165705

Lawler, E. E., III. (1967). Secrecy about management compensation: Are there hidden costs? *Organizational Behavior and Human Performance, 2*(2), 182–189.

Lawler, E. E., & Porter, L. W. (1967). The effect of performance on job satisfaction. *Industrial Relations, 7*(1), 20–28.

Le Beau, C. (2019, May 2). How knowing your colleague's salary could hurt you. Quartz. https://finance.yahoo.com/news/knowing-colleague-salary-could-hurt-154941944.html

Lee, K., Duffy, M. K., Scott, K. L., & Schippers, M. C. (2018). The experience of being envied at work: How being envied shapes employee feelings and motivation. *Personnel Psychology, 71*(2), 181–200. https://doi.org/10.1111/peps.12251

Lewis, R. L., Eandi, S. E., & Kurnatowska, M. K. (2018). Global efforts to advance gender pay equity. Bureau of National Affairs. https://www.bakermckenzie.com/-/media/files/expertise/employment/gender_pay_equity.pdf

Li, M. (2013). Using the propensity score method to estimate causal effects: A review and practical guide. *Organizational Research Methods, 16*(2), 188–226. https://doi.org/10.1177/1094428112447816

Lim, J. H., Tai, K., Bamberger, P. A., & Morrison, E. W. (2020). Soliciting resources from others: An integrative review. *Academy of Management Annals, 14*(1), 122–159. https://doi.org/10.5465/annals.2018.0034

Lind, E. A. (2001). Fairness heuristic theory: Justice judgments as pivotal cognitions in organizational relations. In J. Greenberg & R. Cropanzano (Eds.), Advances in *organizational justice* (pp. 56–88). Stanford University Press.

Lind, E. A., Greenberg, J., Scott, K., & Welchans, T. D. (2000). The winding road from employee to complainant: Situational and psychological determinants of wrongful-termination claims. *Administrative Science Quarterly, 45*(3), 557–590.

Lind, E. A., Kulik, C. T., Ambrose, M. L., & de Vera Park, M. (1993). Individual and corporate dispute resolution: Using procedural fairness as a decision heuristic. *Administrative Science Quarterly, 38*(2), 224–251.

Lind, E. A., & Van den Bos, K. (2002). When fairness works: Toward a general theory of uncertainty management. *Research in Organizational Behavior, 24*, 181–223.

LinkedIn. (2019). *Global talent trends.* https://business.linkedin.com/content/dam/me/business/en-us/talent-solutions/resources/pdfs/global_talent_trends_2019_emea.pdf

Littman, M. (2001, July–August). The silent treatment. *Working Woman*, p. 39.

Mackey, J., & Sisodia, R. (2014). *Conscious capitalism: liberating the heroic spirit of business.* Harvard Business Review Press.

Mannheim, K. (1970). The problem of generations. *Psychoanalytic Review, 57*(3), 378–404.

Marasi, S., & Bennett, R. J. (2016). Pay communication: Where do we go from here? *Human Resource Management Review, 26*(1), 50–58. https://doi.org/10.1016/j.hrmr.2015.07.002

Marasi, S., Wall, A., & Bennett, R. J. (2018). Pay openness movement: Is it merited? Does it influence more desirable employee outcomes than pay secrecy? *Organization Management Journal, 15*(2), 58–77.

Marijn, P., Janssen, O., Van Yperen, N. W., & Van de Vliert, E. (2007). Achievement goals and interpersonal behavior: How mastery and performance goals shape information exchange. *Personality and Social Psychology Bulletin, 33*(10), 1435–1447. https://doi.org/10.1177/0146167207305536

Mas, A. (2006). Pay, reference points, and police performance. *Quarterly Journal of Economics, 121*(3), 783–821.

Mas, A. (2008). Labour unrest and the quality of production: Evidence from the construction equipment resale market. *Review of Economic Studies, 75*(1), 229–258. https://doi.org/10.1111/j.1467-937X.2007.00461.x

Mas, A. (2016). *Does disclosure affect CEO pay setting? Evidence from the passage of the 1934 Securities and Exchange Act.* Princeton University. https://www.princeton.edu/~amas/papers/CEODisclosureMandate.pdf

Mas, A. (2017). Does transparency lead to pay compression? *Journal of Political Economy, 125*(5), 1683–1721. https://doi.org/10.1086/693137

Matherly, W. (1926). The evolution of personnel management. *Industrial Management, 72*(4), 256–257.

Maurer, R. (2018, August 6). *Salary is most important part of job ad.* SHRM. https://www.shrm.org/resourcesandtools/hr-topics/talent-acquisition/pages/salary-most-important-part-job-ad.aspx

Mayer, R. C., & Davis, J. H. (1999). The effect of the performance appraisal system on trust for management: A field quasi-experiment. *Journal of Applied Psychology*, *84*(1), 123–136.

Mayer, R. C., Davis, J. H., & Schoorman, F. D. (1995). An integrative model of organizational trust. *Academy of Management Review*, *20*, 709–734. https://doi.org/10.5465/AMR.2007.24348410

Mercer. (2020). *Israel to expand gender pay gap reporting*. Retrieved April 11, 2021, from https://www.mercer.com/our-thinking/law-and-policy-group/israel-to-expand-gender-pay-gap-reporting.html

Merluzzi, N. (2016, June 14). *These businesses are taking the equal pay pledge*. Whitehouse. Gov. https://obamawhitehouse.archives.gov/blog/2016/06/14/businesses-taking-equal-pay-pledge.

Milkman, R. (2017). A new political generation: Millennials and the post-2008 wave of protest. *American Sociological Review*, *82*(1), 1–31. https://doi.org/10.1177/0003122416681031

Milkovich, G. T., & Anderson, P. H. (1972). Management compensation and secrecy policies. *Personnel Psychology*, *25*(2), 293–302. https://doi.org/10.1111/j.1744-6570.1972.tb01105

Milkovich, G. T., Newman, J. M., & Gerhart, B. (2013). *Compensation* (11th ed.). McGraw-Hill Irwin.

Milkovich, G. T., & Stevens, J. (2000). From pay to rewards: 100 years of change. *ACA Journal*, *9*(1), 6–18.

Miller, D., Le Breton-Miller, I., & Scholnick, B. (2008). Stewardship vs. stagnation: An empirical comparison of small family and non-family businesses. *Journal of Management Studies*, *45*(1), 51–78.

Miller, D. T., & Effron, D. A. (2010). Psychological license: When it is needed and how it functions. *Advances in Experimental Social Psychology*, *43*, 115–156.

Mishel, L., & Wolfe, J. (2019, August 14). *CEO compensation has grown 940% since 1978: Typical worker compensation has risen only 12% during that time*. Economic Policy Institute. https://www.epi.org/publication/ceo-compensation-2018

Montag-Smit, T. A., & Smit, B. W. (2021). What are you hiding? Employee attributions for pay secrecy policies. *Human Resource Management Journal*, *31*(3), 704–728.

Moyal, A., & Ritov, I. (2020). The effect of contest participation and contest outcome on subsequent prosocial behavior. *PLoS One*, *15*(11), e0240712. https://doi.org/10.1371/journal.pone.0240712

Naylor, J. C., Pritchard, R. D., & Ilgen, D. R. (1980). *A theory of behavior in organizations*. Academic Press.

Newman, J. M., Gerhart, B., & Milkovich, G. T. (2016). *Compensation*. McGraw-Hill.

Nisbett, R., & Ross, L. (1980). *Human inference: Strategies and shortcomings of social judgment*. Prentice-Hall.

NLRB v. Babcock & Wilcox Co., 736 F.2d 1410 (10th Cir. 1984).

NLRB v. Truitt Manufacturing Co., 351 U.S. 149 (1956).

Obloj, T., & Zenger, T. (2017). Organization design, proximity, and productivity responses to upward social comparison. *Organization Science*, *28*(1), 1–18.

Obloj, T., & Zenger, T. (2022). The influence of pay transparency on (gender) inequity, inequality and the performance basis of pay. *Nature Human Behaviour*, *6*(5), 646–655.

O'Connell, B. (2020, April 14). How transparent can managers be about pay? SHRM. https://www.shrm.org/resourcesandtools/hr-topics/people-managers/pages/pay-transparency-and-managers.aspx

Ohlmer, I. V., & Sasson, A. (2018, July). Showing your cards: Pay transparency and overall pay dispersion. *Academy of Management Proceedings, 2018*(1), 16544.

Organ, D. W., & Paine, J. B. (1999). A new kind of performance for industrial and organizational psychology: Recent contributions to the study of organizational citizenship behavior. International Review of Industrial and Organizational Psychology, 14, 337–368.

Organ, D. W., & Ryan, K. (1995). A meta-analytic review of attitudinal and dispositional predictors of organizational citizenship behavior. *Personnel Psychology, 48*(4), 775–802. https://doi.org/10.1111/j.1744-6570.1995.tb01781

Organisation for Economic Co-operation and Development. (2021). *Collective bargaining coverage.* https://stats.oecd.org/Index.aspx?DataSetCode=CBC

Oxfam. (2019). *Mind the gap: The state of employment in India in 2019.* https://www.oxfamindia.org/Mind-Gap-State-of-Employment-in-India

Parrott, W. G., & Smith, R. H. (1993). Distinguishing the experiences of envy and jealousy. *Journal of Personality and Social Psychology, 64*(6), 906–920.

Patchen, M. (1961). A conceptual framework and some empirical data regarding comparisons of social rewards. *Sociometry, 24*(2), 136–156. https://doi.org/10.2307/2786063

Payscale. (2017). *PayScale research shows many employers still ask about salary history but refusing to answer has different outcomes for candidates depending on gender.* http://www.marketwired.com/news-release/2017/06/27/1052580/0/en/PayScale-Research-Shows-Many-Employers-Still-Ask-About-Salary-History-but-Refusing-to-Answer-Has-Different-Outcomes-for-Candidates-Depending-on-Gender.html

Payscale. (2020a, July 29). *2022 State of the Gender Pay Gap Report.* https://www.payscale.com/research-and-insights/gender-pay-gap/

Payscale. (2020b). *2020 compensation best practices.* https://v2-wp-staging.payscale.com/cbpr

Peeters, G., & Czapinski, J. (1990). Positive–negative asymmetry in evaluations: The distinction between affective and informational negativity effects. *European Review of Social Psychology, 1*, 33–60.

Perez-Truglia, R. (2020). The effects of income transparency on well-being: Evidence from a natural experiment. *American Economic Review*, 110(4), 1019–54.

Peterson, K. (2014, March 5). At Whole Foods, paychecks are public. CBS News. https://www.cbsnews.com/news/at-whole-foods-paychecks-are-public

Pfeffer, J., & Langton, N. (1993). The effect of wage dispersion on satisfaction, productivity, and working collaboratively: Evidence from college and university faculty. Administrative *Science Quarterly, 38*(3), 382–407.

Pham, L. D., Nguyen, T. D., & Springer, M. G. (2021). Teacher merit pay: A meta-analysis. *American Educational Research Journal, 58*(3), 527–566.

Ployhart, R. E., Nyberg, A. J., Reilly, G., & Maltarich, M. A. (2014). Human capital is dead; Long live human capital resources. *Journal of Management, 40*(2), 371–398.

Podsakoff, P. M., Ahearne, M., & MacKenzie, S. B. (1997). Organizational citizenship behavior and the quantity and quality of work group performance. *Journal of Applied Psychology, 82*(2), 262–270. https://doi.org/10.1037/0021-9010.82.2.262

Pollen. (2021). *Why we went pay transparent.* https://pollen.co/blog/why-we-went-pay-transparent

Porath, C. L., & Erez, A. (2007). Does rudeness really matter? The effects of rudeness on task performance and helpfulness. *Academy of Management Journal, 50*(5), 1181–1197. https://doi.org/10.2307/20159919

PYMNTS. (2018). *The challenge of culture and compensation at Whole Foods, post-Amazon acquisition.* PYMNTS.com. https://www.pymnts.com/news/retail/2018/whole-foods-amazon-acquisition-ecommerce-employees-union/

Queen's Printer of Acts of Parliament. (2010). *The Equality Act 2010 (gender pay gap information) regulations 2017* [Legislation]. https://www.legislation.gov.uk/ukdsi/2017/9780111152010

Quicklet. (2019, December 26). Amazon and Whole Foods: A tale of two companies. https://www.qlicket.com/amazon-whole-foods-tale-two-companies

Rainey, C. (2018, February 1). It's reportedly becoming "normal" to see Whole Foods employees cry at work. *Grub Street.* https://www.grubstreet.com/2018/02/whole-foods-inventory-system-reportedly-making-employees-cry-at-work.html

Ramachandran, G. (2012). Pay transparency. *Penn State Law Review, 116*(4), 1043–1080.

Riskin, A., Bamberger, P., Erez, A., & Zeiger, A. (2020). Discrete incivility events and team performance: A cognitive perspective on a pervasive human resource (HR) issue. In *Research in personnel and human resources management.* Emerald.

Robles, B., & McGee, M. (2016). *Exploring online and offline informal work: Findings from the Enterprising and Informal Work Activities (EIWA) survey* [Finance and Economics Discussion Series]. Divisions of Research & Statistics and Monetary Affairs, Federal Reserve Board.

Rosenfeld, J. (2017). Don't ask or tell: Pay secrecy policies in U.S. workplaces. *Social Science Research, 65,* 1–16. https://doi.org/10.1016/j.ssresearch.2017.01.009

Rosenfeld, J. (2021). *You're paid what you're worth and other myths of the modern economy.* Harvard University Press.

Rosenfeld, J., & Denice, P. (2015). The power of transparency: Evidence from a British workplace survey. *American Sociological Review, 80*(5), 1045–1068. https://doi.org/10.1177/0003122415597019

Ross, M., & Sicoly, F. (1979). Egocentric biases in availability and attribution. *Journal of Personality and Social Psychology, 37*(3), 322. https://doi.org/10.1037/0022-3514.37.3.322

Rousseau, D. M. (2005). *I-deals: Idiosyncratic deals employees bargain for themselves.* Sharpe.

Rousseau, D. M., Ho, V. T., & Greenberg, J. (2006). I-deals: Idiosyncratic terms in employment relationships. *Academy of Management Review, 31*(4), 977–994. https://doi.org/10.5465/AMR.2006.22527470

Rynes, S. L. (1987). Compensation strategies for recruiting. *Topics in Total Compensation, 1,* 285–296.

Sackett, P. R., & DeVore, C. J. (2001). Counterproductive behaviors at work. In. N. Anderson, D. S. Ones, H. K. Sinangil, & C. Viswesvaran (Eds.), *The SAGE handbook of industrial, work and organizational psychology* (pp. 145–164). SAGE.

Sadler, T. R., & Sanders, S. (2016). The 2011–2021 NBA collective bargaining agreement. *Managerial Finance, 42*(9), 891–901. https://doi.org/10.1108/MF-02-2016-0048

Schall, M., Martiny, S. E., Goetz, T., & Hall, N. C. (2016). Smiling on the inside: The social benefits of suppressing positive emotions in outperformance situations. *Personality and Social Psychology Bulletin, 42*(5), 559–571. https://doi.org/10.1177/0146167216637843

Schnaufer, K., Christandl, F., Berger, S., Gollwitzer, M., & Meynhardt, T. (2018, July). Pay transparency in the field: Envy-inducing social comparisons may reduce job satisfaction. *Academy of Management Proceedings, 2018*(1), 14338.

Schneider, B. (1987). The people make the place. *Personnel Psychology, 40*(3), 437–453.

Schurr, A., & Ritov, I. (2016). Winning a competition predicts dishonest behavior. *Proceedings of the National Academy of Sciences of the USA, 113*(7), 1754–1759. https://doi.org/10.1073/pnas.1515102113

Schuster, J. R., & Colletti, J. A. (1973). Pay secrecy: Who is for and against it? *Academy of Management Journal, 16*(1), 35–40. https://doi.org/10.2307/255040

Shalvi, S., Eldar, O., & Bereby-Meyer, Y. (2012). Honesty requires time (and lack of justifications). *Psychological Science, 23*(10), 1264–1270.

Shaw, J. D. (2014). Pay dispersion. *Annual Review of Organizational Psychology and Organizational Behavior, 1*(1), 521–544.

Shaw, J. D., Delery, J. E., Jenkins, G. D., & Gupta, N. (1998). An organization-level analysis of voluntary and involuntary turnover. *Academy of Management Journal, 41*, 511–525. https://doi.org/10.2307/256939

Shaw, J. D., & Gupta, N. (2007). Pay system characteristics and quit patterns of good, average, and poor performers. *Personnel Psychology, 60*, 903–928. https://doi.org/10.1111/j.1744-6570.2007.00095.x

Shaw, J. D., Gupta, N., & Delery, J. E. (2002). Pay dispersion and workforce performance: Moderating effects of incentives and interdependence. *Strategic Management Journal, 23*(6), 491–512. https://doi.org/10.1002/smj.235

Sheen, R. (2019, October 21). Why your company needs to implement pay equity audits now. *Harvard Business Review.*

Sheen, R. (2022). *Gender pay inequity starts at beginning of career.* Retrieved January 6, 2022, from https://trusaic.com/blog/gender-pay-inequity-starts-at-beginning-of-career

SHRM. (2020). *Black workers still earn less than their White counterparts.* Retrieved April 11, 2021, from https://www.shrm.org/ResourcesAndTools/hr-topics/compensation/Pages/racial-wage-persistence-poses-challenge.aspx

SimanTov-Nachlieli, I., & Bamberger, P. (2021). Pay communication, justice, and affect: The asymmetric effects of process and outcome pay transparency on counterproductive workplace behavior. *Journal of Applied Psychology, 106*(2), 230–249. https://doi.org/10.1037/apl0000502

SimanTov-Nachlieli, I., & Bamberger, P. (2022). *The automatic implications of pay transparency on employee integrity: Taking social mindfulness into account* [Working paper]. Tel Aviv University.

Simmons, C. H., Wehner, E. A., Tucker, S. S., & King, C. S. (1988). The cooperative/competitive strategy scale: A measure of motivation to use cooperative or competitive strategies for success. *Journal of Social Psychology, 128*(2), 199–205. https://doi.org/10.1080/00224545.1988.9711363

Smit, B. W., & Montag-Smit, T. (2018). The role of pay secrecy policies and employee secrecy preferences in shaping job attitudes. *Human Resource Management Journal, 28*(2), 304–324. https://doi.org/10.1111/1748-8583.12180

Smit, B. W., & Montag-Smit, T. (2019). The pay transparency dilemma: Development and validation of the Pay Information Exchange Preferences Scale. *Journal of Applied Psychology, 104*(4), 537–558.

Smith, H. J., Pettigrew, T. F., Pippin, G. M., & Bialosiewicz, S. (2012). Relative deprivation: A theoretical and meta-analytic review. *Personality and Social Psychology Review*,
16(3), 203–232. https://doi.org/10.1177/1088868311430825

Spector, P. E., Fox, S., Penney, L. M., Bruursema, K., Goh, A., & Kessler, S. (2006). The
dimensionality of counterproductivity: Are all counterproductive behaviors created
equal? *Journal of Vocational Behavior*, *68*(3), 446–460. https://doi.org/10.1016/
j.jvb.2005.10.005

Steele, F. (1975). *The open organization: The impact of secrecy and disclosure on people and
organizations*. Addison-Wesley.

Stiglitz, J. E. (2002). Information and the change in the paradigm in economics. *American
Economic Review*, *92*(3), 460–501. https://doi.org/10.1257/00028280260136363

Tannenbaum, A. S. (1982). J. C. Naylor, R. D. Pritchard, D. R. Ilgen: A theory of behavior
in organizations. New York: Academic Press, 1980. *Behavioral Science*, *27*(2), 194–195.
https://doi.org/10.1002/bs.3830270212

Tetlock, P. E. (1985). Accountability: The neglected social context of judgment and choice.
Research in *Organizational Behavior*, *7*, 297–332.

Thaler, R. H., & Sunstein, C. R. (2009). *Nudge: Improving decisions about health, wealth,
and happiness*. Penguin.

Trachtman, R. (1999). The money taboo: Its effects in everyday life and in the practice of
psychotherapy. *Clinical Social Work Journal*, *27*(3), 275–288. https://doi.org/10.1023/
A:1022842303387

Trotter, R. G., Zacur, S. R., & Stickney, L. T. (2017). The new age of pay transparency.
Business Horizons, *60*(4), 529–539. https://doi.org/10.1016/j.bushor.2017.03.011

Trusaic. (2022). *The pay equity definitive guide: 2022 edition*. Retrieved August 23, 2022,
from https://trusaic.com/pay-equity-definitive-guide

Tversky, A., & Kahneman, D. (1983). Extensional versus intuitive reasoning: The conjunc-
tion fallacy in probability judgment. *Psychological Review*, *90*(4), 293–315.

U.S. Bureau of Labor Statistics. (2020, September 1). *Employment by major industry sector*.
https://www.bls.gov/emp/tables/employment-by-major-industry-sector.htm

U.S. Equal Opportunity Commission. (2020). *Dell sued by EEOC for violation of equal pay
laws*. Retrieved February 23, 2021, from https://www.eeoc.gov/newsroom/dell-sued-
eeoc-violation-equal-pay-laws

Van den Bos, K. (2005). What is responsible for the fair process effect? In J. Greenberg &
J. A. Colquitt (Eds.), *Handbook of organizational justice: Fundamental questions about
fairness in the workplace* (pp. 274–300). Erlbaum.

Van den Bos, K., & Lind, E. A. (2002). Uncertainty management by means of fairness
judgments. *Advances in Experimental Social Psychology*, *34*, 1–60. https://doi.org/
10.1016/S0065-2601(02)80003-X

Van den Bos, K., Wilke, H. A. M., & Lind, E. A. (1998). When do we need procedural fairness? The role of trust in authority. *Journal of Personality and Social Psychology*, *75*(6),
1449–1458. https://doi.org/10.1037/0022-3514.75.6.1449

Van Dijk, E., & Zeelenberg, M. (2003). The discounting of ambiguous information in
economic decision making. *Journal of Behavioral Decision Making*, *16*(5), 341–352.
https://doi.org/10.1002/bdm.450

Van Doesum, N. J., Van Prooijen, J. W., Verburgh, L., & Van Lange, P. A. (2016). Social
hostility in soccer and beyond. *PLoS One*, *11*(4), e0153577.

Van Knippenberg, B., Van Knippenberg, D., & Wilke, H. A. (2001). Power use in cooperative and competitive settings. *Basic and Applied Social Psychology*, *23*(4), 291–300.
https://doi.org/10.1207/S15324834BASP2304_5

Van Lange, P. A. M., & Van Doesum, N. J. (2015). Social mindfulness and social hostility. *Current Opinion in Behavioral Sciences*, *3*, 18–24. https://doi.org/10.1016/j.cob eha.2014.12.009

Vecchio, R. (2005). Explorations in employee envy: Feeling envious and feeling envied. *Cognition and Emotion*, *19*(1), 69–81.

Veldman, T. (2017). *Pay transparency in the EU*. Publications Office of the European Union.

Vermunt, R., Wit, A., Van den Bos, K., & Lind, A. (1996). The effect of inaccurate procedure on protest: The mediating role of perceived unfairness and situational self-esteem. *Social Justice Research*, *9*, 109–119.

Visser, J. (1991). Trends in trade union membership. *Employment Outlook*, *1991*, 97–134.

Vroom, V. H. (1964). *Work and motivation*. Wiley.

Wanasika, I., & Adler, T. (2011). Deception as strategy: Context and dynamics. *Journal of Managerial Issues*, *23*(3), 364.

Webb, S., & Webb, B. (1897). *Industrial democracy*. Longman.

Weissman, C. G. (2017, June 20). Whole Foods CEO hints at a more Amazon-like approach to company culture. *Fast Company*. https://www.fastcompany.com/4041293/whole-foods-ceo-hints-at-a-more-amazon-like-approach-to-company-culture

Westfall, B. (2019, September 10). Pay transparency, explained. Talent Management.

Whitman, D. S., Caleo, S., Carpenter, N. C., Horner, M. T., & Bernerth, J. B. (2012). Fairness at the collective level: A meta-analytic examination of the consequences and boundary conditions of organizational justice climate. *Journal of Applied Psychology*, *97*(4), 776–791. https://doi.org/10.1037/a0028021

Whyte, W. F. (1955). *Money and motivation: An analysis of incentives in industry*. Harper.

Williamson, O. E. (1975). *Markets and hierarchies, analysis and antitrust implications: A study in the economics of internal organization*. Free Press.

Willis Towers Watson. (2018a). *2018 getting compensation right*. https://www.willistower swatson.com/en-US/Insights/2018/06/2018-getting-compensation-right-survey-glo bal-findings-report

Wood, J. V. (1996). What is social comparison and how should we study it? *Personality and Social Psychology Bulletin*, *22*(5), 520–537.

Wong, M., Chung, B., Lam, L. W., & Bamberger, P. A. (in press). Pay transparency as a moving target: A multi-step model of pay compression, I-deals, and collectivist shared values. *Academy of Management Journal*. https://journals.aom.org/doi/abs/10.5465/amj.2020.1831

Workplace Justice. (2020). *Promoting pay transparency to fight the gender wage gap: Creative international models*. National Women's Law Center. https://nwlc.org/resource/promoting-pay-transparency-to-fight-the-gender-wage-gap-creative-intern ational-models

WorldatWork–Mercer. (2020). *Pay transparency study*. https://worldatwork.org/resour ces/research/pay-transparency-study

Worstall, T. (2014). Apple, Google, Intel, Adobe escape cheaply from the engineers' class action suit. *Forbes*. https://www.forbes.com/sites/timworstall/2014/04/27/apple-goo gle-intel-adobe-escape-cheaply-from-the-engineers-class-action-suit/?sh=7f7d0 9e34847

Zenger, T. (2016). The case against pay transparency. Harvard Business Review Digital Articles, 1–6.

Zitek, E. M., Jordan, A. H., Monin, B., & Leach, F. R. (2010). Victim entitlement to behave selfishly. *Journal of Personality and Social Psychology*, *98*(2), 245–255. https://doi.org/10.1037/a0017168

Index